Effective Investig
Child Homicide an
Suspicious Deaths

Effective Investigation of Child Homicide and Suspicious Deaths

David Marshall, QPM

Foreword by
Lord Laming, CBE, DL

Contributions from Professor Tony Risdon, Dr Martin Weber,
Professor Neil Sebire, Dr Lizzy Dierckx, Russell Wate QPM,
Nadine Tilbury, Tony Osborne, and Chloe Hawkins

OXFORD
UNIVERSITY PRESS

OXFORD

UNIVERSITY PRESS

Great Clarendon Street, Oxford OX2 6DP

Oxford University Press is a department of the University of Oxford.
It furthers the University's objective of excellence in research, scholarship,
and education by publishing worldwide in

Oxford NewYork

Auckland Cape Town Dar es Salaam Hong Kong Karachi
Kuala Lumpur Madrid Melbourne Mexico City Nairobi
New Delhi Shanghai Taipei Toronto

With offices in

Argentina Austria Brazil Chile Czech Republic France Greece
Guatemala Hungary Italy Japan Poland Portugal Singapore
South Korea Switzerland Thailand Turkey Ukraine Vietnam

Oxford is a registered trademark of Oxford University Press
in the UK and in certain other countries

Published in the United States
by Oxford University Press Inc., NewYork

Cover photos: © ImageSource / Punchstock; StockDisc / Punchstock; Shutterstock; ImageState /
Punchstock; Up The Resolution (uptheres) / Alamy; Shutterstock; Shutterstock; Justin Kase / Alamy;
Chris George / Alamy; © DigitalVision / Punchstock; DigitalVision / Punchstock; Dominic Harrison /
Alamy; Up The Resolution (uptheres) / Alamy; Photodisc / Punchstock

First published 2012

British Library Cataloguing in Publication Data

Data available

Library of Congress Cataloging in Publication Data

Data available

Typeset by Cenveo, Bangalore, India
Printed in Great Britain
on acid-free paper by
CPI Group (UK) Ltd, Croydon, CR0 4YY

ISBN   978-0-19-963917-5

10 9 8 7 6 5 4 3 2

Foreword

I am delighted to have been given the opportunity to contribute in this very small way to this most informative and timely book. We all can contribute to the safety and proper development of children but Parliament has placed on each of the key statutory services a range of duties that are unique to their particular service. These duties cannot be delegated to any other organization. This is because Parliament has long recognized that children are not simply small adults. Rather, the physical frailty or innocence of youth may make them potentially vulnerable to abuse, neglect, or exploitation by the adults they should be able to rely on for love and protection. The law goes well beyond the detection and prosecution of deliberate harm by making clear that the welfare of each child is of paramount importance.

Clearly most parents want the best for their children and society has a direct interest in supporting families to help children become fulfilled and able adults. But sadly the reality also is that some parents, either because of inadequacy or malice, take advantage of the relative weakness of young children. Some adults for their own selfish needs can go to great lengths to exploit childhood innocence or vulnerability. As a result, children can be robbed of their childhood and may well be blighted for life.

Some of the evidence to the Victoria Climbié Inquiry made clear that the work undertaken by the Police Child Protection Teams was not always given a priority. Indeed, in some quarters it was referred to in rather disparaging terms. Since then there is clear evidence that it is now more generally recognized that this work demands not only the highest specialist police and investigative skills but also personal qualities such as persistence, determination, and even courage. None of us like to think that there are adults who deliberately seek to harm and exploit children. It is against that background that well informed knowledge and skill often have to be employed in situations in which the suspect is likely to be devious, manipulative, or threatening.

Over and above the ability to demonstrate high quality police work, those engaged in safeguarding the wellbeing of children and young people have to develop an even wider range of qualities that comes from the essential need to work successfully across organizational boundaries. No other police work demands the requirement often to work intensively in multi-agency teams but those able to do this are frequently rewarded by an even higher level of worthwhile results and professional satisfaction.

Therefore, the authors of this book are to be congratulated on the quality of their research and sound practical guidance. This is a book specially designed to promote good practice and better outcomes for children and families. It is as readable as it is instructive. I hope it becomes essential reading for all those involved in the safeguarding of children, be they managers or practitioners.

The government deserves great credit for making clear on the face of the Police Reform and Social Responsibility Bill currently before Parliament the requirement to exercise those 'duties in relation to the safeguarding of children and the promotion of child welfare that are imposed on the chief constable by sections 10 and 11 of the Children Act 2004'. Parliament could not make it clearer that this work must be a priority in every service.

To help secure a good outcome and better life chances for every child, I have no hesitation in commending most warmly this clearly written and very practical book.

The Lord Laming CBE. DL.

Preface

This is the book I always wanted to have as a Senior Investigating Officer. For eight years up to my retirement in 2010 I was responsible for the investigation of intra-familial child homicides and suspicious deaths in London. Prior to this role I had been involved in the investigation of what was perceived by my colleagues as 'really serious crime', including kidnaps, contract killings, and adult homicides in London and abroad. However, I came to realize, commencing with my posting to the Paedophile Unit at New Scotland Yard, that crimes against children are some of the most serious and demanding investigations a detective can investigate. I discovered that it is an extremely specialized crime area with its own legislation, stated cases, guidance, and crucial multi-agency working. I would have liked a book that brought together all the key legislation, guidance, policies, and procedures along with operational options and background information on areas such as post-mortems in one volume. It would not just have reproduced the related guidance but highlighted the key points, signposting the reader to the source documents and other references including web sites.

In the last ten years, the deaths of children have continued to feature in the media with high profile cases illustrating the tragic and fatal impact they can have, not only on the child victims, but also in relation to parents and carers who have been accused of unlawfully killing children in their care—with real and perceived miscarriages of justice being reported.

High profile cases from Victoria Climbié to 'Baby P' continue to feature, prompting new legislation, statutory requirements, reviews, guidance, and procedures. Conflicting expert medical evidence has been a key feature in this forensic environment as has media reporting, multi-agency failures, resourcing, and information on how and why children die.

For a child, the first year of life is a vulnerable time period, with many children sadly dying from known and unknown medical causes, but some in circumstances that research suggests may be covert homicides.

It is in this highly sensitive area that the police and other partner agencies including children's social care, social services, health, and education have to operate. They have to make fast responses to circumstances that could be one of the most tragic incidents that could ever befall the child and their parents, or one where the parent or carer is criminally responsible for the death. Decisions made early on can seriously impact on the outcome of an investigation into the cause of death of a child. The breach of the deceased child's ultimate right to life has to remain paramount but their parents' and family's right to a sensitive but thorough examination of the facts to establish a cause of death is also very high on the agenda.

It was at the time of the Victoria Climbié Inquiry and the restructuring of child abuse investigation under one command in London that I had, as a DCI, responsibility for one of three major investigation teams dealing with complex child abuse. Three teams became two and the teams then had the additional responsibility for investigating intra-familial child homicides and suspicious deaths in London, separate and distinct from the homicide command that dealt with adult homicides. In 2005, the Child Abuse Investigation Command became responsible for dealing with what was then termed 'cot deaths'. This provided a fantastic link within a single command for additional resources and expertise when a sudden and unexpected death of a child was considered suspicious. A few years later, the two major investigation teams became one—it was this team that I was responsible for up to my retirement. This team was responsible for investigating all intra-familial child homicides and suspicious deaths in London—in some years there were as many as 12 homicides, several suspicious deaths, and on average about 90 cot deaths. Team is a key word, as I worked with a number of fantastic officers and police staff in the Metropolitan Police and other forces during this period. I have orchestrated the writing of this book, and set out many sections in my words, but my comments have been hugely influenced by learning I gained from my colleagues in this operational environment. I have also included valuable contributions and material from these colleagues and others who I have had the privilege to meet and work with.

In childhood death, the post-mortem examination of the deceased child is a key area and is reflected in this book by the inclusion of three pathologists as main contributors. In London we were very fortunate to be able to utilize the services of pathologists at Great Ormond Street Children's Hospital and, whilst not used exclusively, the majority of my cases' post-mortems were carried out there. Over the years (including one year I will not forget where two separate post-mortem examinations for homicides were undertaken late on Christmas Eve at Great Ormond Street Hospital), a very valuable and appreciated professional relationship evolved with these pathologists, to such an extent that I was able to persuade them to contribute considerably to this book.

Specializing in this field of serious crime, I became involved with others undertaking a similar role from around the country on the ACPO Homicide Working Group sub-group on child deaths, and for several years with the NPIA Investigating Sudden Childhood Death Programme that originated from the work of this sub-group. This course, originally delivered nationally by the NPIA, but now also delivered locally by individual forces, examines in detail through practical scenarios and presentations from professionals many of the areas covered in this book. I continue to assist in delivering this course. It is the influence of all those involved in these various areas that has informed the remit and contents of the book. Although primarily written for police officers tasked with these investigations, the contributions from others impacted by childhood death, including parents and professionals, has hopefully made the book relevant to a far wider readership.

This book is not police guidance: much is based on police and other agency guidance, legislation, etc, but the comments and suggestions are my personal views, having had several years of utilizing this material in an operational context. It should be seen as advice to be considered and, if appropriate, taken, but, if not, put to one side, perhaps for future consideration.

The SIO has to ultimately make professional judgements based on the individual circumstances of a specific case, taking into consideration the relevant law and guidance, together with their experience, always documenting their decisions and rationale. This book hopefully throws light on the many complexities and areas within the child death continuum in order to assist SIOs and others when making those challenging but necessary professional judgements.

Guidance helps when negotiating unknown territory including generic points to consider, processes to follow, and investigative options advocated by those who have gone before. Every case in some way will be unique but include common features, such as legal boundaries, but every child who dies is a unique individual deserving special consideration of their specific circumstances to answer the question 'why did they die?' This case-specific approach informed by historic operational learning with the child victim at the centre is the one advocated in this book.

Lord Laming, who has written the foreword to this book, greatly influenced the way I now perceive crimes against children. Recommendation 97 from the Victoria Climbié Inquiry report provided me with a support basis for many discussions with my managers regarding resourcing for investigations. It simply says:

> Chief Constables must ensure that the investigation of crime against children
> is as important as the investigation of any other form of serious crime. Any
> suggestion that child protection policing is of a lower status than other forms
> of policing must be eradicated.

My desire is that this book illustrates in a powerful way how important and demanding the investigation of childhood death is and that it becomes a useful resource for those tasked with this challenging but essential work.

Dave Marshall QPM

Acknowledgements

Many people have contributed to this book, either directly with written sections or diagrams, or indirectly with advice, comment, or over the past years in their role and participation in investigations and related discussions in various forums. There is not room to outline in full all of these contributions but I am very conscious that this book is a 'team' effort so I would like to express my appreciation to several groups of contributors without whom this book would have failed to materialize.

Keeping the deceased children at the forefront, I would like to acknowledge all the children whose cases inspired this book project and some of whom feature in the cases referred to. May they always be remembered and investigators continue to keep the deceased child at the centre of investigations.

I would like to thank two very courageous ladies who shared their experiences in relation to their child's death, providing a valuable insight into how an investigation affects the child's parents and family.

Sophie Bissmire shared the story about the short life and sudden death of her daughter Neave Sophie Bissmire who was born on 23 August 1999—and died on 24 November 1999 aged 13 weeks and 2 days.

Joanne Early provided her honest and challenging perspective as a mother whose husband was charged with the murder of one of their twins and of also seriously injuring the other twin.

Illustrations and other material in the chapters and appendices were provided by Dr Chris Wright (child death continuum diagram), Dave Law (GMP) (comments on samples from parents, consistent messages for parents/carers), Dr Diana Jellinek (rapid response diagram and GM procedures), Jeff Boxer (evaluating factors diagram), GMP, MPS, NPIA, CC Brian Moore (NDM model), Home Office (homicide figures from Supplementary Volume 2 to Crime in England and Wales).

The main contributors—Professor Tony Risdon, Dr Martin Weber, Professor Neil Sebire, Dr Lizzy Dierckx, Russell Wate QPM, Nadine Tilbury, Tony Osborne, and Chloe Hawkins—all exceptionally busy people who, despite this, found the time to write key sections of this book, provide encouragement, and comment on draft chapters.

My critical friends including those above together with John Fox, Tony Cook, Dr N Cary, James Vaughan, Geoff Wessell, Sonya Baylis, and members of the ACPO HWG CHD sub-group.

The Metropolitan Police Service (MPS)—I spent nearly 30 years in the MPS and learned from many during that period, but over the last ten years the following in one way or other supported encouraged or increased my knowledge and appreciation of investigating childhood death. There is insufficient space to detail their respective roles but hopefully you all appreciate what you did and that I enjoyed the privilege of working with and learning from you. I am also grateful for access to templates and information after I had retired for inclusion in this book.

Central to my time in the MPS were SCD5(6) Major Investigation Team police officers and police staff whose teamwork, tenacity, dedication, and commitment over many years investigating child homicides and suspicious deaths produced tremendous results and with whom it was a real pleasure to work. In particular I would like to thank Norman Inniss, Keith Braithwaite, Colin Burgess, Paul Maddocks, Ian Hughes, Colin Welsh, Paul Clack, and Michael Orchard.

There are others within SCD5 child abuse investigation command who I worked with conducting research and supported childhood death investigations, including Alison Brown, Jenny Mayes, Charlotte Llombard-Vigouroux, Anthony Joy, Sam Upton, Dick Henson, Reg Hooke, Gordon Briggs, Terry Sharpe, Caroline Bates, Chris Bourlet, Alistair Jeffrey, Peter Spindler, Dave Shephard, Derrick Kelleher, Alan Gibson, Mick Thurley, Alistair Horne, Dave Byford, and Steve Ranson.

There are many others from other agencies including Moya Reed (CPS), Karen Squibb-Williams (CPS), counsel in the central trials unit at the Central Criminal Court, and the many medical experts who gave evidence in the cases my team investigated.

Graeme Lannigan, Gary Crawford, and Andy Paddison provided information on childhood death investigations in Scotland, Northern Ireland, and Wales.

I have been fortunate to contribute to and present on the NPIA Investigating Childhood Death programme, an initiative from the ACPO Homicide Working Group Childhood Death sub-group chaired by Russell Wate. The course is focused on the police response and was designed to assist SIOs and those tasked with investigating childhood deaths in this specialized crime area. The key contributors included Jeff Boxer, John Fox, and Helen Hopwood, supported by Andy Kay. Much of my learning and views have been influenced by this course along with cases, comments, and questions from several students, trainers, and presenters on the NPIA course run centrally and locally by individual forces. Those who made a particular impression included Dr Phil Cox, Bernie Bradshaw, Alison Towersey, Martin Compton, Sarah Blunn, Liz Gilvear, Toran Wybrow, and Nick Duffield.

My wonderful, very supportive (some may say long suffering) and understanding wife Margaret, and masters of the reality check Tim and Hannah, as always endeavoured to keep me on track and allowed me to make room for my writing—I couldn't have produced this book without their support.

Lord Laming is one of my heroes, so for him to agree to write the foreword for this book was a tremendous surprise. He is exceptionally busy so I am very grateful that he managed to find the time to write the foreword but also to send me emails in response to completed chapters I sent him with words of encouragement—thank you.

Sir Paul Beresford for his work and Private Member's Bill that would extend the offence of familial homicide to include causing or allowing the death or serious physical harm to a child or vulnerable adult.

Oxford University Press—Lucy Alexander, Peter Daniell, Emma Hawes, and others involved for their support, guidance, and patience in the writing of this book.

The national police charity Child Victims of Crime—my team utilized their services on several occasions and to help continue their tremendous support for child victims of crime, including their siblings and family, all royalties from the sale of this book will go to this charity. Full details of CVOC can be found on their website: <http://www.cvoc.org.uk/>.

I welcome any comments or information on developments in relation to any areas covered in this book and can be contacted via email: djm@davemarshall-consultancy.co.uk.

Contents

Contents

APPENDICES

Contributors

Pathology

Professor Tony Risdon has been a Consultant Histopathologist since 1972, practising General Histopathology at Addenbrooke's Hospital, Cambridge and at the Royal London Hospital. He was Senior Lecturer in Paediatric Pathology at Great Ormond Street from 1972–5, and Professor from 1982 until his retirement from the NHS practice in 2004. For the past two decades he has taken a particular interest in sudden death in the first year of life from both natural and unnatural causes. The department at Great Ormond Street hospital of which he was head does more than 200 examinations per annum and over one-third of the autopsies for Sudden Unexpected Death in Infancy (SUDI) in the UK. He has taken responsibility for suspected infant homicides including those due to inflicted injuries. Because of the need for this service, he took the Diploma in Medical Jurisprudence, acquired further training in Forensic Medicine, and was granted Home Office Registration. On his retirement from the NHS he was given honorary status at Great Ormond Street hospital and continues to do autopsies for the police using the special autopsy laboratory and radiological services available at this tertiary referral hospital. He is a partner in Forensic Pathology Services.

Dr Martin Weber was a Consultant Paediatric Pathologist at Great Ormond Street Hospital, London. He undertook his MD Thesis studying post-mortem examination of Sudden Unexpected Death in Infancy (SUDI) and has published several peer-reviewed papers in this field.

Professor Neil Sebire is currently Professor of Paediatric Pathology at Great Ormond Street Hospital, London. He has a research interest in understanding the causes of infant deaths and runs a research programme in this area. He has published over 350 scientific papers in scientific peer-reviewed journals.

Paediatrician's perspective and rapid response

Dr Lizzy Dierckx trained as a doctor at St Mary's Hospital Medical School, Paddington. She has worked in several major children's hospitals across the country including King's College Hospital (London), St James' Hospital (Leeds), John Radcliffe Hospital (Oxford), and the Royal Manchester Children's Hospital. She is currently a Consultant Community Paediatrician in Central Manchester. Part of this role is to act as the Lead for the Rapid Response Team for Greater Manchester investigating Sudden Unexpected Child Death.

Police—stranger murders, reviews, and SCR

Russell Wate QPM is a former police officer having spent most of his service in crime investigation. His last six years were spent as Detective Chief Superintendent for Cambridgeshire Police. Prior to this he dealt with the deaths of Holly Wells and Jessica Chapman, and was also the Senior Investigating Officer (SIO) for the Bichard Public Inquiry. He was the ACPO lead for investigating child deaths, and was a member of the ACPO child protection working group and the Homicide Working Group, and vice chair of the family liaison national executive board. Russell worked for the Department of Education on the 'Munro' review of child protection and he is the independent chair of Hammersmith & Fulham LSCB.

Law on parallel proceedings

Nadine Tilbury was a Senior Crown Prosecutor and Senior Policy Advisor for the CPS, and the CPS policy lead on safeguarding children and on the family/criminal interface. She was a contributing author to the Law Society publication, *Related Family and Criminal Proceedings: A Good Practice Guide.* Prior to joining the CPS, she worked in local authorities and in private practice, where she gained extensive experience of legal issues relating to children.

CATCHEM database

Tony Osborne joined the Derbyshire Constabulary in 1979, and spent the majority of his service engaged on major crime investigations. In 1995, he became involved with the CATCHEM database and developed an interest in updating and analysing the data. He assisted the database custodian, DI Chuck Burton OBE, in support of child sexually-motivated homicide and suspicious missing person cases. In 2003 he was seconded to the National Crime Faculty, taking over as custodian of the database, providing support to many high profile cases throughout the UK. In 2009 he took up a position with the NPIA continuing to manage the CATCHEM database, combining this role with that of NPIA's national advisor for suspicious missing person cases.

NPIA National Injuries Database

Chloe Hawkins has been working as an adviser at the National Injuries Database for seven years, assisting both police and medical experts in the interpretation of injuries through provision of search reports and facilitation of independent expert opinions. Within the National Injuries Database team, Chloe holds a portfolio for paediatric cases. Prior to joining the National Injuries Database in 2004, Chloe graduated with a degree in Psychology from the University of Surrey and had spent time working for the Home Office in the field of serious crime research, specifically focusing on the police investigation of Sudden and Unexpected Deaths in Infancy (SUDI).

Special Features

This book contains several special features that it is hoped will make it more helpful to the reader. These are defined and explained below.

Key points

Information requiring particular emphasis is summarized in key points.

Definitions

Definitions of specific terms are provided where this is useful.

Case studies/Good practice

Where these are appropriate, the material in the text will be related to case study examples to give an indication of how the issue relates to the practical business of policing.

Further information and reading

These boxes provide the reader with additional information and direct the reader towards additional reading that will elaborate upon points discussed in the text.

There are also multiple diagrams and flowcharts for ease of illustration and presentation.

History and Background to Child Death Investigation

1.1 **Introduction**

Investigating child homicides and suspicious deaths necessitates a co-ordinated multi-agency response, and presents unique challenges for those tasked with this extremely complex, specialized, and sensitive crime area. These often protracted investigations, operating in what can be a highly emotive and distressing environment, require professionals from a number of disciplines to work together to safeguard the interests of the deceased child, their siblings, and any future children, whilst maintaining a supportive and empathetic position in relation to the child's parents, carers, and other family members. There are now well established policies, procedures, and statutory guidance in place to provide a framework for these professionals to operate, with the police being the lead agency in child homicides and suspicious deaths, eg Chapter 7 of *Working Together* (2010).

The current investigative environment has been influenced considerably by past failures in protecting the right to life of children and is still an area where controversy amongst different affected groups, eg in relation to the causation of the death, continues, with the arguments often being played out in courts and the media.

The processes of child homicide and suspicious deaths have evolved through episodes of history to their current position. However, before considering these it is important to examine the nature and extent of this tragic phenomenon, where vulnerable children are unlawfully killed, sometimes by those in the greatest position of trust and responsibility for their safety and wellbeing—their own parents and carers.

1.2 **Facts and figures surrounding homicides**

The latest figures published by the *Home Office Statistical Bulletin* in January 2011 for 2009/2010 showed that 52 child victims under the age of 16 years were victims of murder, manslaughter, or infanticide (the total number of victims including adults was 615), and a further two were victims of familial homicide (causing or allowing the death of a child or vulnerable adult). This equates to a child being unlawfully killed in England and Wales on average once a week. The most vulnerable age group was for those under one when figures for the period 2007/08 to 2009/10 were examined.

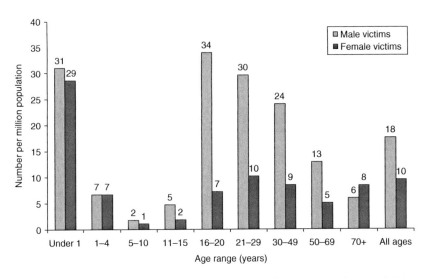

Figure 1.1 Offences currently recorded as homicide per million population by age of victim, combined years 2007/08 to 2009/10

Reproduced from Smith, et al, *Home Office Statistical Bulletin. Homicides, Firearm Offences and Intimate Violence 2009/10. Supplementary Volume 2 to Crime in England and Wales 2009/10* (London: Home Office) with permission.

As can be seen in Figure 1.2, these statistics also showed that in 69 per cent (36) of the cases recorded in these homicide figures for this period the perpetrator was a parent, in 19 per cent (10) of the cases at the time of recording there was no known suspect, in 6 per cent (3) of the cases a stranger had been responsible, and in the remaining 6 per cent (3) of cases the perpetrator was known, so that in 75 per cent (39) of the cases the victims had been acquainted with the main suspect. For these figures, the definition of 'suspect' refers to people who had been arrested and charged with a homicide offence or would have been if they had not died or committed suicide.

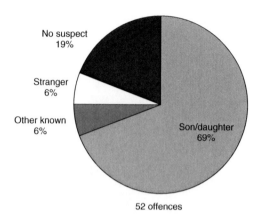

52 offences

Figure 1.2 Victims under 16 years of age, by relationship of victim to principal suspect, 2009/10

Reproduced from Smith, et al, *Home Office Statistical Bulletin. Homicides, Firearm Offences and Intimate Violence 2009/10. Supplementary Volume 2 to Crime in England and Wales 2009/10* (London: Home Office) with permission.

These figures of recorded homicides, when combined with the following facts and figures for other measures in relation to childhood death, present a troubling picture in relation to the true scale of child homicide in England and Wales for whom the data is available, but with lessons for the UK as well.

Not all child deaths are homicides or suspicious; sadly many children die from natural causes, medical conditions, and accidents. The Foundation for the Study of Infant Death (FSID) has produced information on *Cot Death Facts and Figures* (last updated August 2010, available from their website <http://www.fsid.org.uk>), illustrating that over 300 babies still die every year as cot deaths in the UK.

Definition of 'cot death' by FSID

'Cot death is the sudden and unexpected death of a baby for no obvious reason. The post mortem examination may explain some deaths. Those that remain unexplained after post mortem examination may be registered as sudden infant death syndrome (SIDS), sudden infant death, sudden unexpected death in infancy, unascertained or cot death'.

The FSID figures cover the period 2000 to 2008 and include England and Wales, Scotland, and Northern Ireland. Figures are broken down for each individual year in this period, for each country, to include totals for children aged from birth to one year and also for babies over 12 months old.

The figures for children up to a year show a reduction in numbers from 2000 to 2008, from a UK total of 374 in 2000, with 334 in England in Wales, and an overall UK rate (per 1000 live births) of 0.55, down to a UK total of 312 in 2008, with 281 in England and Wales, and an overall UK rate (per 1000 live births) of 0.39.

The figures for cot deaths amongst babies aged over twelve months ranged from a UK total of 19 in 2000, with 17 in England and Wales, down to a UK total of 11 in 2008, with 8 in England and Wales, with only 3.4 per cent of cot deaths in the UK in 2008 being amongst babies over one year old.

FSID also point out that, since the launch of the Reduce the Risk campaign in England and Wales in 1991, with the positive encouragement of safer sleeping practices for babies, the sudden infant death number has fallen dramatically by around 70 per cent.

An article in the journal *Archives of Disease in Childhood* (Sidebotham, et al, 2011) looked at changes in rates of violent child deaths in England and Wales between 1974 and 2008, using an analysis of national mortality data (including data on causes of death from the Office of National Statistics (ONS) and on recorded homicides published by the Home Office). While explaining that, in the context of as many as 53,000 children dying worldwide each year through homicide, with the possibility that due to the nature of the crime there may be under-reporting including covert homicides, they concluded that, over the past 30 years in England and Wales, the rates of violent death in infancy (less than one year) and middle childhood (1 to 14 years) had fallen, but that, in contrast, rates in adolescence (15 to 19 years) had remained static or even risen over the same period. They suggest that 5 to 15 infants, 15 to 45 children, and 32 to 117 adolescents die violent deaths each year, with the true figures likely to be at the higher end of these ranges. The variation in numbers highlighted in the study results from different data sets, recording periods, age bands, registration criteria, and classifications within them. However, in the past three years absolute numbers of child deaths (0 to 19 years) from assault have varied from 48 to 58, which the authors argue represent a minimum estimate of the numbers of children dying violent deaths, as the true number of violent child deaths in England and Wales is not known.

To the figure of 54 child victims from the Home Office figures for 2009/10, consideration must also be given to the number of possible covert homicides. Researchers in another article in the journal *Archives of Disease in Childhood* (2004) (supported by Vaughan and Kautt, 2009), suggest that between five and ten per cent of the 300 sudden and unexpected deaths in infancy a year may be covert homicides.

This may suggest that the true figure for child homicides could have been between 69 and 84 victims for the year (2009/10). It is this possibility that makes child homicide investigation so difficult and different from other forms of homicide, where the cause of death is far more certain and clear from the outset. In a child-centred, victim-focused investigation, this possibility of a covert homicide has to at least be considered, but in a very compassionate and sensitive manner, maintaining an open mind in the search for the truth.

Sidebotham, et al (2011) make a key point in their conclusion in relation to their research, suggesting a welcome reduction in violent child deaths that supports the other statistics cited and ethos running throughout this book, and is worth repeating here.

KEY POINT

'These reductions [in violent child deaths] ... appear to reflect real improvements in protecting children from severe abuse. However, there is no cause for complacency while at least one child or young person per week dies as a result of assault. Within this context, it is important that professionals, policy makers and the public continue to learn lessons from violent child deaths and to recognise that we all carry a responsibility to ensure children's safety.'

1.3 Important landmarks in child death investigation

The previous sections have explained that we now have specific guidance on investigating childhood death (to be covered in depth in subsequent chapters), and that the child death figures appear to be improving; but how have we arrived at this current position? The following section on the history of child death investigation illustrates how the current position evolved through a number of cases and issues over many years, showing that the timing and the sequence of events had a key impact on the continuing chronology, with many issues reoccurring and having a lasting effect on future childhood death investigations.

It is essential when examining any aspect of criminal investigation to look at the context in which the specified offence is committed, not only for that specific case but also the investigative context in more generic terms. A key feature or element of any context will be the history: what has occurred previously that has impacted on this particular area and, crucially, what lessons are to be learned from previous cases, to inform good practice but also to negate repeating previous errors? The history of childhood death investigation presents a very diverse and challenging picture with some disappointingly tragic cycles of failure. In some areas the investigative issues have moved on, although in others they have remained constant, with many continuing to present unique challenges to those tasked with the responsibility of determining how a child has died.

The period we will focus on in this chapter is between 1945 and 2010, examining the events and their position in the sequence of events of the overall chronology. It is essential to understand how the investigation of childhood death has developed and evolved over this key time frame. However, before looking at that key period in the history of childhood death investigation, we will look at a story of a childhood death investigation from a much earlier period, that in a simple way will focus our minds on some key themes that are still central to today's investigations, but which are not unique, having been evident in society for over thousands of years.

This story is one of the earliest records of a childhood death investigation that can be dated to around 930 BC and has been the subject of paintings by famous artists including Raphael, William Blake, and Gustave Doré, as well as providing the basis for film and TV drama storylines, eg the BBC Soap drama, EastEnders.

Discussion point

As the following story unfolds what are the key issues or themes that are still evident today?

1.3.1 **Early child death story**

Now two prostitutes came to the king and stood before him. One of them said, 'My lord, this woman and I live in the same house. I had a baby while she was there with me. The third day after my child was born, this woman also had a baby. We were alone; there was no-one in the house but the two of us.

During the night this woman's son died because she lay on him. So she got up in the middle of the night and took my son from my side while I your servant was asleep. She put him by her breast and put her dead son by my breast. The next morning, I got up to nurse my son-and he was dead! But when I looked at him closely in the morning light, I saw that it wasn't the son I had borne.'

The other woman said, 'No! The living one is my son; the dead one is yours.'

But the first one insisted, 'No! The dead one is yours; the living one is mine.' And so they argued before the king.

The king said, 'This one says, "My son is alive and your son is dead," while that one says, "No! Your son is dead and mine is alive."'

Then the king said, 'Bring me a sword.' So they brought a sword for the king. He then gave an order: 'Cut the living child in two and give half to one and half to the other.'

The woman whose son was alive was filled with compassion for her son and said to the king, 'Please, my lord, give her the living baby! Don't kill him!'

But the other said, 'Neither I nor you shall have him. Cut him in two!'

Then the king gave his ruling: 'Give the living baby to the first woman. Do not kill him; she is his mother.'

When all Israel heard the verdict the king had given, they held the king in awe, because they saw that he had wisdom from God to administer justice. (© NIV)

This story contained in historic documents effectively illustrates the following key points for consideration.

KEY POINTS FOR CONSIDERATION

- How the elation of giving birth can be short lived and followed by the depths of grief at the loss of that newborn child—opposite ends of the emotional spectrum.
- The issues presented when there are a limited number of witnesses to the event and conflicting accounts—the 'Which of you did it?' scenario.
- Difficulty in establishing the cause of death.
- Death caused by a parent or carer overlaying a child and the challenging emotions that can pervade when there is the realization that the parent's actions may have contributed to the death.
- The different ways parties to the events can react to the death of a child.
- The extreme spectrum of emotions that can be experienced, from bitterness and resentment to compassion and empathy, by those directly and indirectly involved.
- Other opposites of deceit versus truthfulness in providing accounts and answering questions. The methods used to establish the truth.
- The difficult decisions that those investigating the circumstances of a death or administering justice have to make, as regards not only as to what has happened to the deceased child, but also as to how to deal with any surviving children. The resources deployed to answer these questions.
- The various methods that can be utilized to establish the truth.

Investigating childhood death continues to be extremely difficult and fraught with challenges that, as illustrated in this case, often require the 'wisdom of Solomon'—the king in this account—to arrive at a just outcome.

1.4 **Chronology of child death investigation**

Within more recent history there have been several key events that have come to be seen as defining moments in the investigation of child deaths and which have impacted on the investigative process. These will be briefly outlined in the following sections of this chapter, to give a fuller understanding of how the investigation of childhood death has developed. Some events will be discussed in greater detail in subsequent chapters. Generally, the events will follow a chronological order, but sometimes there is an overlap of events, with several key events occurring within the same time period. Hopefully, the outline of these important episodes in history will illustrate the developing background against which childhood deaths have been investigated and show how we have arrived in the current investigative environment, in which future deaths will be examined.

As will be clear from the chronology, these events are not limited solely to the police but cut across all those impacted by a child death, including the child victim, siblings, parents and carers, medical expert witnesses, and partner agencies, eg Social Services and healthcare.

Other cases and events may have occurred within this time period, but the events identified have been included as they illustrate the drivers for changes in perception and professional practice, as well as how issues can reoccur.

1.4.1 Public Inquiries (1945–1999)

Between 1945 and 1999, there were a large number of Public Inquiries into the deaths of children, where the actions of the carers and the professionals responsible for the welfare of the deceased children (often including their siblings) came under considerable scrutiny in a public forum. The findings of these inquiries would invariably lead to criticism of the various parties, and become the drivers for new or revised guidance, policies, and procedures, and even new legislation.

Case study—1945: Dennis O'Neill

Dennis O'Neill, aged 13 years, was starved and beaten to death by his foster father, Reginald Gough. Key issues at the Home Office inquiry included failures by agencies and staff, resourcing, and communication.

Case study—1973: Maria Colwell

Maria Colwell, aged seven years, was starved and beaten to death by her stepfather, William Kepple. Although having been fostered, she had been returned to her mother with insufficient evidence to justify this. All agencies were criticized in the inquiry, which ascertained that the family had been visited 50 times by social workers, police, health visitors, and housing officers.

The *Report of the Committee of Inquiry into the Care and Supervision Provided in Relation to Maria Colwell* published in 1974, and chaired by Judge Thomas Field-Fisher, QC, identified three key areas that would sadly continue to feature in subsequent enquiries.

- Lack of communication between those agencies involved
- Inadequate training for those involved, and
- Changes in the makeup of society and how children's place within it was perceived.

Case study—1984: Jasmine Beckford

Jasmine Beckford, aged four years, was starved and beaten to death by her stepfather, Maurice Beckford, who was convicted of manslaughter, and her mother, Beverley Lorrington, convicted of neglect. Despite Jasmine being known to Social Services for two and a half years and Beckford having been convicted of assaulting her younger sibling, she was seen only once in ten months by her social worker.

Case study—1984: Tyra Henry

Tyra Henry, aged 21 months, was beaten to death by her father after his release from prison for seriously assaulting her brother. Tyra's injuries included 50 bite marks on her body. The inquiry highlighted a lack of communication, training, resources, supervision, and experience, together with a failure to recognize and respond to the warning signs.

Mr Louis Blom-Cooper, the Jasmine Beckford Inquiry chairman, made some interesting comments, stating that, with the exception of the Tyra Henry Inquiry, to be held shortly, the Beckford Inquiry, which cost more than £300,000 'could well be the end of a series' which stretches back through more than 20 inquiries to the Maria Colwell case in 1973. He considered that 'We have got to the stage where the child abuse system has been sufficiently refined.' He explained that:

- a new code of practice for social workers was to be introduced,
- the child's interests must come first, and
- that the government was
  - consulting on how child abuse inquiries should be set up,
  - producing fresh guidance on the handling of child abuse cases and
  - that the issue of family courts was under review.

He said:

> 'I don't think we are going to see any major issues of principle in handling child abuse come up in the future. There will still be cases. This is a high risk game and there will be disasters. But I suspect they will be individual failures rather than something very fundamental.'

This is included as an appropriate challenge to our mind sets when we think we have identified and resolved all the key issues only to be met by a future case where, sadly, history is repeated, as will be evident from the following public inquiries in the 1980s and 90s, and more recent, current-day child deaths, eg Victoria Climbié, Baby P, and Kyra Ishaq.

Case study—1984: Heidi Koseda

Heidi Koseda, aged four years, was starved to death in a cupboard in a locked room by her stepfather and mother. A health visitor, despite having made 16 attempts to see Heidi at her home, never managed to actually see her in person.

Case study—1986: Kimberley Carlile

Kimberley Carlile, aged four years, was starved and beaten to death by her stepfather, Nigel Hall, and her mother. The Inquiry found that her death was avoidable and criticized social work and health staff.

Case study—1987: Doreen Mason

Doreen Mason, aged 16 months, who, despite being on the at risk register from birth, died from neglect having been beaten, burnt, and her leg fractured and received no treatment for her injuries. Her mother, Christine Mason, and her boyfriend, Roy Aston, were convicted of manslaughter and cruelty.

Case study—1992: Leanne White

Leanne White, aged three years, was beaten to death by her stepfather, Colin Sleate, who had inflicted over 100 injuries including repeated blows to the stomach that resulted in internal bleeding. Sleate was convicted of murder and her mother, Tina White, of manslaughter. The Inquiry considered that, if Social Services had responded appropriately to the concerns of her grandparents and neighbours, her death would have been preventable.

Case study—1994: Rikki Neave

Rikki Neave, aged six years, with two of his sisters, was beaten and burnt by his mother Ruth Neave, a drug addict. Despite his mother asking several social workers to take Rikki into care, he was left in her custody and found strangled in a wood.

Case study—1999: Chelsea Brown

Chelsea Brown, aged two years, was beaten to death by her father, Robert Brown, who had a history of violence against children. Despite numerous visits by her social worker and a paediatrician who examined her and found deliberately-inflicted injuries, no referral to police or case conference was held. Her father was convicted of murder and her mother of child cruelty.

This is just a snapshot from a number of inquiries, with over 70 since the introduction of the Children Act 1948. (See Hopkins (2007), 'What have we learned? Child death scandals since 1944', *Community Care*, 11 January, and Batty (2003), 'Catalogue of cruelty', *Society Guardian*, 27 January.)

As can be seen from the chronology of these highlighted public inquiries, the identification of key issues is essential, although only a part of the process; necessary safeguards have to be adopted, implemented, and adequately resourced to reduce the risk of similar circumstances reoccurring in the future. It would be impossible to totally eliminate the risk, as several of the contributing factors are outside of everyone but the perpetrator's control; the need for robust prevention and risk identification initiatives must be a priority.

Even though these inquiries were in relation to the deaths of the children, there were also far reaching implications for child protection and child abuse investigation that are inextricably linked. Children do not always die from abuse, but the investigative environment is identical in many ways, with only a fine line between survival and death distinguishing the two. Although this book's focus is on child homicide and suspicious deaths, it will, out of necessity, also include aspects of child abuse investigation, as unlawful child death is at the end of the spectrum of child abuse per se.

1.4.2 **The Children Act 1989**

This legislation, whilst not directly applicable to child deaths, as it is preventative legislation to protect and safeguard children, was a key milestone in child protection that is still central to that area today. It is clearly applicable and relevant for surviving siblings and future children of child homicide perpetrators. Its basis for introduction grew out of the startling findings from the above enquiries and also the 1988 *Cleveland Inquiry Report* by Dame Butler-Sloss, an inquiry into a complex child abuse investigation. A number of children had been taken into care in questionable circumstances, with many of their parents having been accused of child abuse, where a particular medical examination was utilized to detect sexual abuse. The issues that arose during the inquiry including the diagnosis of sexual abuse, the interviewing of children, and consideration of their views, as well as communication between different agencies, were considered in relation to proposed new legislation before Parliament and ultimately informed the 1989 Children Act.

The Children Act 1989 provided a primary legislative framework in relation to the prevention and investigation of child abuse and included the following key sections:

- **Section 17**—Identifies a child in need and the actions to be taken in relation to safeguarding and promoting their welfare.
- **Section 27**—Outlines the specific duty for services to co-operate in the interests of the child in need.

- **Section 44**—Emergency protection orders.
- **Section 46**—Police protection powers where otherwise a child is likely to suffer significant harm.
- **Section 47**—Identifies action to be taken if a child is suffering or is likely to suffer significant harm.
- **Section 53**—In relation to sections 17 and 47 emphasizes the need to take into account the child's wishes in relation to any suggested action to be taken in relation to them.

These procedures and legislation are important for child homicide and suspicious death investigations as in many cases the deceased child will have siblings. These may be witnesses, but in addition be subject to actions in relation to the above procedures. The two avenues of enquiry, childhood death and child protection procedures, as previously explained, will invariably run in parallel and often be inextricably linked.

1.4.3 **Child death milestones**

There then followed a number of milestones that all impacted in some way on the investigation of childhood death. They challenged society's perception regarding the extent and nature of the issues affecting it, including the inescapable fact that parents and carers were capable of killing children in their care. These milestones included the following:

Case study—1991: Beverley Allitt: 'The Angel of Death'

Between 21 February and 22 April 1991, a state-enrolled nurse at a Lincolnshire hospital, Beverley Allitt, murdered four children and injured nine children, whose ages ranged from seven weeks up to 11 years. She had killed the children by injecting them with potassium chloride or insulin. The term 'Munchausen syndrome by proxy' was a condition identified by Professor Sir Roy Meadow in 1977 as a form of child abuse and which describes the behaviour of this serial killer, who, whilst in a position of responsibility, betrayed that trust by killing or injuring children in her care. The many newspaper headlines describing her as 'the angel of death' perhaps illustrate the difficulty of society in accepting how a professional dedicated to saving lives could in reality be capable of destroying lives.

On another level, this level of unbelief that allowed Beverley Allitt to go undetected for some time is mirrored where friends and family do not believe that a family member would be capable of killing a child. There is a huge psychological barrier to be overcome, often requiring considerable evidence, before many people will accept the possibility that people do unlawfully kill children—and that the image of an evil monster is not the only one portrayed. (At the current time the term 'fabricated or induced illness' is the preferred term to describe this offending behaviour and is covered in Chapter 6.)

Case study—1991: The 'Back to sleep campaign'

In the same year, 1991, the Department of Health's 'Back to sleep campaign' is credited with saving the lives of thousands of babies, who, prior to the campaign's launch, may have become victims of what was referred to at that time as 'cot death'—the sudden and unexplained death of a child, usually under the age of a year, and more commonly under six months.

The simple messages of the campaign in relation to the best way for your baby to sleep included:

- Lie your baby on his or her back.
- Use layers of sheets and blankets rather than a duvet.
- The best place is in a cot next to your bed.
- Cover just to the shoulders.
- Feet just touching the foot of the cot.
- Do not use a pillow.
- Offer a dummy.

This advice continues to be advocated and has resulted in the reduction in child deaths, continuing at the improved level. In this chronology where invariably the picture is very bleak and challenging, this is a 'good news' story that continues to have a positive impact on the rates of childhood death.

Case study—1986–1994: Professor David Southall: Covert Video Recordings of Life-threatening Child Abuse

Between 1986 and 1994, at hospitals in North Staffordshire and London, Professor Southall ran a research project in which children aged between two and 44 months' old, considered to be at risk from their parents, were covertly observed whilst in hospital. The patients were covertly monitored by hospital staff to establish the truth of the medical symptoms reported by their parents. Of the 39 children who were covertly observed, 33 were seen on camera to be intentionally suffocated, poisoned, or seriously assaulted (including a deliberate fracture) and this led to their parents being prosecuted for criminal offences. Also of interest is that the 39 patients undergoing covert surveillance had 41 siblings, 12 of whom had died suddenly and unexpectedly, 11 of which deaths had been classified as sudden infant death syndrome. However, following the surveillance, four parents admitted to suffocating eight of these siblings and another sibling was found to have been deliberately poisoned with salt. The project, despite its findings and staggering results, subsequently received some criticism from parents and other interested parties of the way it was managed, the methods it utilized, and in relation to issues of confidentiality.

Issues from this era still reverberate, with Professor David Southall continuing to be the subject of a campaign by parents who felt they were wrongly accused of child abuse wanting Professor Southall to be disciplined by the General Medical Council (GMC), charged with child abuse related offences in relation to the treatment of their children whilst in hospital under his care, and struck off the medical register. This campaign by the parents and other interested parties continues to this day and has impacted not only on their lives and their children's lives, but also on Professor Southall, who maintains his position that everything he did was, in his belief, in the best interests of the children in question. He is also limited in answering his critics, as much of the information on which decisions were made is confidential Family Court material that is against the law for him to disclose. It has also had a negative impact over the last 20 years on other paediatricians and medical experts' willingness to give evidence in similar cases, in view of the sensationalized media coverage that the ongoing actions have sometimes generated.

Case study—1997: Louise Woodward case in the USA and 'shaken baby syndrome'

1997 was the year that saw the issue of shaken baby syndrome come to the public notice with the prosecution of an English nanny, Louise Woodward, who was working in Boston and accused of killing the baby in her care by fatally shaking him. The case received considerable international media coverage and there was widespread support for Louise Woodward from friends and family, who did not accept that she was responsible for inflicting the fatal injuries referred to as 'the triad'. They, like the defence medical experts, believed there was an alternative causation for the injuries. Louise Woodward was convicted of killing the child in her care, Matthew Eappen, aged eight months. The original conviction of second degree murder was reduced on appeal to involuntary manslaughter.

There is still some debate over the causation of the triad of injuries, comprising retinal haemorrhages (bleeding into the linings of the eye), subdural haemorrhages (bleeding beneath the dural membrane covering the brain), and encephalopathy (damage to the brain affecting function) which, in the absence of any other evidence for an alternative plausible explanation, would be considered indicative of a non-accidental head injury. The issues surrounding 'shaken baby syndrome' continue to reverberate in the criminal justice and family court arenas. It is interesting to note that, whilst several still remember the name of the defendant, Louise Woodward, far fewer remember the name of the eight-month-old victim, Matty Eappen.

Case study—1991–2000: The legacy of Victoria Climbié

In 1998, for a better education, Victoria was flown from the Ivory Coast to France and then England where she lived for 11 months in the care of a great aunt and her boyfriend. On 25 February 2000, Victoria died in hospital from hypothermia, having suffered systematic abuse, where the perpetrator's belief in spirit possession was a factor, and at the time of her death she had 128 separate injuries.

On 12 January 2001, Victoria's carers were convicted of her murder, and on 20 April 2001 an Independent Inquiry was set up under the leadership of Lord Laming.

This was a real watershed case illustrating that, despite a considerable number of public inquiries, and changes in legislation and procedures, it was sadly still possible for history to repeat itself and for a child to die in horrific circumstances, where those who had the responsibility for safeguarding them failed in areas that had been highlighted in the Maria Colwell case of 1973.

The *Victoria Climbié Inquiry Report* was published in January 2003, and concluded that there had been 'a gross failure of the system' by the police, Social Services, and the health service. There were a total of 108 recommendations including a key one for the police, Recommendation Number 97, which stated:

> Chief Constables must ensure that the investigation of crime against children is as important as the investigation of any other form of serious crime. Any suggestion that child protection policing is of a lower status than other forms of policing must be eradicated.

This again illustrates the inseparability of child homicide and child abuse, which are just different points on the child abuse continuum.

1.4.4 High profile court cases reported miscarriages of justice—Clark, Cannings, and Patel (2003)

In 2003 there were successful Appeal Court judgments in the cases of Sally Clark and Angela Cannings, and a 'not guilty' verdict in the related trial of Trupti Patel. All three woman had more than one of their own children die in their care and been charged with their murder.

Case study—Sally Clark

Sally Clark, who had two children die, was convicted in 1999 of their murders but in a second Court of Appeal case hearing in 2003 had her conviction quashed, as the Court felt the conviction was unsafe. The two main issues in the second appeal centred on the discovery of previously undisclosed results of post mortem samples that suggested one of the deaths may have been from natural causes. The second was in relation to a statistic extrapolated by Professor Sir Roy Meadow from a 'Confidential Enquiry into

Sudden Death in Infancy' (CESDI) study entitled *Sudden Unexpected Deaths in Infancy* (SUDI), that made him come to the conclusion that the chances of two infant deaths within such a family being sudden infant death syndrome (SIDS) would be one in 73 million. The Court of Appeal thought that this statistic had misled the jury, although neither the prosecution nor the defence had suggested the deaths were as a result of SIDS. Injuries had been discovered on both children, some that were suggested to be the result of shaking and asphyxiation, and the prosecution had also suggested a number of similarities between the two deaths.

Case study—Angela Cannings

Angela Cannings had three children die and a fourth child suffer from an apparent life threatening event (ALTE). She was convicted in 2002 of two counts of murder in relation to two of the children's deaths. Her conviction was quashed in 2003 as the Appeal Court concluded that it was also unsafe. The Crown's case was that she had smothered her children resulting in either death or an ALTE. The defence case was that all the deaths were as a result of SIDS.

Case study—Trupti Patel

Trupti Patel, who had three children die and a fourth suffer from an ALTE, was charged in relation to their deaths, but after a six-week trial, the jury returned verdicts of 'not guilty'. There was significant media coverage of these three cases and some headlines even suggested 'Prosecution of mothers for baby deaths "will cease"'.

Personal criticisms of the eminent paediatricians Professor Sir Roy Meadow and Professor David Southall, including official complaints to the GMC in relation to the Sally Clark case, saw a change in the way medical experts were viewed and portrayed in the media. This often negative portrayal by the media became more pronounced over the following years and resulted in a detrimental impact on medical experts' willingness to give evidence at court in relation to child abuse and homicide cases.

At one stage both Professor Sir Roy Meadow and Professor David Southall were found guilty of serious professional misconduct and had their names erased from the register by the GMC. However, after many years and legal battles including in the Court of Appeal, both had the GMC's findings reversed and were reinstated to the register. Their cases were a protracted and complex process that it is not appropriate to cover in detail here, but they are succinctly explained in 'The Trouble with Paediatricians' by Catherine Williams (2010) in *Medical Law Review* (details in 'Further information and reading' at the end of this chapter).

Further information and reading

For free access to legal judgments like the Appeal Court cases cited go to
<http://www.bailii.org>, the website for the British and Irish Legal Information
Institute.

1.4.5 **Which of you did it? (2003)**

In 2003, following on from a seminar of the same title in 2000, the NSPCC,
working with partner agencies, highlighted several issues related to the investigation of child death, including the 'Which of you did it?' scenario. This scenario related to the situation where a child had been unlawfully killed in a
domestic environment and there were a limited number of suspects who could
have been responsible for the death, usually the parents. However, neither
parent would admit responsibility or apportion blame. Where both had previously been charged jointly with an offence of homicide, the prosecutions failed
because of an Appeal Court judgment in the case of *R v Lane and Lane* (1987) 82
Cr App R 5. This judgment held that, in the 'Which of you did it?' scenario, if
both suspects were charged, the circumstances could be such that it could result
in the unfair conviction of an innocent person if there was uncertainty as to
who was present and responsible for the fatal injuries. This had meant that
there were cases where there was no dispute that a child had been unlawfully
killed, but no one was prosecuted for the offence, albeit the Family Court may
have taken action in relation to surviving siblings and future children born to
the parents. The published findings of this multi-agency group advocated a new
offence to cater for this lacuna in the law.

This theme was continued in April 2003 with the Law Commission (Law
Com. No. 279), *Children: Their Non-accidental Death or Serious Injury (Criminal
Trials). A Consultative Report*, and in September 2003 with the Law Commission
(Law Com. No. 282) report of the same title with their recommendations.

1.4.6 **Reports and Legislation—(2003/4)**

Following on from the previously mentioned *Victoria Climbié Inquiry Report*
published in 2003, there were a number of additional relevant documents and
legislation published that added to the landscape of child death investigation
and child protection. These included:

- A Green Paper—*Every Child Matters*—the government's response to the *Victoria
  Climbié Inquiry Report* (8 September 2003).
- The *Bichard Inquiry Report* (2004)—in relation to managing intelligence and
  sharing information following the murders in Soham of two schoolgirls,
  Holly Wells and Jessica Chapman, by Ian Huntley. The Inquiry examined the
  problems of not sharing information, managing intelligence, and poor

communication which wrongly allowed Ian Huntley to be employed in a post at a school.

- Legislation—The Children Act 2004—this would underpin the expectations of *Every Child Matters*, placing a statutory duty on local authorities and partner agencies to co-operate to improve the well being of children. Section 11 was central to this, placing a duty on both organizations and individuals to ensure functions are discharged with regard to the need to safeguard and promote the welfare of children.

1.4.7 Research—one in ten cot deaths may be murder or child neglect (2004)

In this highly emotive environment, with reported 'miscarriages of justice' and criticism of medical experts, two researchers, Dr Sarah Levene and Dr Christopher Bacon, from FSID, published an article in the journal *Archives of Disease in Childhood* suggesting that one in ten cot deaths may be murder or child neglect. This finding suggested that up to 30 to 40 cot deaths a year could in fact be covert homicides and accepted the fact that sometimes parents do kill their children. These findings are supported by other research (Vaughan and Kautt, 2009).

1.4.8 Sudden unexpected death in infancy—the report of a working group chaired by The Baroness Helena Kennedy QC (September 2004)

This seminal report was a multi-agency protocol for the care and investigation of sudden unexpected deaths in infancy. The eminent group of professionals who produced it was convened by The Royal College of Pathologists and The Royal College of Paediatrics and Child Health, initiated as a response to the acquittal of Sally Clark in January 2003. Members of the working group, in addition to representatives from the two colleges, also included representatives from FSID, the police, coroners, Department of Health, and Social Services. The multi-agency protocol advocated by this report has become the basis for current guidance on the investigation of sudden unexpected death in infancy and childhood.

1.4.9 The Attorney General's Review (2004)

Following the successful appeal of Angela Cannings, the Attorney General ordered a review of 297 cases from the previous ten years where children under two had died and a person had been convicted in relation to their death, especially where the conviction relied almost entirely on medical experts' evidence. Of the 297 cases reviewed, 28 were considered for referral to the Criminal Cases Review Commission and, where appropriate, referred to the Court of Appeal.

One of only two people to have their conviction for killing their children quashed after successful appeals as a result of this review was Donna Anthony who was convicted in 1998 in relation to the deaths of two of her children and was released from prison in 2005. It is interesting to see the comments from the Appeal Court judgment (*R v Anthony* [2005] EWCA Crim 952 (11 April 2005)) shown below:

> As the summary of events demonstrates, the conviction did not depend exclusively, or almost exclusively, on a disagreement between distinguished and reputable experts. There was indeed cogent and disturbing evidence, additional to the expert medical evidence, which supported the allegations made against the appellant and her own account of events was inconsistent and at times self-contradictory. (para.76)
>
> Notwithstanding the presence of disturbing features about the appellant's behaviour and her account of events, we have concluded that if the evidence available in the unchallenged form in which it is available to us had been available at trial, the decision of the jury might well have been different, and, in any event, if the judgment of the Court in *Cannings* had been available to the judge he would have ensured that the evidence given by the experts would have taken a different route, and would inevitably have summed the case up differently. In these circumstances, we are persuaded that the convictions are unsafe and must be quashed. (para. 97)

1.4.10 The Domestic Violence, Crime and Victims Act 2004

On 21 March 2005, section 5 of the above Act came into force, creating the new offence of 'Causing or allowing the death of a child or vulnerable adult'. This was in response to the issues raised in the NSPCC *Which of you did it?* report published in 2003, along with the Law Commission reports in the same year. This legislation is discussed in more detail in Chapter 3. The new offence recognized the special relationship and responsibility that carers and household members had to their children, introducing special procedural measures in support of this. In specific circumstances, it allowed the prosecution of both the person suspected of 'causing' the unlawful death of a child, together with any person who recognized that there was a risk of significant harm to a child, failed to take reasonable steps to protect the child from the risk, and the child died from an unlawful act in circumstances that they should have reasonably foreseen, and so 'allowed' the death to occur.

1.4.11 Appeal Court cases —issue of 'shaken baby syndrome' and 'the triad' (2005)

The Appeal Court ruling in the combined cases of *R v Harris, Rock, Cherry, and Faulder* examined in detail the medical evidence relating to the triad of injuries and, in particular, a defence theory for their causation described as the 'unified hypothesis theory'—Geddes et al, 2003—which suggested that the injuries of the triad could be caused by a severe lack of oxygen which led to brain swelling rather than inflicted trauma. This theory, that in the court proceedings was accepted to be only a hypothesis by Dr Geddes, was not endorsed by the Court of Appeal which stated (para. 69):

> In our judgement, it follows that that the unified hypothesis can no longer be regarded as a credible or alternative cause of the triad of injuries.

However, whilst accepting that the triad did exist, the conclusion regarding future prosecutions was that it would be considered unlikely to mount a prosecution based solely on the presence of the triad of injuries without any other supporting evidence. Guidance was also given in relation to medical expert evidence and in the Criminal Procedure Rules regarding case management.

1.4.12 Working Together to Safeguard Children (2006, superseded) (2010)

This multi-agency guidance, deriving its statutory basis for several chapters from the Children Acts of 1989 and 2004, included Chapters 7 and 8 which relate directly to child deaths. **Chapter 7** outlines two related child death review processes that became compulsory on 1 April 2008 and were to be followed when a child died in the Local Safeguarding Children Board's area. The first process relates to a rapid response by a group of key professionals who come together for the purpose of enquiring into and evaluating each unexpected death of a child. The second involves an overview of all child deaths in the area and is undertaken by a multi-agency Child Death Overview Panel (CDOP).

Chapter 8 related to Serious Case Reviews—a multi-agency review on lessons to be learned where abuse or neglect of a child is known or suspected and either the child has died or the child has been seriously harmed, and there is cause for concern as to the way in which the authority, their Board partners, or other relevant persons have worked together to safeguard the child. The guidance was updated in 2010.

1.4.13 The death of Baby Peter Connelly (2007–2009)

Peter Connelly, aged 17 months, who had been on the child protection register for eight months, was unlawfully killed in August 2007 and found to have sustained over 50 injuries including a broken back. This death received unprecedented publicity and occurred in Haringey, London, the same area as the death of Victoria Climbié in 2000, with several of the same issues including communication, training, and the way society perceives children being identified again. The child's mother, Tracey Connelly, her boyfriend, Steven Barker, and his brother, Jason Owen, were all convicted in 2009 of 'Causing or allowing the death of a child or vulnerable adult' receiving indeterminate sentences.

Haringey Council's leader and a cabinet member resigned whilst the Director of Children's services was dismissed in the aftermath of public scrutiny and uproar. (In August 2011, the Supreme Court upheld an earlier Appeal Court judgment that they had been unfairly dismissed.)

1.4.14 The Protection of Children in England: A Progress Report (2009)

In 2009, following on from the death of Peter Connolly, Lord Laming, who had conducted the Victoria Climbié Inquiry, was asked to prepare a progress report into the protection of children in England. His report, *The Protection of Children in England: A Progress Report*, was published in March 2009, and one quote in particular perhaps provides an explanation as to why the lessons identified in the Maria Colwell Inquiry in 1973 were tragically repeating themselves.

He stated that policies, procedures, and structures are important 'but more so the robust and consistent implementation of these policies and procedures which keeps children and young people safe'.

He also stated that 'managers must lead by example by taking a personal and visible interest in frontline delivery'.

These statements are not, in my view, limited to child protection but also are equally valid to all those tasked with investigating child homicides and suspicious deaths, when sadly those child protection policies, procedures, and structures have failed. They have the duty and responsibility of implementing the child death policies and procedures to establish the circumstances of the death and, if any criminal offences are disclosed, establishing who was responsible. Investigations will be far more effective when managers, the investigating officers, and especially the Senior Investigating Officer (SIO) lead by example, taking a personal and visible interest in frontline delivery and a determination to succeed that the death of any child deserves. The responsibility also extends further as the consequences for other siblings or children yet to be born, of an inadequate or ineffective investigation, are potentially catastrophic.

1.4.15 Further issues with 'the triad'—appeals of *R v Henderson and others* (2010)

The issue of the triad and expert medical evidence again became the focus of a number of appeals that were heard together. One of these cases concerned Keran Henderson who was convicted in 2007 of the manslaughter of Maeve Sheppard, aged 11 months. Like the Louise Woodward case ten years earlier, there was considerable media coverage of the support she was receiving from her friends and family who just could not accept that she would be capable of inflicting the fatal injuries that resulted in the death of Maeve. However, the Court of Appeal upheld the conviction and commented unfavourably on the conduct of some of the defence medical experts. These Appeal Court cases are included in this chronology as they:

- Highlight the circular way in which history can repeat itself;
- Demonstrate the reliance placed on expert medical evidence;
- Illustrate the psychological impact of these types of cases;
- Reveal the varying levels of acceptance of the possible causes of death; and
- Show the relevance of the surrounding circumstances in child deaths.

There are also lessons to be learned by both the prosecution and defence in the management of these cases for future trials: we must learn from history and be open to alternative explanations, recognizing that all the genuine evidential jigsaw pieces do fit into the true picture.

1.5 Investigative features—and how they differ from other homicide investigations

Having explained the evolving history of childhood death investigation, this section will consider how there are a number of features which are sometimes unique and not apparent in other homicide investigations. However, whilst there will be many aspects of the investigation that will be the same and be covered in the standard guidance in the ACPO *Murder Investigation Manual* (MIM), this book will seek to identify those areas where child homicide investigation presents unique or different challenges and develop the guidance to cater for these investigative challenges. However, the 'five building block principles' will continue to underpin the investigative processes.

KEY POINTS

The Five Building Block Principles of Investigations

- Preservation of life;
- Preserve scenes;
- Secure evidence;
- Identify victim/witnesses, and;
- Identify suspects.

1.5.1 Investigative differentials

The investigative process and how it sometimes differs from other homicide investigations will be examined in detail in subsequent chapters, and in particular Chapters 4, 5, and 6. However, it will be useful here in a checklist to just identify from the outset several areas for future consideration where the investigation of child homicide is different to that of adult homicides.

Checklist—Key areas for consideration where child homicide investigations differ from adult homicides

1. **Less attributable as a homicide from outset**—Where the initial circumstances show no obvious cause of death being immediately apparent or even after post-mortem.

2. **Hidden nature of child homicide**—Due to the vulnerability of very young children it is possible to obscure the cause of death and the circumstances, eg asphyxiation in young children as tell tale signs visible in adult cases are sometimes absent.

3. **Sensitive management**—Due to the tragic nature of child death and period of uncertainty in establishing cause of death and circumstances.

4. **Specialist knowledge**—Serious crime area in an unique investigative environment.

5. **Natural death v crime?**—This is not always obvious from the outset and may take some time to establish.

6. **Paediatric pathologist**—Specialized post-mortem procedures.

7. **Dealing with and access to body**—Issues of parents handling the deceased child if any suspicions in relation to circumstances and cause of death that would not arise in adult cases.

8. **Faith and child rearing practices**—For example, belief in spirit possession, bed sharing practices.

9. **Highly emotional nature of child deaths**.

10. **Risk for siblings if child is unlawfully killed by carer.**

11. **Multi-agency response**—This is essential and advantageous but there can be issues in relation to conflicting priorities, sharing of information, and communication.

12. **Suspect within the family**—This can present real issues for family liaison strategy.

13. **Reliance on experts**—Particularly medical experts where limited witnesses to circumstances surrounding the death, eg inflicted injury versus accidental.

14. **Special offences**—Serious crime area with criminal offences relating solely to children.

15. **Parallel proceedings in the Criminal and Family Courts**—May create issues, eg in relation to disclosure and access to siblings who may be witnesses.

16. **Limited forensic opportunities**—For example, closed circuit television (CCTV) or DNA comparisons that are so useful in adult homicide cases but are sometimes of limited value when a family member is responsible for the death.

17. **Media reporting**—Can impact on the investigation, eg timing of enquiries, reluctance of medical experts to give evidence.

As the book progresses other differences may become evident but these examples are included to stimulate consideration of these identified areas and where this differential may impact on the investigation. These specific areas will be examined in more detail in subsequent chapters.

1.5.2 **Investigative perceptions**

A useful way to perhaps consider the various perceptions of the different groups of people impacted by childhood death is to answer the following question.

Question: Rank in order of seriousness the following offences:

(a) A gang related murder.
(b) A domestic murder, eg husband kills his wife.
(c) A child murdered by their carer.
(d) A child murdered by a stranger.
(e) A terrorist-related murder.
(f) A rape or serious sexual assault of a child.
(g) A cat thrown into a wheelie bin.
(h) A dog kicked by its owner.

But then consider how they may be ranked by different groups who would consider the offences from varying perspectives. Consider the following groups:

---

1. Police
2. Public
3. Partner Agencies
4. Press
5. Parents and family
6. Judicial system including CPS, lawyers, barristers, and judiciary

---

What factors would be appropriate to consider when trying to determine the respective ranking results for each group to the question?

No definitive answer will be given to the question but just completing the exercise will hopefully illustrate yet another facet of childhood death investigation and the environment in which investigations are conducted. A few comments may assist with the exercise and show how the question may be answered by the different groups.

KEY POINTS TO CONSIDER WHEN ANSWERING THE QUESTION

- What level of resources do the police deploy to the respective investigations?
- What level of media coverage do the respective offences receive?
- What sentences do the respective perpetrators receive when convicted?
- Is the sentence commensurate with the level of seriousness?
- How highly is the life of a child victim valued and is that reflected in the sentences received?
- What emphasis should be placed on the behaviour and motivation of the offender?
- Is there more empathy shown to people who kill their own children as opposed to strangers who kill a child?
- What place should the special position of responsibility a parent has for their child have in this process?
- Should the vulnerability of the victim be a factor?
- Does the fact that older victims have more of a 'life story' and an 'identity' affect how their loss is perceived?
- Should a distinction be drawn between a parent who, under a number of stressors, 'cracks' and fatally assaults their child compared to someone who derives a sadistic pleasure from inflicting injuries on a child?
- Are animals viewed in a similar way to children or do they receive preferential consideration?
- Where is the focus when cases are reported—is it on the victim or someone else, eg parents?

In concluding this chapter, perhaps the answer to where child homicide ranks on the seriousness rankings could incorporate features from the following:

- Each case is unique and, although there may be common themes, each should be considered on a case by case basis;
- Different groups may have a different perspective that will affect their response to childhood death; and
- There may be no definitive answer as to whether or not a child murder is the most serious offence but, even if child homicide is not considered the most serious, it could still be argued undoubtedly that it was equally as serious and, therefore, deserved a similar priority and allocation of resources, whether human or physical, to investigate it.

KEY POINT

It is essential to remember and emphasize that any investigation into a childhood death involves professionals from many different agencies who all have distinct roles but who complement each other by working together to establish how and why the child died, most crucially by sharing information and professional knowledge.

The majority of childhood deaths will not result in criminal proceedings as there will be other natural and medical explanations for the deaths, which are equally as important outcomes, eg establishing a natural cause of death from a health perspective or other factors for social care when considering options in relation to any siblings and Family Court proceedings.

Childhood death investigation operates in a very challenging and thought pro-voking environment—one that needs very careful consideration, sensitivity, management, and professional knowledge-based judgements that hopefully this book will help inform.

This brief history of childhood death, and consideration of how it differs from other forms of homicide investigation, provides the background and sign-posts key areas for the subsequent chapters that will develop some of these issues in more detail. It will examine the continuum of child death investiga-tion from the non-suspicious sudden unexpected death in infancy (SUDI), through suspicious child deaths to child homicide at the other end of the spec-trum. These chapters will also consider legislation and guidance, case manage-ment, and future considerations.

Further information and reading

ACPO (2006), *Murder Investigation Manual* (London: NPIA).

A Local Authority v S [2009] EWHC 2115 (Fam) (8 May 2009).

Children Act 1989 (London: HMSO).

Children Act 2004 (London: HMSO).

HM Government (2010), *Working Together to Safeguard Children. A guide to inter-agency working to safeguard and promote the welfare of children* (Nottingham: DCSF Publications).

Kennedy, H (2004), *Sudden Unexpected Death in Infancy. The report of a working group convened by The Royal College of Pathologists and The Royal College of Paediatrics and Child Health* (London: The Royal College of Pathologists and The Royal College of Paediatrics and Child Health).

Laming, Lord H (2003), *The Victoria Climbié Inquiry. Report of an Inquiry by Lord Laming*, Cm 5730 (London: The Stationery Office).

Levene, S, and Bacon, C (2004), 'Sudden unexpected death and covert homicide in infancy', *Archives of Disease in Childhood*, 89, 443–447.

R v Anthony [2005] EWCA Crim 952 (11 April 2005).

R v Angela Cannings [2004] EWCA Crim 01 (19 January 2004).

R v Sally Clark [2003] EWCA Crim 1020 (11 April 2003).

R v Harris, Rock, Cherry, and Faulder [2005] EWCA Crim 1980 (21 July 2005).

R v Henderson, Butler, and Oyediran [2010]. EWCA Crim 1269 (17 June 2010).

Smith, K, Coleman, K, Eder, S, and Hall, P (2011), *Home Office Statistical Bulletin. Homicides, Firearm Offences and Intimate Violence 2009/10*.

Supplementary Volume 2 to Crime in England and Wales 2009/10 (Home Office: London).

Southall, P, Plunkett, C, Banks, M, Falkov, A, and Samuels, M (1997), 'Covert Video Recordings of Life-threatening Child Abuse: Lessons for Child Protection', *Paediatrics*, 100(5), 735–760.

Vaughan, J, and Kautt, P (2009), 'Infant death Investigations Following High-Profile Unsafe Rulings: Throwing Out the Baby with the Bath Water?', *Policing*, 3(1), 89–99.

Williams, C (2010), 'The Trouble with Paediatricians', *Medical Law Review*, 18(3).

NOTES

NOTES

NOTES

The Investigative Focus and Mindset in Childhood Death

2.1 **Introduction**

Having examined in the first chapter the many significant milestones in the history and development of childhood death investigation and highlighted how the investigation of childhood death can be so different from other homicides, this chapter will concentrate on the investigative focus for all sudden and unexpected childhood deaths.

2.2 **The diagnostic and investigative continuum**

Sudden and unexpected deaths in childhood can be usefully considered as falling into three broad groups that overlay a diagnostic and investigative continuum extending from a natural death at one end of the continuum to an un-natural death, featuring criminal intent and homicide, at the opposite end. Two closely-related terms in relation to childhood death—SUDI and SUDC—will be regularly mentioned so it is useful to define them at this early stage.

Definition of 'Sudden and Unexpected Death of an Infant (SUDI) or Child (SUDC)'

Unexpected death is defined as the death of an infant (under one year) or child (less than 18 years old) which:

- Was not anticipated as a significant possibility, eg 24 hours before the death; or
- Where there was a similarly unexpected collapse or incident leading to or precipitating the events which led to the death.

KEY POINTS

The three broad investigative groups:

- SUDI/SUDC—no concerning factors and includes SIDS, natural, or medical causes.
- SUDI/SUDC—suspicious child deaths that may feature criminal offences other than the four homicide offences below.
- Homicide—feature criminal offences of murder, manslaughter, infanticide, and familial homicide.

Each of these groups will be considered in more detail in their respective chapters. It is not always clear from the outset which of the broad groups the deaths falls in to, although an initial view, eg SIDS, may subsequently be found to be correct. However, and this is a key factor, the initial view may be incorrect and the reality may be that it falls somewhere else on the continuum. Inappropriate actions based on an incorrect assessment, however well founded at that time, may lead to essential evidence being lost and justice denied for the parties affected.

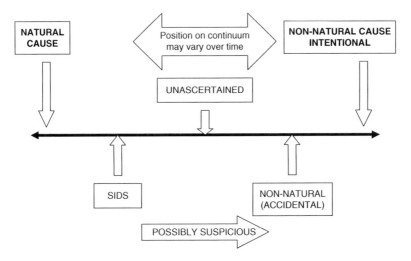

Figure 2.1 Diagnostic and investigative continuum
Based on model by Dr Chris Wright, 2011

Case study

A death initially considered as a very 'straightforward' SIDS, and dealt with as such, resulted in the coroner releasing the body to the undertakers. Toxicology sample results were then received by the pathologist and unusual levels of a controlled drug discovered in the child. Further investigation revealed that the deceased child had been poisoned and that a surviving sibling had also been poisoned. Their mother was convicted of causing the death of the child and poisoning the sibling.

KEY POINT

No SUDI/SUDC should ever be considered as 'straightforward'; that may be one of the investigative hypotheses with a probable cause of death, but it is essential to keep an open mind in the search for the truth of what has actually occurred.

It is important to note that in child deaths there is understandably an eagerness to release the body to the family as soon as possible. Although this is a decision for the coroner, it is imperative that police and others involved in the investigation provide and update any information that will have a bearing on this decision. Likewise, an initially suspicious death may, after a thorough investigation, be ascertained to be non-suspicious. The classification of 'suspicious death' and factors associated with it will be dealt with in Chapter 5.

Case study

Paramedics who examined a young baby at its home considered that the baby had been dead for some period of time, had unusual bruising with blood near its mouth and, because in addition the parents (who were drug addicts) had provided apparently inconsistent accounts, they considered the death so suspicious that they left the body in situ. The police dealt with the death as suspicious and both parents were arrested on suspicion of murder. The post mortem results subsequently revealed that the child had died from an infection and no criminal offences were disclosed.

As previously explained, these childhood deaths cover a complex and involved continuum of causation from natural causes all the way through suspicious deaths to intentional non-natural causes that incorporate homicide.

KEY POINT

The majority of SUDI will NOT be the consequence of a criminal act but will be one of the most devastating events that any parent or family may experience. Whilst retaining an open mind, those tasked with investigating the death have to balance the rights of the deceased child with those of the parents, surviving siblings, and family. This is why these investigations are probably some of the most difficult deaths to investigate.

The unique challenge faced is that it is invariably some time before the position on this continuum is established and so the investigative strategy has to cater for this unknown, and incorporate contingencies for changes in information bearing on the cause and circumstances of death. Managing the investigation in this problematic area of the unknown can be assisted by adopting the correct investigative focus and mindset. Invariably it will result in all investigations, irrespective of where they eventually feature on the continuum, being inextricably linked in method and content from the outset, but adapted on a flexible case-by-case basis as the investigation progresses. Professional judgement and experience will also play a key part in the implementation of investigative strategies.

2.3 **The investigative focus**

Above the main doors of the Central Criminal Court (the 'Old Bailey'), City of London, inscribed in the stonework and in the shadow of the woman holding the Scales of Justice are the words:

Defend the children of the poor and punish the wrongdoer

A child-focused investigation with the deceased child and any siblings at the forefront, with adverse outcomes hopefully only impacting on those found guilty of wrongdoing, has to be the goal everyone involved strives for. Keeping the deceased child as the central and primary focus of the investigation together with any siblings, but with an empathetic secondary, but still essential focus, on the parents and family will help in the investigative decision-making process. Some notorious cases highlight the pitfalls of reversing this focus and putting the parents/carers at the centre, eg Baby Peter Connelly and Kyra Ishaq. In both cases, the children, Peter and Kyra, were of secondary consideration in many areas until sadly they became the focus of homicide inquiries.

Achieving this objective is supported by utilizing consistent investigative parameters for all investigations. Any childhood death investigation should be a **search for the truth**, an investigation to answer the following four questions.

Four key questions in any childhood death investigation

1. Why did this child die?

2. What was the cause of the death and the circumstances?

3. Are any criminal offences disclosed?

4. If so—who was/were responsible for committing those offences?

This rationale is supported by the following statements from Baroness Kennedy *SUDI Working Group Report 2004* (Appendix IV, para. 1.2, p. 66):

> Every child who dies deserves the right to have their sudden and unexplained death fully investigated in order that a cause of death can be identified, and homicide excluded.
>
> Apart from anything else, this will help to support the grieving parents and relatives of the child. It is also important to enable medical services to understand the cause of death and, if necessary, create interventions to prevent future deaths in children.
>
> The police have a key role in the investigation of infant and child deaths, and their **prime responsibility** is to the child, as well as siblings and any future children who may be born into the family concerned.

GOOD PRACTICE

Regardless of the anticipated outcome for any sudden unexpected childhood death investigation it is essential to:

Keep a record of key decisions and the information available at that time on which they were based. Ideally this should be in a Policy Book.

And that:

The recorded investigative strategy incorporates the fact that the investigation will be a 'search for the truth' in endeavouring to answer the four key questions and list them.

2.4 **The rights of the child**

There is a legal and moral basis that supports this investigative position which is contained within the United Nations Convention on the Rights of the Child (1989) and also the Human Rights Act 1998. In support of the basis for your investigative strategy, it is worth considering highlighting the relevant rights applicable to a specific case in the Policy Book. The main rights that may be applicable to childhood death investigations are listed below, as many may be unfamiliar with some of the rights but also to emphasize the rationale for this suggested investigative mindset.

2.4.1 **United Nations Convention on the Rights of the Child (1989)**

This is a legally binding international instrument that includes a total of 54 Articles of Rights and aims to provide protection for all children under the age of 18 years. They cover all aspects of child protection, but the key Articles in relation to childhood death investigation are listed below, some of which are not reproduced in full but contain sufficient information for this chapter. UNICEF has produced a useful *Fact Sheet: A summary of the rights under the Convention on the Rights of the Child.*

Article 2 (Non-discrimination): The convention applies to all children, whatever their race, religion or abilities; whatever they think or say, whatever type of family they come from. It doesn't matter where children live, what language they speak, what their parents do, whether they are boys or girls, what their culture is, whether they have a disability or whether they are rich or poor. No child should be treated unfairly on any basis.

Article 3 (Best interests of the child): the best interests of children must be the primary concern in making decisions that may affect them. All adults should do what is best for children. When adults make decisions, they should think about how their decisions will affect children. This particularly applies to budget, policy and law makers.

Article 4 (Protection of rights): Governments have a responsibility to take all available measures to make sure children's rights are respected, protected and fulfilled.

Article 6 (Survival and development): Children have the right to live. Governments should ensure that children survive and develop healthily.

Article 12 (Respect for the views of the child): When adults are making decisions that affect children, children have the right to say what they think should happen and have their opinions taken into account.

Article 16 (Right to privacy): Children have a right to privacy. The law should protect them from attacks against their way of life, their good name, their families and their homes.

Article 19 (Protection from all forms of violence): Children have the right to be protected from being hurt and mistreated, physically or mentally. Governments should ensure that children are properly cared for and protect them from violence, abuse and neglect by their parents or anyone else who looks after them.

2.4.2 The Human Rights Act 1998

The Convention rights set out in Schedule 1 to the Human Rights Act 1998 apply to everyone, not just children, but the following are especially pertinent to childhood death investigations.

Article 2—Right to Life: Everyone's right to life shall be protected by law.

This is supported by the case of *Osman v UK* (2000), that emphasized a positive obligation to take all reasonable steps to safeguard life.

Article 3—Prohibition of Torture: No one shall be subjected to torture or to inhuman or degrading treatment or punishment.

The case of *Z and others v UK* (2001), a child neglect case, provided a mandate to prevent this occurring in a private setting making it very relevant to child abuse investigation.

Article 6—Right to a Fair Trial.

This is primarily aimed at anyone charged with a criminal offence and so directly impacts on any investigation to ensure that it is a balanced and fair search for the truth, but it is morally also a right that any deceased child is entitled to. Any investigation and subsequent trial should ensure that the circumstances of their death are professionally and thoroughly investigated to ensure justice for them. The voice of the deceased child and their rights should permeate all childhood death investigations.

Articles 8 and 14 are self-explanatory but set out rights that must be central to child death investigations:

Article 8—Right to Respect for Private and Family Life: Everyone has the right to respect for his private and family life, his home and his correspondence.

There shall be no interference by a public authority with the exercise of this right except such as in accordance with the law and is necessary in a democratic society in the interests of national security, public safety or the economic well-being of the country, for the prevention of disorder or crime, for the protection of health or morals, or for the protection of the rights and freedoms of others.

Article 14—Prohibition of Discrimination : The enjoyment of the rights and freedoms set forth in this Convention shall be secured without discrimination on any ground such as sex, race, colour, language, religion, political or other opinion, national or social origin, association with a national minority, property, birth or other status.

2.5 Investigative development

Having established the focus of a childhood death investigation the following chapters will consider the processes involved and issues impacting on them from initiation to conclusion. Whilst the ACPO (2006) *Murder Investigation Manual* (MIM) provides generic guidance in relation to homicide and major incident investigations, this book's specific focus will be in relation to child homicide. It will not simply reiterate the standard guidance in the MIM but seek to develop it where child homicide investigation presents unique or different challenges. However, the 'five building block principles' will continue to provide the foundation.

Checklist—The Five Building Blocks (MIM, 2006)

- Preservation of life;
- Preserve scenes;
- Secure evidence;
- Identify victim/witnesses;
- Identify suspects.

2.6 Multi-agency involvement in investigation

It is also essential to remember and emphasize that any investigation into a childhood death involves professionals from many different agencies, who all have distinct roles but who complement each other by working together to establish how and why the child died, most crucially by sharing information and professional knowledge. The majority of childhood deaths will not result in criminal proceedings as there will be other natural and medical explanations for the deaths which are equally as important outcomes, eg establishing a natural cause of death from a health perspective or other factors for social care when considering options in relation to any siblings and Family Court proceedings.

Childhood death investigation operates in a very challenging and thought provoking environment—one that needs very careful consideration, sensitivity, management, and professional knowledge-based judgements to 'defend the children of the poor and punish the wrongdoer' in the search for the truth.

Further information and reading

ACPO (2006), *Murder Investigation Manual* (London: NPIA).
UNICEF, *Fact Sheet and information on UN Convention on the Rights of the Child.* Available at <http://www.unicef.org>.

NOTES

NOTES

Guidance and Legislation

3.1 **Introduction**

The legislation and guidance relating to child homicides, suspicious, and sudden and unexpected childhood deaths will of necessity reflect the specialist and unique environment in which they occur. Whilst some of the legislation and guidance will also apply to adult deaths, and have features in common, eg offence of murder and the role of HM Coroner, there is also guidance and legislation specifically created to cater for child death. To be in a position to ensure a thorough and professional investigation, it is imperative that investigators are not solely aware of the guidance for sudden and unexpected childhood deaths, but also have an understanding of the possible criminal offences that may have been committed in the much smaller percentage of cases where criminal acts may have resulted in or contributed to unlawful deaths. These are all key factors when considering the four key questions of any sudden and unexpected childhood death.

1. Why did this child die?
2. What was the cause of the death and the circumstances?
3. Are any criminal offences disclosed?
4. If so—who was/were responsible for committing those offences?

An examination of these areas will provide a strong foundation for considering both the guidance and legislation in subsequent chapters when the three main areas on the childhood death continuum of: (a) natural non-suspicious, (b) suspicious, and (c) unlawful unnatural deaths are looked at in more detail. Some of the guidance will also have a wider application in relation to related procedures, eg Serious Case Reviews, that will be covered in later chapters.

In this chapter a concise working knowledge summary identifying the key points will be provided together with signposts to all the key legislation and guidance. This will provide a basis of understanding to appreciate their application in the differing but related contexts that follow in the future chapters.

3.2 *Working Together to Safeguard Children* (2010)

Working Together to Safeguard Children (2010) (referred to as *Working Together*) is a guide to inter-agency working to safeguard and promote the welfare of children in accordance with the Children Acts of 1989 and 2004. Its contents have been greatly influenced by the tragic deaths of Victoria Climbié and Peter Connolly with their respective Public Inquiry and Review, both undertaken by Lord Laming.

Two chapters are especially significant in relation to child death. In Chapter 7 of *Working Together* (pp. 208–231) is guidance in relation to the Child Death Review Processes. Chapter 8 of *Working Together* (pp. 231–256), which will be covered in more detail in Chapter 7 of this book, relates to Serious Case Reviews of certain child deaths with a view to improving the ways people work individually and together to safeguard and promote the welfare of children. Both chapters are designated as statutory guidance which is underpinned by section 16 of the Children Act 2004, and means that those to whom the guidance applies:

> Must take the guidance into account and, if they decide to depart from it, have clear reasons for doing so. (*Working Together*, 2010: para. 26)

KEY POINT

The police are statutory partners with the Local Safeguarding Children Board (LSCB) and as such *Working Together* applies to them, and so it is essential information to be aware of and understand.

POINT TO NOTE

As a result of the publication *A child-centred system: the Government's response to the Munro review of child protection*, published in July 2011, some of the processes within *Working Together* may be revised. Although methodology and emphasis may change it is likely that the essential elements and rationale will remain; so for example there will still be Serious Case Reviews but the way they are undertaken may change. It is anticipated that all of the key points summarized below will still be applicable.

Definition of 'safeguarding'

Safeguarding and promoting the welfare of children is a central theme within *Working Together* and can be defined as:

- protecting children from maltreatment;
- preventing impairment of children's health or development;
- ensuring that children are growing in circumstances consistent with the provision of safe and effective care; and
- undertaking that role so as to enable those children to have optimum life chances and to enter adulthood successfully.

(*Working Together*, 2010: para. 1.20)

Central to *Every Child Matters*, a set of reforms outlined in the government's response to the Public Inquiry into the death of Victoria Climbié, incorporated into *Working Together* and supported by the Children Act 2004, are five key outcomes.

> ## Checklist—The five key outcomes (*Working Together*, 2010: para. 1.1)
>
> The aim is for every child, whatever their background or circumstances, to have the support they need to:
> - S = stay SAFE
> - H = be HEALTHY
> - E = ENJOY and achieve
> - E = achieve ECONOMIC well-being
> - P = make a POSITIVE contribution

Whilst this book's focus is sadly on children who have died, another important theme inextricably linked is the safety of deceased children's siblings and any future children born into the family, as emphasized by Baroness Kennedy in her report into *Sudden Unexpected Death in Infancy* (2004).

The crucial outcome of the five key outcomes in this particular context is staying SAFE which is further emphasized by a further five common principles, specifically pertinent to childhood deaths and especially so when having contact with family members.

> ## Checklist—Five common principles
>
> 1. Being caring and sensitive particularly to those who are grieving.
> 2. An inter-agency response—working together and sharing information.
> 3. Keeping an open mind and adopting a balanced approach.
> 4. Ensuring a proportionate response to the circumstances.
> 5. Preservation of all potential evidence.

The safeguarding legislation in England and Wales, concentrated within the Children Acts of 1989 and 2004 and encompassing the overarching themes of the Human Rights Act 1998 and the United Nations Convention on the Rights of the Child 1989, emphasize a 'DUTY' for organizations and individuals to safeguard children. It is important that everyone impacted by the legislation sees it as a 'duty' and **not** as an optional extra if resources permit.

The key 'duties' are summarized below.

1. The Children Act 1989
   - s. 17 duty on Local Authority (LA) to safeguard and promote the welfare of child in need.
   - s. 27 duty to co-operate with LA and other organizations.

2. The Children Act 2004
    - s. 10 duty on LA to make arrangements to promote co-operation between organizations to improve the well-being of children.
    - s. 11 duty for organizations including the police to ensure their functions are discharged with regard to the need to safeguard and promote the welfare of children.

3.3 **Chapter 7 child death review processes**

These linked processes, which became compulsory on 1 April 2008, operate across England but are co-ordinated on a local geographical basis, within the Local Safeguarding Children Board (LSCB) and Child Death Overview Panel (CDOP) areas. Wales, Northern Ireland, and Scotland have similar processes. The processes fall into the following two categories:

1. **Rapid Response Process**—including a professionals' meeting and multi-agency collaboration following the sudden and unexpected death of a child, and
2. **The Child Death Overview Panel (CDOP) process**—a sub-committee of the LSCB whose function is to review all child deaths in their area against national criteria to inform local strategic planning on how best to safeguard and promote the welfare of the children in their area.

There is a difference between them in that the CDOP reviews **ALL** deaths of children whilst the Rapid Response Process **ONLY** caters for sudden and unexpected child deaths.

> The term 'child' encompasses children and young people up to the age of 18 years but excludes 'both those babies who are stillborn and planned terminations of pregnancy carried out within the law'. (*Working Together*, 2010: para. 7.1)

The authors of *Working Together*, in echoing the sentiments expressed by Baroness Kennedy (2004), state that;

> An appropriate balance should be drawn between the forensic and medical requirements and the family's need for support.

But that:

> In all cases, enquiries should
> - Seek to understand the reasons for the child's death,
> - Address the possible needs of other children in the household,
> - Consider the needs of all family members, and also
> - Identify any lessons to be learnt about how best to safeguard and promote children's welfare in the future.

It emphasizes that:

> Families should be treated with sensitivity, discretion and respect at all times, and professionals should approach their enquiries with an open mind. (*Working Together*, 2010: para. 7.5)

The guidance also specifically mentions children with life-limiting (LL) or life threatening (LT) conditions. Whilst accepting that these can be very carefully and sensitively managed, eg end of life care plans may be in place, it explains that if the death of a child with an LL or LT condition should occur unexpectedly, then this 'should be managed [in the same way] as for any other unexpected death so as to determine the cause of death and any contributory factors'. (*Working Together*, 2010: para. 7.6)

For ease of reference a reminder of the definition of an unexpected death of a child is:

Definition of 'unexpected death'

Unexpected death is defined as the death of an infant or child (less than 18 years old) which:

- Was not anticipated as a significant possibility for example, 24 hours before the death; or
- Where there was a similarly unexpected collapse or incident leading to or precipitating the events which led to the death.'

(*Working Together*, 2010: para. 7.21)

3.3.1 **The Rapid Response Processes**

These processes, as the term 'rapid' implies, are intended to take place as soon as possible after the unexpected death of a child or young person and to be a multi-agency led response to inquire into and evaluate that death. The results of this process are then fed into the CDOP process, which is less time-specific in comparison and further explained below.

Communication and sharing information are crucial in establishing the cause of death together with its surrounding circumstances. Ideally, each LSCB/CDOP area should have an existing protocol, incorporating an 'on call' rota, of all relevant professionals in order to respond in line with this statutory guidance. It is important to emphasize that an integral element of any protocol will include the coroner, who has the independent judicial authority and obligation to investigate the cause and circumstances of:

(a) Any violent or unnatural death or
(b) Any sudden death for which the cause of death is unknown.

The questions they will try to answer are:

- Who died?—The identity of the deceased and certain registration details.
- When, where, and how did they die?

They are not responsible for apportioning blame if there is a question as to who was criminally responsible or legally liable: that will usually be determined in the criminal or civil courts.

The coroner's authority (derived from the Coroners Act 1988 and Coroners Rules 1984) is also required when dealing with deceased person's bodies in relation to a number of key areas including movement, samples, post-mortem examinations, tissue/sample retention, property, and release of the body. Each coroner will have coroner's officers who represent the coroner's interests in many of the practicalities concerned, including the important liaison with the deceased family. Where possible, it is useful to have a standing general approval for the measures agreed to in the protocol by the coroner to reduce the need to obtain specific approval on each occasion, eg taking samples in accordance with standard sets for sudden unexpected death in infancy or for other types of death presentation.

3.3.2 Rapid Response Meeting

Whilst the professionals concerned in any child death may have distinct roles and responsibilities in relation to specific duties associated with their area of expertise, the guidance envisages them all coming together at an early stage (usually within 24 hours) in a multi-agency meeting to share information bearing on the death and its circumstances. This meeting is usually co-ordinated and chaired by a local designated paediatrician responsible for unexpected deaths in childhood. The makeup of those attending the rapid response meeting may include the following professionals:

Table 3.1 Potential Rapid Response Meeting attendees

Designated Paediatrician (Chair)		
GP	Health Visitor	Police
Nurse	Midwife	Social Worker
Mental Health Professional	Substance Misuse Worker	Probation Officer

but each meeting's members will be determined ultimately on a case-by-case basis, and individual involvement of professionals from other specialist agencies, eg hospice support worker, children's community nurse, education, prison staff, pathologist, ambulance staff, A&E department staff, coroner's officer, faith leaders, fire fighters, included when appropriate.

The joint responsibilities of the professionals at the Rapid Response Meeting as set out in *Working Together* (2010: para. 7.50) include:

- Responding quickly to the unexpected death of a child;
- In agreement with the coroner, making immediate inquiries to try and ascertain the circumstances and reasons for the death;
- Each of the represented professionals undertakes inquiries that relate to their specific role and obligations in relation to a child dying unexpectedly;
- Liaison with those who have ongoing responsibilities for other family members;
- Providing support to the bereaved family;
- Maintaining contact throughout the childhood death processes to ensure that the family members and other professionals who have ongoing responsibilities for other family members are kept up to date with relevant information about the child's death.

The meeting may be a useful forum to discuss whether the death should be referred to the LSCB for consideration of initiating the Serious Case Review process as outlined in Chapter 8 of *Working Together* if there are concerns that the cause of death may have been the result of abuse or neglect.

GOOD PRACTICE

If there are concerns about the siblings of the deceased child warranting a strategy meeting to discuss whether to initiate section 47 Children Act 1989 inquiries, then it sometimes happens that the Rapid Response Meeting and a multi-agency child protection Strategy Meeting are combined. The rationale put forward may be to save time and duplication of information-sharing between parties who would be included at both meetings if held separately. However, whilst expediency may be a valid reason, care has to be taken over the subsequent disclosure of information, eg minutes of meetings, as they have been created for two different, albeit related, processes. Different organizations have different responsibilities in the two meetings, eg if a crime is suspected then the police become the lead agency, or there may be information in relation to one meeting that is not relevant for the other and vice versa, although, hopefully, professional common sense will prevail. Ideally, one meeting should follow on from the other and the two processes be kept separate.

The Rapid Response Meeting is only one of the processes in relation to the response to an unexpected child death; many of the professionals who subsequently attend the Rapid Response Meeting will have contributed to the immediate response itself. The main actions within this immediate response will have occurred more often than not at a hospital, but on occasions the deceased child may not be transferred to hospital, eg if the child had an end of life plan they will not normally be considered to have died unexpectedly, or if the child has had their death confirmed but the circumstances are considered suspicious and they are left in situ because of forensic considerations.

3.3.3 **Immediate response actions (a summary based on** ***Working Together***, **2010)**

These may include the following:

- Children who die at home or in the community should normally be taken to an A&E department and resuscitation should always be initiated unless clearly inappropriate. Children should not be taken immediately to the mortuary.
- If the death is suspicious there may be forensic reasons for the body to be left in situ at the location of their death.
- As soon as practicable after arrival at the hospital, the child should be examined by the on call consultant paediatrician or consultant in emergency medicine, as appropriate, depending on the age of the child.
- The paediatrician (on call or designated) should initiate an immediate preliminary information-sharing and planning discussion between lead agencies (health, police, Local Authority Children's Social Care) to decide what will happen next and who will do what. This may be by telephone, quickly convened at the hospital, or a combination.
- A detailed and careful history of events leading up to and following the discovery of the child's collapse should be taken from the parents/carers using a suitable template to capture a nationally-agreed data set. The paediatrician should carefully record the examination findings and history in the hospital notes. This may be jointly taken with a police officer in some circumstances.
- Appropriate investigative samples should be taken immediately on arrival and after death is confirmed with the authority of the coroner or, where the coroner is not involved, with the consent of the parents.
- Depending on the age of the child, a full skeletal survey should be considered (for babies and young children it is accepted good practice to undertake a full skeletal survey, whereas for older children it may not be so relevant).
- When a child is pronounced dead the consultant clinician should inform the parents and explain the processes that will follow, including police and coroner involvement, and coroner's authority to order a post-mortem. The issue of tissue retention requiring parental consent may also be explained.
- The coroner should be informed.
- Other notifications of death completed, eg National Patient Safety Agency (NHS Providers) or Care Quality Commission.
- The consultant clinician who has seen the child should inform the designated paediatrician with responsibility for unexpected deaths.
- Consideration should be given to allowing the parents to be with and hold their child in an appropriate location with a nurse or other professional maintaining a discreet presence at all times.

- Mementos such as a photograph, lock of hair, or hand and footprints may be offered to the family unless there are clear reasons not to. (This topic will be addressed in more detail in Chapter 4.)
- Support and contact details of relevant professionals should be provided to the parents.
- Consideration should be given to a joint home or location of death visit by the police and paediatrician or other healthcare professional within 24 hours. This visit enables professionals to talk with parents/carers and evaluate the circumstances in the environment where the child died. This should be standard for SUDI.
- The well-being of any siblings should be considered, including bereavement support and appropriate action taken if there are any concerns.
- The police will initiate an investigation into the unexpected death of a child on behalf of the coroner, including producing a report of the circumstances and enquiries made.
- When a child with a known life limiting or life threatening condition dies in a manner or time that was not anticipated, the rapid response team should liaise closely and promptly with a member of the medical, palliative, or end of life care team who knows the child and family, to jointly determine how best to respond to the child's death. (*Working Together*, 2010: para. 7.59)
- If a child dies away from their normal place of residence, a joint decision is required between the two rapid response teams for the respective areas as to who will lead the investigation. Usually it will be the area where the child normally resides but the team should liaise closely with the team for the area where the child died.
- If a child dies whilst they are abroad, then it will be investigated by the relevant agencies in that jurisdiction. However, when the information is known, the CDOP in the area where the child usually resides should still review the information.

3.3.4 **Actions after the initial response**

In most cases of unexpected child deaths, the coroner will order a post-mortem examination. Where the death may be unnatural, or is as yet undetermined, the coroner will also hold an inquest.

A further meeting will be usually held between the pathologist, police, local authority children's social care, paediatrician, and relevant healthcare professionals to discuss the preliminary post-mortem findings and review any additional information.

When the final post-mortem findings are known, a case discussion will be held and its format will largely depend on the cause of death and the age of the child as to who attends. It will be chaired by the designated paediatrician, and the LSCB child death core data set will be completed for the CDOP process. If the cause of death is natural, then the coroner will not hold an inquest.

KEY POINT

These rapid response actions relate only to unexpected deaths of children. If the child died from a natural cause and a doctor is able to issue a medical certificate of the cause of death, then the coroner's involvement and these processes will not apply. However, the CDOP processes will still apply as they apply to all child deaths.

In cases where there are suspicions regarding the cause of death and there is a criminal investigation, there will be implications for the processes, and decisions between the senior investigating officer and the other agencies will determine further actions. These may include access to the body, but the main issue will be in the timing of the release of information to parents and others if this may have an adverse impact on the investigation and possibly the course of justice, eg if the parents are due to be interviewed or arrested. Whilst in consultation with the CPS and partner agencies it is hoped that these difficulties can be overcome, as the information will be provided but just delayed; the police should also be aware that the coroner is required to disclose certain information to 'interested parties' which will include the parents. To negate any adverse impact this might have on an investigation, it is essential that police inquiries are as expeditious as possible, and close liaison is maintained with the coroner through his officer or directly if appropriate. The above is a summary of the key processes and generic issues, the detailed police response within these processes will be examined in more detail in the following chapters.

KEY POINT

In summary, the role of rapid response could be summed up as:

1. To establish cause of death.
2. To explicitly consider safeguarding of siblings.
3. To co-ordinate support for families.
4. To gather information for CDOP.

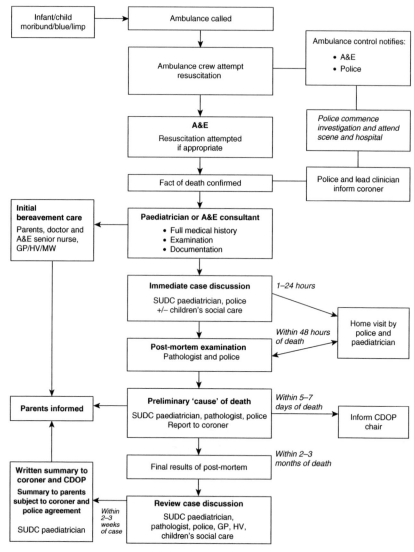

Figure 3.1 Rapid response—recommended sequence of events
(As shown in GM SUDC procedures)

3.3.5 **Child Death Overview Panels**

All the review processes in relation to child homicides and suspicious deaths will be considered together in Chapter 7 of this book but it will be useful in understanding the *Working Together* guidance in Chapter 7 to briefly explain the key points in the CDOP's processes and how they are linked with the Rapid Response Processes.

KEY POINTS

From *Working Together* (paragraph numbers in brackets)

The Local Safeguarding Children's Board should use the aggregated findings from all child deaths collected according to the nationally agreed minimum data set to inform local strategic planning on how best to safeguard and promote the welfare of the children in their area. (7.2)

They will achieve this through the CDOP processes.

They must also have mechanisms to involve and inform parents/families in both CDOP and Rapid Response Processes that their child's death will be subject to review. (7.7)

However,

Parents and family members should be assured that the objective of child death review process is to

- Learn lessons in order to improve the health, safety and well being of children and
- Ultimately, hopefully, to prevent further such child deaths.
- The process is NOT about culpability or blame. (7.9)

3.3.6 The CDOP key facts

Relevant *Working Together* paragraph numbers are shown in brackets.

- A sub-committee of the LSCB(s) (7.2)
- Responsible for reviewing the available information on all child deaths (7.2)
- Includes deaths of all children and young people from birth up to age of 18 years (excludes babies who are stillborn and planned legal terminations) (7.2) and is
- Accountable to the LSCB chair (7.2)
- Parents do not attend the CDOP meeting (7.10)
- All cases are anonymized prior to discussion at CDOP (7.11)
- CDOP produce an annual report which is a public document (7.11)
- CDOP will make arrangements for families to meet with relevant professionals when necessary to help answer their questions in relation to their child's death (7.12)
- The process is a paper based review (7.25)
- Fixed core multi-agency membership (7.25)
- Regular meetings (7.25)
- Review professional's response and involvement before and after death (7.25)

- Consider relevant environmental, social, health, and cultural aspects (7.25)
- Consider how deaths may be preventable in the future (7.25)
- Determine whether or not the death was deemed preventable (ie modifiable factors in family, environment, parenting capacity, or service provision, may have contributed to the death)—Decision must await outcome of other investigations, eg SCR, post-mortem, inquest, criminal proceedings, but should not stop preventable action being implemented in the meantime (7.25)
- Make recommendations to LSCB or relevant bodies so that prompt action can be taken to prevent future such deaths (7.25)
- Identify patterns or trends in local data and report to LSCB (7.25)
- Co-operate with regional and national initiatives—to identify lessons on the prevention of child deaths (7.36)

The reason so much emphasis has been placed on Chapter 7 of *Working Together* is because it forms the basis and structure for all child death investigations, with additional or more detailed investigations being undertaken depending on the individual circumstances and where they feature on the child death continuum.

3.3.7 **National data collection forms**

There are a number of templates for recording the data for the Chapter 7 child death review processes, including a *Notes for Users* available on the Department for Education website <http://www.education.gov.uk>.

Table 3.2 National templates for recording Chapter 7 processes

National Templates for Recording Chapter 7 Processes			
Form A	Notification of child death	Form A1	Case processing
Form B	Agency report	Form B 2	Neo-natal < 28days
		Form B 3	Death of a child with a known life limiting condition
		Form B 4	SUDI
		Form B 5	RTA
		Form B 6	Drowning
		Form B 7	Fire and burns
		Form B 8	Poisoning
		Form B 9	Other non-intentional injury
		Form B 10	Substance misuse
		Form B 11	Apparent homicide
		Form B 12	Apparent suicide
		Form B 13	Summary of autopsy findings
Form C	Analysis proforma		
Form D	Audit tool for rapid response		
Form E	Audit tool for CD overview		

3.4 **Police guidance**

The police response will be examined in detail in relation to child deaths in non-suspicious, suspicious, and in suspected homicides in the following chapters. In addition to complying with *Working Together*, in particular Chapter 7 (summarized in generic terms above), the police response will also rely heavily on specific police guidance and joint guidance with partner agencies.

This additional guidance will be referred to in relevant sections of this book but will not generally be reiterated; instead key points particularly pertinent to child death will be highlighted and the reader signposted to the original guidance document if they require further information.

3.4.1 **ACPO (2006), *Murder Investigation Manual* (MIM)**

This document and accompanying CD (containing supplementary reading in PDF format) examines all aspects of a homicide investigation, focusing on the Senior Investigating Officer's (SIO) role and perspective. Within the 300-page manual it provides generic strategic and operational advice based on accumulated shared learning from numerous homicide enquiries. There is additional guidance in relation to specific types of homicide and aspects of homicide investigation on the accompanying CD. However, the manual and CD were produced in 2006 and, whilst the majority of information is still very applicable, some of the additional resources have now been updated so it is worth confirming that any specific advice is the most up to date before relying on it. Many police guidance documents are now web-based so that they can be updated online, eg the POLKA website currently managed by the NPIA contains a number of documents in a web-based library. On the CD are the *Infant deaths— ACPO guidelines* (2006); this is one of the resources that has recently been updated and its replacement summarized below.

3.4.2 **ACPO (2011), Homicide Working Group, *A Guide to Investigating Child Deaths***

This guidance provides up to date information that is intended to support the delivery of policing services in England, Wales, and Northern Ireland in relation to the police response to and investigation of child deaths, superseding the 2006 guidelines. It is not intended to be prescriptive but to be applied on a case-by-case basis considering the specific circumstances and resources available.

3.4.3 **Local child death procedures**

Many areas will have their own specific child death procedures specially tailored to meet the local demographics and requirements of the professionals and authorities involved. A good example would be the *London Child Protection*

Procedures (4th edn, April 2011) including Chapter 12 that specifically relates to 'Death of a child'. These can be accessed and a copy downloaded from the London Safeguarding Children Board website: <http://www.londonscb.gov.uk/procedures>.

Whilst *Working Together* applies to England, both Wales and Northern Ireland have their own guidance and child protection procedures that are very similar in nature and content. In 2003, in Northern Ireland, the Department of Health, Social Services and Public Safety published *Co-operating to Safeguard Children* and the Police Service of Northern Ireland *Service Procedure (SP 2/2010) Sudden Unexpected Death in Infancy* in relation to investigating childhood death.

In Wales, there are the *All Wales Child Protection Procedures* (2008) and Public Health Wales has recently published *Procedural Response to Unexpected Deaths in Childhood* (PRUDiC). In Scotland, the ACPOS (2008) *Scottish Investigators' Guide to Sudden Unexpected Deaths in Infancy (SUDI)* applies.

KEY POINT

An awareness of Chapter 7 or the equivalent guidance is not sufficient: it is also important to be aware of and know the local protocols for investigating childhood death in your area.

3.4.4 ACPO (2011), Homicide Working Group, *An SIO's Guide to Investigating Unexpected Death and Serious Untoward Harm in Healthcare Settings*

Unfortunately some children, like many adults, die in a healthcare setting. Whilst the majority of cases involve no criminal negligence or culpability in relation to their care, there may on occasions be a requirement for the police to investigate the circumstances of the death. This may be as a result of a referral from the NHS, coroners, relatives and their representatives, other agencies, concerned informants, or Inspectorates and regulators. This guidance, like the specific ACPO investigating child deaths guidance, supplements the ACPO *Murder Investigation Manual* and additionally signposts readers to further important and relevant related guidance.

3.5 Legislation

As outlined in the initial chapter, childhood death presents such unique legal aspects and challenges that the resolution of these has led to the creation of a number of specific criminal offences designed to cater for them. In this section homicide and related offences will be examined together in the context of child death—some offences apply to everyone but others relate solely to childhood death. The four homicide offences will be examined initially and then the related offences. This will provide an overview and background against which the various scenarios and issues that will become apparent in the subsequent chapters can be considered.

GOOD PRACTICE

In relation to your continual professional development it is important to keep up with judgments from the Court of Appeal and any new or amended legislation.

The following web-based resources of :

1. The National Archives 'The official home of UK legislation' website: <http://www.legislation.gov.uk>.
2. The 'Police National Legal Database' (PNLD) website: <https://www.pnld.co.uk>.
3. The British and Irish Legal Information Institute (BAILII) website: <http://www.bailii.org>.
4. The Crown Prosecution Service website: <http://cps.gov.uk/legal_resources.html>.

are excellent sources of legal information that provided invaluable signposts for information in relation to the legislation covered in this section.

The term 'homicide' simply means the killing of a human being by another human being and can be either 'lawful' or 'unlawful'. For a homicide to be considered lawful it would have to be:

1. In the execution of a legal duty or advancement of justice;
2. In defence of property or self defence;
3. To prevent a serious crime; or
4. Misadventure—where no negligence is associated with the act.

The term 'unlawful' will cater for the four offences we will consider below: of murder, manslaughter, infanticide, and familial homicide. These and the related offences will be briefly explained and sometimes illustrated with anonymized case studies to aid understanding.

3.5.1 **Murder**

This is a Common Law offence:

> Where a person of sound mind and discretion unlawfully kills any reasonable creature in being and under the Queen's peace, with intent to kill or cause grievous bodily harm

Penalty: Life imprisonment

Case study

Father, in violent row with mother of a young baby that she was holding, grabbed the baby from her and forcibly threw the baby head first to the ground causing the baby to suffer a fatal head injury including multiple fractures to the skull. He pleaded guilty to murder.

3.5.2 Attempted murder

This offence is contrary to section 1(1) of the Criminal Attempts Act 1981 and in reality may be harder to prove than murder, as it will be necessary to prove that the person charged intended to kill the intended victim not just inflict grievous bodily harm. The action that they took to attempt to murder their intended victim must be more than merely preparatory.

Penalty: Life imprisonment

Case study

A mother, having written a suicide note, took her three young children and gave them medication in order to help them sleep. She placed them into her car having already secured a washing machine hose from the exhaust into the car. With the car engine running, she took some medication herself, secured the car, and waited for them all to die from carbon monoxide poisoning. Fortunately someone was suspicious of her actions and alerted the emergency services and everyone survived after having medical treatment. She was convicted of attempting to murder all three of her children.

3.5.3 Manslaughter

There are two categories within this Common Law offence, namely 'voluntary manslaughter' and 'involuntary manslaughter'.

Penalty (Manslaughter): Life imprisonment

Voluntary manslaughter

The category of voluntary manslaughter applies when all the constituents of murder are present, ie an intention to kill or cause grievous bodily harm, but the 'level of culpability' is reduced by the defences of loss of control, diminished responsibility, or if the death was in pursuance of a suicide pact.

Case study

A mother suffering from a mental illness repeatedly stabbed her young child resulting in her death. She attempted to commit suicide by stabbing herself but, because of the interventions of a police officer in rendering first aid, survived. She was convicted and found to be 'not guilty' of murder but 'guilty' of manslaughter on the grounds of diminished responsibility.

'Diminished responsibility' as a defence to murder is explained in section 2 of the Homicide Act 1957, and would apply where the defendant is suffering from an abnormality of mental functioning that is a recognized medical condition which substantially impaired their ability to understand the nature of their conduct, to form a rational judgement, or to exercise self control. Whilst being a defence to murder if substantiated, the defendant would be found guilty of the alternative charge of manslaughter.

Involuntary manslaughter

'Involuntary manslaughter' occurs where someone has been unlawfully killed but the perpetrator's 'guilty mind' or 'mens rea', ie an intention to kill or cause grievous bodily harm, is absent and the death results from: (a) an unlawful act, (b) through gross negligence involving a breach of duty, or (c) by recklessness.

(A) 'Unlawful' means:
  • The death must be the result of an unlawful act not omission;
  • An objective view would be that the act would put the victim at risk of suffering some physical harm (includes shock); and
  • It is not required to prove that the accused knew that the act was unlawful, dangerous, or that they intended to cause harm.
(B) 'Gross negligence' arises when a person who owes a duty of care to another breaches that duty of care resulting in the death of the other person, and that the conduct of the person who owes a duty of care is considered to be so bad or 'reprehensible' as to be criminal. This level of proof may mean that even serious mistakes or errors of judgement do not reach this threshold if the person was doing their best and made an 'honest' mistake in a very difficult environment, eg an emergency life-saving situation.

To assist in answering this difficult issue, the *Adomako* test (*R v Adomako* (1994) 99 Cr App R 362) provides a four-stage objective test:

1. Was a duty of care in existence to the deceased?
2. Was there a breach of that duty of care?
3. Did the breach of that duty cause the death of the deceased?
4. Was the breach of that duty sufficient to be considered as gross negligence and therefore a crime?

(C) 'Reckless' can overlap with gross negligence but is a subjective test, in that the person realized that in the circumstances a risk existed or would exist, or they were aware that their actions carried with them a risk of an outcome occurring as a result of them, and in both cases it would be considered unjustified or unreasonable to take that risk.

KEY POINT

The situation where an allegation of manslaughter through gross negligence may arise would be in a hospital setting where medical staff make an error in relation to the administration of a drug in an emergency situation. The *Adomako* case quoted above relates to an anaesthetist who was convicted of manslaughter through gross negligence as he failed to notice a patient's oxygen supply had become disconnected for nine minutes despite a blood pressure alarm going off. The patient who was undergoing an eye operation suffered a fatal cardiac arrest.

The ACPO (2011) Homicide Working Group—*An SIO's Guide to Investigating Unexpected Death and Serious Untoward Harm in Healthcare Settings*—is a useful resource when investigating these types of allegation.

3.5.4 **Corporate manslaughter**

The Corporate Manslaughter and Corporate Homicide Act 2007 offence of 'corporate manslaughter' ('corporate homicide' in Scotland) relates to organizations including the police, NHS, and private health care sector. If the way an organization's activities are managed or organized causes a death, there was a relevant duty of care by the organization to the deceased, and a gross breach of that duty (including the way those activities were organized or managed by senior management) resulted in the death of a person, then they may be guilty of corporate manslaughter.

Penalty (Corporate manslaughter): A fine
There may be additional offences under Health and Safety legislation, eg The Health and Safety at Work Act etc 1974.

3.5.5 **A special verdict of 'not guilty' of murder by reason of insanity**

This verdict can apply to any case if the criteria based on the case law from the 1843 *McNaghten* case are met. The accused at the time of the offence has to have been suffering from 'such a defect of reason from a disease of the mind' to such an extent that they:

• Did not know what they were doing, or
• Did know what they were doing but did not know it was wrong.

In a case where this is applicable and there is no dispute to the actual facts of the case, the jury in what is termed a *McNaghten* hearing, after hearing expert medical evidence supporting the defence of 'insanity' will be asked to return a verdict of 'not guilty by reason of insanity'. If this verdict is given, the defendant would be detained until they no longer presented a danger to themselves or members of the public and probably be subjected to a Hospital Order (section 37) and a Restriction Order (section 41) under the Mental Health Act 1983.

Case study

A wealthy and accomplished businessman, who was devoted to his family, including his young daughter, had returned home from an exhausting conference abroad with little sleep over a 72-hour period. Having spent the evening with his daughter and family, they all went to bed. With no warning whatsoever and completely out of character, early the following morning he picked up his young daughter and in a mad frenzy, smashed her head against the wooden floor of the flat in front of his wife. The assault was so severe that it caused multiple fractures of the skull and severe brain injury from which his daughter died two days later in hospital. Medical opinion suggested that he was suffering from an acute psychotic disorder in which at the time of the assault he was hallucinating, hearing voices, and believed he was killing a satanic entity. The jury returned a verdict of not guilty of murder by reason of insanity. He was placed under a Hospital Order and Restriction Order and was detained in hospital for treatment without limit of time.

3.5.6 Familial homicide—Causing or allowing the death of a child or vulnerable adult

This offence under section 5 of The Domestic Violence, Crime and Victims Act 2004 will be considered in some detail, as it is relatively recent legislation (2004). This Act specifically legislates for the situation where a child or vulnerable adult is unlawfully killed, there are a limited number of persons suspected of having been responsible (usually the parents/carers), but no one is prepared to accept responsibility or apportion blame for the death. It was introduced to limit occasions where this scenario, ie 'Which of you did it?', arose and no one was convicted of an offence, despite a child or vulnerable adult having been unlawfully killed. A ruling in a case of *R v Lane and Lane* (1987) 82 Cr App R 5, had decided that it was not correct to charge them both with being jointly responsible for manslaughter, for example, as that process could result in one of them being wrongly convicted of manslaughter when in fact that person had actually played no part in the offence. The newer offence of 'familial homicide' in the way the legislation is drafted recognizes the special position of responsibility which parents, carers, and household members hold in respect of their children, and the duties they have to their children.

The offence under section five provides that members of a household who have frequent contact with a child under 16 or a vulnerable adult will be guilty of the offence if they either:

1. 'Caused' the death

or

2. 'Allowed' the death, if the following three conditions are met:
   - They were aware—or ought to have been—that the victim was at significant risk of serious physical harm (amounting to grievous bodily harm

61

under the Offences Against the Person Act 1861) from a member of the household;

- They failed to take such steps as they could reasonably have been expected to take to protect that person from the above risk;
- The person died from the unlawful act of a household member in circumstances that the defendant foresaw or ought to have foreseen. The term 'act' includes a course of conduct and also includes an omission.

Definitions

'Child' means a person under 16 years;

'Serious' harm means harm that amounts to grievous bodily harm for the purposes of the Offences Against the Person Act 1861;

'Vulnerable adult' means a person aged 16 or over whose ability to protect themselves from violence, abuse, or neglect is significantly impaired through physical or mental disability or illness through old age or otherwise (this may be a temporary or permanent vulnerability);

'Unlawful' act is one that constitutes an offence, or would constitute an offence but for being the act of:

A person under 10 years, or

A person entitled to rely on a defence of insanity.

'Household' is intended to be given its ordinary English meaning and will be unlikely to cover care homes or professional nurseries.

The offence is stated in section 5 with 'special procedures' set out in section 6. Additional guidance on the offence can be found in the Act's 'Explanatory Notes' and in Home Office Circular 9 of 2005. Below is a useful summary of the key points, but for a detailed understanding it is advisable to read the source documents and, in particular, the Home Office Circular. This is the offence for which the three people responsible for the death of Baby Peter Connelly were convicted in 2008.

KEY POINTS

- The prosecution does not have to prove which element of the offence is applicable. In other words, which element of 'caused' or 'allowed' the death applies to the respective defendants: both are charged with 'causing or allowing the death'.
- The offence, unfortunately, is not retrospective, so it does not apply to offences committed before 21 March 2005.

- Suspects can be additionally charged with offences of murder and/or man-slaughter if they are suspected of 'causing the death'.
- Where the defendant is charged both with familial homicide and murder or manslaughter, the case will await the close of evidence on both charges, provided that the prosecution has successfully established a case to answer on the charge of familial homicide. This means that the charge of murder or manslaughter is not to be dismissed at 'half time' unless the section 5 offence is dismissed.
- When determining guilt, the jury may draw proper inferences from the defendant's failure to give evidence or refusal to answer a question, but guilt cannot be determined solely on this.
- Unless the person suspected is either the mother or father of the victim, the legislation does not apply to persons under the age of 16 years. However, even if the person who 'caused' the death was under 16, it would not preclude other household members from being charged with 'allowing' the death in respect of their failure to protect the victim. If there is sufficient evidence, a person under 16 could still be charged with murder or manslaughter. This means that a young parent could be charged with the offence but not a sibling or other child in the household who was under 16 years.
- It is important to establish whether any person suspected of familial homicide is aware of a history of violence to a person, or of a history of neglect featuring a risk of serious injury. In this respect, evidence from neighbours (past and present) can be crucial in building up the history of a risk occurring.
- If the unlawful act that resulted in the death of a child or vulnerable adult is an isolated incident with no previous history of abuse, nor any reason to suspect a risk, then familial homicide would not be made out in relation to 'allowing the death'.
- The prosecution would have to rely on other existing legislation in relation to murder, manslaughter, or cruelty, but it will face the same problems that gave rise to the new legislation of familial homicide being introduced: those of establishing which household member was at fault in a 'Which of you did it?' scenario.
- The prosecution must prove that the victim died from 'an unlawful act'. Without this element of the offence, a prosecution under section 5 would fail. It follows that the prosecution must establish causation, ie the cause of death, and be able to link it to the 'unlawful act'.
- Domestic violence often plays a key part in this offence. The Home Office guidance recognizes this, and outlines the potential for a suspect to be a victim of domestic violence and in fear of the perpetrator.

- An objective test on a case-by-case basis in relation to the person who was suspected of 'allowing a death' would consider if they had taken 'reasonable steps to prevent the person coming to harm' including:
  - Told anyone about their concerns for example a GP, Social Services, a teacher, or neighbours;
  - Sought help in relation to drug/alcohol addiction or anger management;
  - Obtained early medical treatment for any previous incidents;
  - Reported their concerns to the police.

GOOD PRACTICE

It is useful to have a copy of Home Office Circular 9/2005 as a reference, particularly when reviewing actions for ongoing investigations and discussions in relation to possible charges.

Home Office Circular 9/2005, *The Domestic Violence, Crime and Victims Act 2004*, is available from <http://www.homeoffice.gov.uk/about-us/publications/home-office-circulars/circulars-2005/009-2005/>.

Penalty (causing or allowing the death of a child or vulnerable adult): 14 years' imprisonment

Case study 1

A couple addicted to crack cocaine, with a history of domestic violence and disputes, had a ten-month-old son who had been placed on a child protection plan due to previous concerns. The child was discovered dead at his home address by paramedics responding to a '999' call from his parents. Despite his parents saying they had recently been feeding him and he had just collapsed, the paramedics found that rigor mortis was present, suggesting he had been dead for some time. A post-mortem examination revealed bruises to his head, healing rib fractures, and a fractured leg, but death was found to have been caused by an intra-abdominal haemorrhage due to a torn mesentery. This internal injury would have resulted from a punch or a kick to the stomach area. Both parents denied any involvement with the injuries and could not account for them. This was a classic 'which of you did it?' scenario and both were charged with 'Causing or allowing the death of a child'. At court on the day of the trial both pleaded guilty to the offence offering the explanation that, whilst having an argument, the mother, who was holding the baby, was punched by her partner but the blow was deflected onto the baby. Although as previously explained the prosecution does not have to prove who 'caused' and who 'allowed' the death in these circumstances, it would appear that the father 'caused the death' by punching his son so hard as to cause the injuries and the mother 'allowed the death'. From the surrounding circumstances and background, she knew her son was at significant risk of serious physical harm from a member of the household, she failed to take reasonable steps to prevent her son coming to harm, and her son died from an unlawful act (assault) by a household member (father) in circumstances that she foresaw or ought to have foreseen. They had obviously neither sought immediate medical help for their son but spent their time tidying up the flat and concocting a story for the paramedics.

There have also been cases where a single parent or carer is convicted of this offence of causing or allowing the death of a child.

(a) A young child was murdered by their mother's boyfriend in an environment that the mother was clearly aware of where child neglect and domestic violence were prevalent. The boyfriend was convicted of murder and the mother convicted of 'causing or allowing the death'—in these circumstances the element of the offence that applied to the mother was 'allowing' the death.

(b) A mother who killed her young baby by poisoning them with a drug in order to make them sleep and also poisoned an older sibling was convicted on her own of 'causing or allowing the death of a child'. In these circumstances the prosecution was relying on the 'causing' element of the offence as, after a thorough investigation, no other persons were suspected of having been involved. However, as previously explained, the prosecution does not have to establish who 'caused' or who 'allowed' the death although in some cases (like these two), the element the defendants fulfilled can be established.

Case study 2

An eight-week-old boy who was in the care of his mother and her boyfriend was rushed to hospital having collapsed at home, and was pronounced dead at hospital. The post-mortem examination revealed numerous fractures inflicted on at least three separate occasions but was unable to ascertain or establish the cause of death. Neither carer would provide an explanation for how the injuries were caused, in a 'which of you did it?' scenario. However, because the cause of death could not be ascertained the required element of an unlawful act—and so the cause of his death—was absent, and so the familial homicide legislation could not be used. Instead both carers were convicted of child cruelty.

Future developments

A recent Private Member's Bill (July 2011) supported by the government, entitled the 'Domestic Violence, Crime and Victims (Amendment) Bill' would extend the current offence to 'Causing or allowing a child or vulnerable adult to die **or suffer serious physical harm**'. Serious harm would encompass grievous bodily harm (sections 18 or 20 of the Offences Against the Person Act 1861) and the penalty for this element of the offence would be ten years'

65

imprisonment. This would cater for offences of grievous bodily harm or where the cause of death of a child cannot be ascertained but would allow those who had inflicted injuries in a 'Which of you did it?' scenario to be prosecuted.

3.5.7 **Infanticide**

This offence is closely related to murder and manslaughter, because if the unique elements of this offence were not additionally present there would still be a case to answer in relation to murder or manslaughter. Infanticide is in effect a defence to murder or manslaughter and an alternative verdict, if the defence requirements are met, to these charges. In addition to infanticide being an alternative verdict to murder or manslaughter, a verdict of 'not guilty by reason of insanity' may also be open to the jury in circumstances where this offence is considered.

Section 1 of the Infanticide Act 1938 states:

> (1) Where a woman by any wilful act or omission causes the death of her child being a child under the age of twelve months, but at the time of the act or omission the balance of her mind was disturbed by reason of her not having fully recovered from the effect of giving birth to the child or by reason of the effect of lactation consequent upon the birth of the child, then, if the circumstances were such that but for this Act the offence would have amounted to murder or manslaughter, shall be guilty of felony, to wit of infanticide, and may for such offence be dealt with and punished as if she had been guilty of the offence of manslaughter of the child.

Penalty (infanticide): Life imprisonment

3.5.8 **Child destruction**

The offence of child destruction, and others relating to abortion, have similar features that may overlap when considering them in relation to possible potential offences. However, in practical terms suspected person(s) will be arrested for the most appropriate offence in relation to the circumstances. If, after a thorough investigation, there is sufficient evidence for a CPS decision then it will invariably be the CPS lawyers and counsel who will make the final decision on the most appropriate charge.

Section 1 of the Infant Life (Preservation) Act 1929 states that:

> (1) ... any person who, with intent to destroy the life of a child capable of being born alive, by any wilful act causes a child to die before it has an existence independent of its mother, shall be guilty of an offence, to wit, of child destruction, and shall be liable on conviction thereof on indictment to imprisonment for life:
>
> Provided that no person shall be found guilty of an offence under this section unless it is proved that the act which caused the death of the child was

not done in good faith for the purpose only of preserving the life of the mother.

(2) For the purposes of this Act, evidence that a woman had at any time been pregnant for a period of twenty-eight weeks or more shall be prima facie proof that she was at that time pregnant of a child capable of being born alive.

A key factor with this offence is the term 'capable of being born alive'. The legislation states that if the child is 28 weeks or more, then it 'is capable of being born alive'. However, issues arise when the child is less than 28 weeks old. In certain circumstances, abortion is legal up to 24 weeks and previous rulings have decided that a foetus of between 18 and 21 weeks is 'not capable of being born alive'. With the advances of medical science and children surviving premature births, these current rulings on ages leaves the period of 22 weeks up to 28 weeks open to further legal and medical debate.

Case study 1

A pregnant mother is assaulted in a domestic assault by her ex-partner and father of the child; she is pushed and kicked and hit with a piece of wood across the stomach. The child sadly dies in the womb and she is induced to give birth. The post-mortem findings suggest that the foetus was between 13 and 15 weeks, incapable of survival outside of the womb, and had no injuries. The pathologist was unable to prove that the assault and the subsequent loss of the child were conclusively linked. This clearly does not meet the age criteria for child destruction but it is still an assault on the mother, and the fact that she was pregnant at the time of the assault with the associated risks perhaps an aggravating factor in its seriousness. It is also questionable whether the piece of wood and how it was used would satisfy a different but related offence of 'using an instrument or other means to procure an abortion or miscarriage'.

Case study 2

The drug Misoprostol, sometimes known as Cytotec (used for the prevention and treatment of gastric ulcers and haemorrhage prevention), is sometimes used illegally to induce an early abortion with the intention of terminating the pregnancy. A young girl who was 27 weeks pregnant took this drug with the intention of terminating her pregnancy but the child was actually born prematurely at 28 weeks and lived for a while. The cause of death was natural causes and the mother was dealt with for procuring an abortion.

This is similar, but significantly different to the case of 'B' where a pregnant mother was stabbed and the baby injured in the womb at about 22–24 weeks. The baby was subsequently born prematurely and lived for 120 days before sadly dying. It was argued that the unborn foetus was part of the mother but the

67

court determined it had a unique status and ruled that, providing it eventually lived independently of the mother, then the principle of 'transferred malice' would apply and 'B' could be convicted of the **manslaughter** of the child. (*Attorney General's Reference (No. 3 of 1994)* [1997] UKHL31). The difference in case study 2 above is that the child died of natural causes but there could no doubt be a debate on the effect of its early birth on its ability to survive. This is a further example of the complexities involved in the area surrounding childhood deaths.

Penalty (child destruction): Life imprisonment

3.5.9 Administering drugs or using instruments to procure an abortion (miscarriage)

Section 58 of the Offences Against the Person Act 1861 states that:

> Every woman, being with child, who, with intent to procure her own miscarriage, shall unlawfully administer to herself any poison or other noxious thing, or shall unlawfully use any instrument or other means whatsoever with the like intent, and whosoever, with intent to procure the miscarriage of any woman, whether she be or be not with child, shall unlawfully administer to her or cause to be taken by her any poison or other noxious thing, or shall unlawfully use any instrument or other means whatsoever with the like intent, shall be guilty of an offence.

Penalty (administering drugs or using instruments to procure an abortion): Life imprisonment

3.5.10 Supplying or procuring poison, noxious thing or any instrument or thing whatsoever to cause an abortion

Section 59 of the Offences Against the Person Act 1861 states that:

> Whosoever shall unlawfully supply or procure any poison or other noxious thing, or any instrument or thing whatsoever, knowing that the same is intended to be unlawfully used or employed with intent to procure the miscarriage of any woman, whether she be or be not with child, shall be guilty of an offence.

Penalty (supplying or procuring poison [etc] to cause an abortion): Life imprisonment

3.5.11 Legal medical termination of pregnancy

To distinguish between legal and illegal terminations of pregnancy it will be useful to briefly look at those which are legal. Section 1 of the Abortion Act

1967, as amended by the Human Fertilisation and Embryology Act 1990, allows in certain circumstances for the legal termination of a pregnancy and states:

Medical termination of pregnancy

(1) Subject to the provisions of this section, a person shall not be guilty of an offence under the law relating to abortion when a pregnancy is terminated by a registered medical practitioner if two registered medical practitioners are of the opinion, formed in good faith—

    (a) That the pregnancy has not exceeded its twenty-fourth week and that the continuance of the pregnancy would involve risk, greater than if the pregnancy were terminated, of injury to the physical or mental health of the pregnant woman or any existing children of her family; or

    (b) That the termination is necessary to prevent grave permanent injury to the physical or mental health of the pregnant woman; or

    (c) That the continuance of the pregnancy would involve risk to the life of the pregnant woman, greater than if the pregnancy were terminated; or

    (d) That there is a substantial risk that if the child were born it would suffer from such physical or mental abnormalities as to be seriously handicapped.

3.5.12 Concealing a birth—by secret disposition of body whether child died before or after birth

Section 60 of the Offences Against the Person Act 1861 states that:

If any woman shall be delivered of a child, every person who shall, by any secret disposition of the dead body of the said child, whether such child died before, at, or after its birth, endeavour to conceal the birth thereof, shall be guilty of a misdemeanour, and being convicted thereof shall be liable, at the discretion of the court, to be imprisoned.

Penalty (concealing a birth): 2 years' imprisonment

Key points in relation to the concealment is whether or not the body is likely to be found, whether it was at a viable age rather than a young foetus, and had the child died before they were concealed. (PNLD, 2011)

An essential question in these cases will be 'Was the child a reasonable creature in being?'—whilst the question of how you define a person for the purposes of legislation, eg murder, has presented moral and philosophical dilemmas. Key factors from Common Law, eg *Rance v Mid-Downs Health Authority* [1991] 1 QB 587 (PNLD D 6758) usefully talk of a child 'having an existence independent of their mother', having independent circulation, and having breathed after birth—simply: Was the child born? Did they live? And, sadly, did they die? These definitions can become very relevant in relation to circumstances where it is not clear that a child has actually lived, eg (a) an unexpected unassisted birth at home by a mother who hadn't realized she was pregnant or had not told anyone and the child does not survive; or (b) an abandoned dead child—foetus or possible stillbirth. In these cases, invariably, a post-mortem will be required and the coroner would have been informed. However, the coroner may not accept jurisdiction if it is clear that the child had not an existence independent of their mother, and issues will then arise regarding the status of the body. It may be that the police consider that they are investigating a possible criminal offence (one of those listed here) and will sensitively seize the body as an 'exhibit' under section 19 of the Police and Criminal Evidence Act 1984. In any case, it will be essential to consult the coroner as a matter of urgency and be guided by their advice and directions.

3.5.13 Preventing lawful burial—conceal corpse—dispose of or destroy dead body

This is a common law offence which is usefully defined in the Court of Appeal judgment in the case of *R v Hunter Atkinson and Mackinder* (1973) 57 Cr App R 773 which states:

> It is still an indictable offence to prevent, or conspire to prevent, the lawful and decent burial of a dead body without lawful excuse. Where there has been an agreement to conceal a dead body and the concealment in fact prevents burial, the offence of conspiracy to prevent burial is complete, although prevention of burial was not the object of the agreement.

Penalty (preventing lawful burial, etc): On indictment—No maximum penalty

Case study

A mother living with her three children had a history of experiencing behavioural issues with her 16-year-old daughter and was also experiencing financial problems that resulted in bailiffs repossessing the house she was living in. When the bailiffs arrived, she informed them that her daughter had died the previous evening. The police were called and discovered the daughter's body under black bin bags in the front room but in a decomposed and putrefying condition. Clearly she had been dead for some time. Due to the decomposition of the body, the pathologist was unable to ascertain a cause of death but considered that the daughter had been dead for about three months. The mother was investigated in relation to the neglect of the other children who had been living in the house during this period and convicted of preventing the lawful burial of her daughter.

A related offence under Common Law is:

Obstructing the coroner in the execution of their duty; this is an indictable only offence with a penalty of imprisonment or a fine.

3.5.14 **Additional supplementary legislation**

There are some situations where the legislation already outlined is not applicable or presents legal difficulties, eg at present if the cause of death is unascertained then, despite a child having suffered injuries, the familial homicide offence would not currently apply, although hopefully this will be remedied in the future.

In these cases the **Children and Young Persons Act 1933** offences may be appropriate. The offences under section 1—child cruelty—could be applied in two different respects.

Section 1 states:

> (1) If a person who has attained the age of sixteen years and has responsibility for a child or young person under that age, wilfully assaults, ill-treats, neglects, abandons, or exposes him, or causes or procures him to be assaulted, ill-treated, neglected, abandoned, or exposed, in a manner likely to cause him unnecessary suffering or injury to health (including injury to or loss of sight, hearing, limb, or organ of the body, and any mental derangement), that person is guilty of a misdemeanour, and shall be liable …[to ten years' imprisonment]

This section might be used in cases where parents/carers knew that their child was ill or injured but they did not obtain medical assistance or take them to the hospital. The term 'wilful' is an important aspect in proving the offence and is a subjective test. There is a less well known section of the offence that may be very relevant to childhood deaths in certain circumstances.

Section 1(2)(b) states:

> Where it is proved that the death of an infant under three years of age was caused by suffocation (not being suffocation caused by disease or the presence of any foreign body in the throat or air passages of the infant) while the infant was in bed with some other person who has attained the age of sixteen years, that other person shall, if he was, when he went to bed, under the influence of drink, be deemed to have neglected the infant in a manner likely to cause injury to its health.

This is an interesting offence as possible overlaying by parents or carers who have been suspected of drinking alcohol or taken drugs is a scenario that does occur. Issues arise, as will be explained later in detail, actually establishing at the postmortem that the child died as a result of suffocation, as without this element the offence cannot be proved. As drafted, this offence appears to relate to alcohol, not drugs, and bed, not sofa or chair. However, there is some debate as to whether, applying the rules of statutory interpretation, the legislation can be said to be just as applicable to overlaying on sofas due to drugs, as it is to overlaying on beds due to alcohol. If such a case arises, discussions should be held with the CPS.

The following offences may also be appropriate in some circumstances:

Maliciously administering poison or noxious thing so as to endanger life—

s. 23 of the Offences Against the Person Act 1861 (Penalty: 10 years' imprisonment)

Unlawfully exposing or abandoning a child under two where life is endangered—

s. 27 of the Offences Against the Person Act 1861 (Penalty: 5 years' imprisonment)

The Criminal Attempts Act 1981 in relation to attempts to commit some of the offences outlined above.

Case study—Exercise

The body of a newborn baby is found at an industrial waste disposal site in a sanitary waste bin from a busy travel terminus. The post-mortem showed that the baby had been born alive and probably breathed a couple of breaths but that their nasal passages were congested. It appeared that the mother may have given birth in the toilet: the child lived briefly but died as a result of the circumstances of the birth, and the mother then put the baby in the sanitary waste bin and left the area without informing anybody.

KEY POINTS

Consider:

What possible offences could have been committed?

Consider all of the offences outlined above utilizing the suggested research resources—there is no definitive answer as there are several unanswered questions (as the mother was never identified).

3.6 Conclusion

It is important to emphasize the importance of the guidance and its utilization in investigations to establish why a child died and stress again that the majority of child deaths are NOT the result of criminal offences. However, it is essential that investigators respond to every child death with an open mind and are sensitively mindful that, in a small proportion of deaths, these offences may have been committed.

Further information and reading

ACPO (2006), *Murder Investigation Manual* (London: NPIA).

ACPO Homicide Working Group (2011), *A Guide to Investigating Child Deaths* [in final stages of approval by ACPO].

Department for Children, Schools and Families, *Why Jason died*. DVD and other childhood death resources at <http://www.education.gov.uk>.

HM Government (2010), *Working Together to Safeguard Children. A guide to inter-agency working to safeguard and promote the welfare of children* (Nottingham: DCSF Publications).

Ministry of Justice (2010), *A Guide to Coroners and Inquests* (Coroners and Burials Division, Ministry of Justice).

NSPCC (2003), *Which of you did it? Problems of achieving criminal convictions when a child dies or is seriously injured by parents or carers* (NSPCC: London).

British and Irish Legal Information Institute (BAILII) website: <http://www.bailii.org>.

National Archives 'The official home of UK legislation' website: <http://www.legislation.gov.uk>.

Police National Legal Database (PNLD) website: <https://www.pnld.co.uk>.

POLKA: POLKA is a secure online space for the policing community currently hosted by the NPIA to share insights, discover ideas, and suggest new ways of working including a DOCUMENT LIBRARY. POLKA can be accessed from the police national network within the Criminal Justice Framework.

NOTES

NOTES

Non-suspicious Child Deaths

4.1 **Introduction**

As previously stated the majority of sudden and unexpected child deaths are non-suspicious in nature and devastating events for the families concerned. The investigative processes outlined in Chapter 7 in *Working Together* for child deaths, as explained in the previous chapter, are multi-agency in nature and in effect, co-ordinated by the designated paediatrician for child deaths, who chairs the rapid response meeting. It will be useful at this juncture to consider the views of those different partners in the investigation process and focus, in particular, on the designated paediatrician, the pathologist, the parent, and the police to obtain their perspective on how the processes will actually work in practice. There are, as previously explained, a number of additional people involved in the investigation who all have an important contribution, eg HM Coroner, Children's Social Care, but hopefully by examining the perspectives of these particular groups in more detail it will highlight some important themes that impact on all of them. It will also emphasize that these are multi-agency investigations where communication and an understanding of each other's perspective is essential in working together to uphold the rights of the deceased child and their siblings, parents, carers, and family.

4.2 **The paediatrician's perspective**

The role of the Sudden Unexpected Death in Childhood (SUDC) paediatrician and the police senior investigating officer (SIO) should be seen as an **equal** partnership. It is essential that, from the outset, there is clear communication of roles and expectations to ensure the best outcomes for families and other professionals. Depending on the nature of the case, other key figures may include the acute doctors at the hospital or children's social care amongst others.

It is vital for all those involved in this process to keep an open mind from the outset until sufficient information is available to make decisions. It is important that professionals do not make assumptions, and understand that the Rapid Response Team will be involved even where a child has a significant underlying disease. Just as a child who is the subject of a child protection plan can die of natural causes, children with underlying disease may have their life deliberately ended prematurely.

When it becomes clearer that a medical cause of death is likely, the balance of who leads the case will shift towards the SUDC paediatrician, who will continue to update police colleagues on any developments. In all but the suspected homicide cases, the SUDC paediatrician will chair the Rapid Response Meeting and the subsequent related meetings with the responsibility for the distribution of action points.

When a case is thought to be homicide, the SUDC paediatrician will defer to their police colleagues. If, however, there remains the possibility of a medical cause of death some police-led enquiries have benefited from the continuing partnership approach, eg police interviews have been conducted including medical-based questions asked by the police officer but prompted by the SUDC paediatrician.

In the past, SUDC paediatricians were involved very little in the homicide enquiries, but in many areas they have increasingly added valuable contributions by chasing background information, helping to explain medical terminology and procedures, and liaising with primary care to support the family, etc.

4.2.1 **Initial actions**

Experience suggests that it assists if the paediatrician talks to the police as soon as possible, perhaps making use of the travelling time on route to the hospital (utilizing hands free technology) to discuss the initial information and start to allocate roles. If this doesn't occur, it is VITAL to sit down before approaching the family to discuss points including:

- Who will lead introductions;
- Who will be present;
- Who will scribe;
- Will the child be examined prior to history taking (as this can help inform professional judgement on whether or not the death is suspicious at an early stage).

KEY POINT

It is important that the professional working environment is such that police officers have the confidence to question medical opinion, but equally the paediatrician and other medical staff are free to ask the police why they are pursuing a particular course of action at that particular time.

Often potential conflicts in priorities and methods can be overcome by cultivating this mutual appreciation of each other's respective roles. It is exceedingly useful to come from two different backgrounds, and talk through a case, to ensure that professional duties are fulfilled in as humane a way as possible.

It is less common now for the initial response to a sudden unexpected child death to be by uniformed officers in marked cars but sometimes operational and resourcing issues may necessitate that. What is very important is that whoever responds does so in a professional and sensitive manner.

In an ideal world the child and family would be seen as soon as possible by the joint Rapid Response Team, which can be best achieved by having a 24/7 on call paediatric consultant-led service. In some areas which have an office hour service, this may be the following day. Another variation is that in some areas the role of the SUDC paediatrician is fulfilled by specially trained health visitors.

4.2.2 Terminology

Terminology is very important, particularly from the grieving parents' perspective. The terms 'search', 'crime scene', and 'scene of crime officer' should be avoided and agreement reached between the paediatrician and police as to suitable terms, eg 'death scene assessment', 'home visit', 'the officer who takes the photos'. Likewise, the police officer can assist by reminding the paediatrician not to use medical jargon, or if they do, to explain it for those present who may not understand it.

4.2.3 Seizing items

When considering 'seizing' items it can be very valuable to have a two-way discussion using the paediatrician as the non-police officer to ask: 'Why does that need to be taken? What may be lost if it wasn't?' It's not the role of the paediatrician to tell a police officer NOT to take something, but it may be appropriate for them to act as an advocate for the family where possible.

4.2.4 Home visit

A distinction needs to be made between a 'home visit' as outlined in Chapter 7 *Working Together* and 'visiting the scene of death' or potential 'crime scene'. In most areas, the homes are visited of children under two years who died (unless from an obvious cause, eg a road traffic collision or overwhelming sepsis) straight from A&E, and preferably with one of the parents if they feel able to. This can be invaluable and provide useful information at an early stage in relation to sleeping position, the general home, whether there is food, clean clothes, etc. It is important to get a 'feel' for safeguarding in relation to any other children in the family.

Some paediatricians can be anxious about the home visit as they may feel they've not been 'trained' to see a 'scene of crime'. It is usually the case that they don't attend if it is actually considered to be a scene of crime, but may review pictures with the police later. If parents have struggled to tell their story in A&E, the paediatrician and police may visit the home to complete the history-taking at a later date. These types of visit would be what paediatricians would regard as home visits. Medical knowledge in relation to prescribed drugs or medication in the premises may prove invaluable.

4.2.5 Taking samples

Each coronial district will have an agreed policy regarding samples taken after death. This can range from restricting the taking of samples outside of the pathology department (so all investigations are performed by the pathologists) to the full Kennedy Protocol for SUDI (see Appendix F) being completed in the

A&E department. It is not the responsibility of police to seize or retain these samples as they are primarily to detect disease or medical abnormalities.

4.2.6 Safeguarding role

Paediatricians are involved daily in considering safeguarding issues for their patients and the siblings of their patients. In order to be confident that there are no child protection concerns regarding a particular family, it is often necessary to seek information from other health care professionals. This can lead to questions about confidentiality, especially when information is requested about other family members (eg the mother's mental health). A balance must be made between: (a) supporting the family and keeping information confidential, against (b) the legal duty to disclose information if relevant to establishing the cause of death of a child or for protecting their siblings. There is GMC guidance for doctors which allows them to share information with the designated paediatrician; they actually have a duty to do so if there may be safeguarding concerns or to allow statutory information to be gathered for the Child Death Overview Panel (CDOP). On some occasions it may be necessary to liaise with legal departments to get access to see medical notes.

4.2.7 Dedicated rapid response team

Many areas are benefiting from a dedicated team of medics being routinely involved with child deaths to acquire a degree of experience in these cases, and also of maintaining a list of useful experts in relation to specialist medical knowledge associated with child deaths, eg eyes, burns, fractures.

Whilst there has always been the potential for the paediatrician to be seen as 'the touchy feely' one, and the police officer the one needing to be 'pulled back by the collar', experience has shown a respectful, mutually beneficial professional relationship.

Policing can be perceived as being very rigid and protocol led. Child death doesn't neatly fit into protocols, so it is of benefit that a fellow professional, someone outside of the police, is able to ask 'why are we doing that?', 'is there a better way for the family?' This role is well suited to paediatricians, who are used to being advocates for the child and their families.

4.2.8 Liaison with HM Coroner

Generally it is the police, not the medics, who liaise more closely with the coroner and his/her liaison team. This requires clear discussion as to who will share what information with families. For example, there are still sometimes issues in ensuring families know where the body of their child is, if it is necessary for them to be moved for post-mortem examination. Each police force may cover several coronial districts, and there may be a different procedure in each of these for who undertakes which role. The principle advocated is that at all times it is clearly agreed whose responsibility it is to keep the family informed of practicalities.

4.2.9 **Mementos**

Mementos by which to remember the deceased child (eg foot and hand prints, lock of hair) are important. Some hospitals offer them for all under-18s and some stipulate that they will be taken only after the post-mortem by the pathology staff, the rationale being that then they are well presented and taken to the family by the Coroners Liaison Officer (CLO), but again this will vary depending on the area.

4.2.10 **Parents' access to the deceased child**

This is a natural response of parents and, provided a professional (eg police/ nurse/social worker) is present, it should be allowed in most cases. In suspicious or homicide cases where forensic considerations will be an issue, the SIO must be consulted before a carer is allowed to handle their baby.

4.2.11 **Welfare of all staff**

Many police officers will have children themselves and (even if they don't) medical deaths can be exceptionally upsetting for them, particularly if they have or know a child of a similar age. It has been said that police officers know how to try to protect their children from crime but are unable to protect them from medical illness, eg meningitis. Medical colleagues should always be available to answer the concerns of police colleagues, and should be sensitive to the fact that, in medical deaths, police officers are often experiencing something that they haven't encountered in training. This is reversed in homicide cases where medical colleagues greatly benefit from the support of police colleagues in an upsetting and unfamiliar situation.

KEY POINT

It is important that arrangements are in place to monitor the effect of dealing with child deaths on all those involved, and to have suitable staff welfare support mechanisms in place.

4.3 **The pathologist's perspective**

With the cause of death being central to any child death investigation, the role of the pathologist is clearly an essential element of the process. With children, the expectation is that the post-mortem or autopsy is undertaken by a paediatric pathologist who specializes in child deaths. If the death is suspicious and the coroner orders a more detailed forensic or 'special post-mortem', this should be performed by: (a) a paediatric pathologist working with a Home Office accredited forensic pathologist, or (b) a Home Office forensic paediatric pathologist. Currently, there is only one Home Office forensic paediatric pathologist in the UK and they are based at Great Ormond Street Children's Hospital in London.

KEY POINT

The role of the pathologist is to investigate on behalf of the coroner the post-mortem findings to establish the cause of death and any other issues from the examination that might have a bearing on the death.

4.3.1 **HM Coroner's permission, licensed premises, and legislation**

Before explaining the detailed role of the pathologist, it is necessary to understand the legal context in which they have to operate. HM Coroner is a very important person within this context as, without their legal authorization, the pathologist is extremely limited in what they can do, particularly when the death is sudden and unexpected. It will, therefore, be of great benefit to understand the duties of the coroner together with the other legal parameters within which the pathologist and fellow professionals undertake their role in child death. This includes the legislation regarding any samples taken during post-mortem examinations and their retention—a very important area to understand for all those involved.

The coroner

The role of the coroner is primarily to facilitate identification of the deceased and to determine how, when, and where that person died. Infant and childhood deaths that should be referred to the coroner include all cases in which:

- The cause of death is unknown, or sudden and unexpected; this includes all SUDI and all SUDC;
- The death occurred during an operation or before recovery from the effects of an anaesthetic;
- The deceased infant or child was not seen by the certifying medical practitioner, either after death or within 14 days of death;
- The death may have been caused by violence or neglect;
- The death may have been due to an accident;

• The death may have been in any other way unnatural or there are suspicious circumstances (This may also include cases in which there is suspicion of possible medical negligence).

(Adapted from the Registration of Births and Deaths Regulations 1987; <http://www.legislation.gov.uk/uksi/1987/2088/contents/made>.)

The coroner will then decide whether to investigate the death further, and whether, as part of the coroner's investigation, a post-mortem examination is required; the latter may not be required in all cases, but the majority of paediatric deaths that are investigated by the coroner will have a post-mortem examination. Most coroners are lawyers; some are doctors with a law degree. The coroner does not carry out the post-mortem examination themselves, but will instruct a pathologist to do so on their behalf. In the case of a paediatric death, this will almost always be a paediatric pathologist, who is a pathologist with specialist expertise in diseases relating to infancy and childhood.

If there are suspicious circumstances, or the death may have been due to violence or neglect, or may have been in any other way unnatural, then the death will be further investigated by the police, who may then request the coroner to sanction a so-called 'special' or forensic post-mortem examination. This is performed by a forensic pathologist, who is a pathologist with specialist expertise in unnatural deaths. As the majority of forensic pathologists do not have specialist expertise in diseases relating to children, most paediatric forensic post-mortem examinations are carried out jointly by a forensic pathologist and a paediatric pathologist.

Samples taken during the course of the post-mortem

When the coroner instructs a paediatric pathologist to carry out a post-mortem examination, parental consent is not required and the coroner's decision overrides that of the parents. All samples collected during, and retained following, the post-mortem examination are done so under the authority of the coroner, and not under the Human Tissue Act 2004 (see below). However, as per the Coroners Rules (as amended), the pathologist may only collect samples that in his/her opinion have a bearing on the cause of death or on the identification of the deceased (<http://www.kcl.ac.uk/depsta/law/research/coroners/1984rules.html> and <http://www.legislation.gov.uk/uksi/2005/420/article/3/made>). The pathologist has a statutory duty to inform the coroner of the samples retained; the coroner will stipulate the time period for retention, which may vary for different samples taken, and will also notify the next-of-kin (parents) of their options relating to the handling of these tissue samples once the coroner's authority has ended, which may be several months (or longer) after the post-mortem examination.

Once the coroner's authority has ended, all tissue samples taken as part of the coroner's post-mortem examination (including so-called blocks and slides, see below) now fall under the jurisdiction of the Human Tissue Act 2004 (see below) and must then be handled according to the parents' wishes.

The parents broadly have three options:

1. They may prefer all samples to be disposed of, which is usually done by the hospital, either by means of incineration separate to other clinical waste, or by cremation; or
2. The parents may wish to have all samples returned to them, usually via their designated funeral director; or
3. The parents may wish to have the samples stored indefinitely by the hospital as part of their child's permanent medical record so that they can be reviewed in the future, either in the light of further medical information or new diagnostic tests. If the parents choose this option, they may also wish to consent to the hospital using these samples for medical education, audit, and quality control, as well as for research which may help other families in the future. All research projects involving human tissue must be approved by a research ethics committee, and samples would be anonymized so that the child cannot be identified.

It is important for parents to realize that, should they choose one of the first two options, subsequent review and further diagnosis will not be possible, which may have implications for the family should the possibility of an underlying genetic disorder be raised at a later date, or in the rare event of a subsequent death of a sibling. Whilst it may be distressing to the family having to make such decisions, it is also important for parents to be informed that, if the family has not communicated a decision to the hospital within three months after the coroner's authority has ended, it is a legal requirement under the Human Tissue Act 2004 that the hospital dispose of the samples. This means, as outlined above, that any subsequent review or further tests will not be possible in the future.

The Human Tissue Act 2004 and licensed premises

The Human Tissue Act 2004 received Royal Assent in November 2004 and came into force on 1 September 2006; its implementation was overseen by the Human Tissue Authority (HTA), an independent statutory regulator that provides advice and guidance relating to the Act, and which is responsible for defining a minimum set of standards, published as Codes of Practice, which are available online (see <http://www.hta.gov.uk>). In addition, the HTA also oversees the licensing of organizations and establishments that deal with human tissue. This not only includes the mortuary, where the post-mortem examination is carried out, but also A&E or Casualty departments, where samples might be taken by a paediatrician immediately after death, usually under the authority of the coroner (see below).

The Act requires consent for the removal, storage, and use of human tissue for so-called scheduled purposes, ie anatomical examination; determining the cause of death; establishing, after a person's death, the efficacy of any drug or other treatment administered to them; obtaining scientific or medical information, which may be relevant to any other person now or in the future; public display; research in connection with disorders, or the functioning, of the human body; transplantation; clinical audit; education or training relating to human health; performance assessment; public health monitoring; and quality assurance. This applies to all tissue removed at post-mortem, including small samples such as blocks and slides (see below), and samples that might be kept as part of the child's medical record. Note that for coronial post-mortem examinations, consent is only required for handling of the tissue samples after the coroner's functions have ceased (see above).

Consent, as defined under the Act, must be both *appropriate* (defined in terms of who may give consent) and *valid* (the conditions that should be met).

Appropriate consent

The Act defines who may give consent, which in the setting of paediatric post-mortem examinations will usually be one or both parents, or person(s) with parental responsibility. For paediatric deaths, it is recommended that, if possible, consent is obtained from the mother, and that, where appropriate, both parents are involved. Under the Act, consent from one parent is sufficient; however, if there is disagreement between the parents, it is recommended that this be sensitively discussed with both parents and that any decision be deferred until such time that an agreement is reached.

Valid consent

Consent is not just a signature on a consent form but should be viewed as an ongoing process in which the parents can discuss the issues fully, ask questions, and make an informed choice, which includes the option of withdrawing consent at a later stage. The Act defines the giving of consent as a positive act; the absence of refusal is not evidence of adequate consent. In order for consent to be valid, it must be given voluntarily by an appropriately informed person who has the capacity to agree to the activity in question.

To give consent, the parents must understand the nature and purpose of what is proposed and be able to make a balanced judgement. In the context of a coroner's post-mortem examination, they should be told about the way tissue and other samples were obtained, how the tissue was used to make a diagnosis, and any possible ways that the samples could be used in the future with their consent; specifically, the use of tissue for clinical audit, quality control, public health monitoring, education and training, and ethically approved research must be discussed, and the consent taker has to ensure that these purposes are fully understood by the parent(s). The consent process must cover the reasons and benefits of consenting to the retention of material, as well as the options for disposal.

Who takes consent?

For consented post-mortem examinations, it is usually the treating clinician's responsibility to seek consent; however, this obviously does not apply to coroner's post-mortem examinations. In the latter, as outlined above, consent only relates to the future handling of the tissue samples that were initially retained under the Coroners Rules, and, in this context, consent is usually obtained by the coroner's officer in charge of the case. There is, however, no statutory duty on the coroner to obtain consent: the coroner has a statutory duty, under the Coroners Rules, merely to *inform* the parents about their options relating to the future handling of the tissue samples once the coroner's functions have ceased; the family, too, has *no* statutory duty to make a decision, and the coroner has *no* statutory duty to communicate the parents' wishes to the pathologist; however, in practice, most coroner's officers readily do this, usually by means of a form signed by the parent(s) which is then forwarded to the pathologist. To ensure that the parents' wishes are communicated to the pathologist, the HTA recommends that local establishments make provision for a so-called *nominated person* whose role is to liaise between the coroner's officer, family, and pathologist. The nominated person could be a bereavement officer, a senior anatomical pathology technologist (APT) (see below), a police family liaison officer, or a coroner's officer. Finally, it is recommended that the person taking consent must be especially careful with families where English is not the first language. As valid consent can only be given if appropriate communication has taken place, information leaflets should be available in different languages for parents whose first language is not English, and interpreters should be used where necessary.

4.3.2 **Pathologist's involvement with rapid response and CDOP**

Although explained in detail in Chapter 3, the following brief summary is a useful reminder and will support an understanding of the pathologist's role. This information is modified from the FSID information leaflet *The Child Death Review. A Guide for Parents and Carers* (<http://fsid.org.uk/document.doc?id=146>).

Rapid response

Unexpected child deaths initiate a so-called rapid response, which broadly includes three stages:

Immediate response

This involves transferring the child to the A&E department, where the child will be examined by a paediatrician or other doctor(s), and blood and other samples may be taken (see below). Preliminary discussions may be held between different professionals, such as the police, the coroner's officer, and the paediatrician.

Early response

This usually takes place within the first week after the death. The pathologist will be asked to carry out the post-mortem examination. All professionals involved share information about the child's death; if the child died at home, the home may be visited by a police officer, with or without an accompanying health care professional.

Later response

This follows on from one week and may take up to several months later. More background information may be gathered during this time, if required, such as reviewing school health records, maternity notes or other relevant information. The coroner will decide whether to hold an inquest and the pathologist will complete the post-mortem report, which is sent to the coroner.

After the post-mortem examination results are available, a final case discussion takes place between the group of professionals that were involved and a report is completed, which is sent to the local Child Death Overview Panel (see below), as well as to the coroner. The purpose of this meeting is to review all the information to identify any factors that may have contributed to the death in order to help prevent future deaths.

Child Death Overview Panel (CDOP)

It is a legal requirement that the death of all children under the age of 18 years be reviewed by a local Child Death Overview Panel (CDOP) on behalf of the Local Safeguarding Children Board (see below). The CDOPs comprise groups of professionals who meet several times a year to review all childhood deaths in their area; the cases are anonymized, as the main purpose is to learn how to prevent future deaths. The panel has representatives from public health, as well as local child health and social care services and the police, in addition to other professionals that may be invited to give specialist advice in selected cases. The panel makes recommendations on the lessons learnt to the Local Safeguarding Children Board, which produces an annual report that is available to the public.

Local Safeguarding Children Board (LSCB)

The Local Safeguarding Children Board (LSCB) has a wider responsibility for safeguarding and promoting the welfare of all children in their area. The board makes sure any recommendations made by the CDOP are sent to those with responsibility for taking them forward. In a small number of child deaths, the LSCB may decide to conduct a more detailed investigation called a Serious Case Review.

The death of a young child, which is often sudden and unexpected, even when it is not suspicious, will result in an investigation by the CDOP and may be the subject of a coroner's inquest. In these circumstances, it is part of the pathologist's duty to provide information to the CDOP and to give evidence at the inquest. When appropriate, the pathologist will often provide further information and advice to the bereaved family, who may not always fully understand the formal proceedings involved in these processes.

4.3.3 Samples taken in A&E for SUDI

The current Kennedy guidelines recommend the taking of various samples immediately after death in A&E or Casualty departments. These include the following samples:

- Blood and cerebrospinal fluid (the fluid around the brain and spinal cord, obtainable by means of a lumbar puncture) for bacteriological investigations (testing for bacteria).
- A nasopharyngeal aspirate for both virological (testing for viruses) and bacteriological investigations.
- Swabs for bacteriology from any identifiable lesions.
- A blood and urine sample (if available) for toxicology.
- Blood spots collected on a Guthrie card for acylcarnitine profiling (to test for fatty acid oxidation disorders, a form of metabolic disorder (see below).
- A skin biopsy and/or muscle biopsy, if the clinical history is suggestive of an underlying metabolic/mitochondrial disorder (a disorder that affects the biochemical processes inside the cells).
- Blood for cytogenetics (chromosome analysis, also known as karyotyping) if there are dysmorphic features (abnormal facial or other external appearances which may suggest an underlying chromosomal disorder).

As outlined above, any establishment, including A&E or Casualty departments, wards, and surgical theatres, where samples from a deceased person are removed for scheduled purposes must be appropriately licensed by the HTA. In this setting, any samples that are collected after the child has been certified dead are almost always taken under the authority of the coroner; it is therefore recommended that local hospital protocols are approved by their local coroner. Furthermore, the results of these investigations must be forwarded to the coroner, who can then make them available to the paediatric pathologist performing the autopsy.

It should be noted that the Kennedy guidelines are recommendations, and that there is no legal requirement for doctors or other health care professionals to collect these samples after death. Moreover, for suspicious deaths that might require a forensic post-mortem examination, it is usually recommended that *no* samples be taken in A&E or, if attempted, that no more than one attempt should be made.

With the exception of samples for metabolic investigations (especially skin and muscle biopsies, if clinically indicated), there is little evidence at present to suggest that the taking of such samples in A&E is superior to collecting samples at post-mortem examination, particularly for microbiological samples for the detection of infection, which in most centres in the UK are routinely collected at autopsy. In a study from Norway, it was shown that the diagnosis of infection is as good at post-mortem and does not require the taking of microbiological samples in A&E, provided the autopsy is performed within 48 hours of death (Lobmaier et al., 2009). One study of over 500 SUDI deaths showed that a prolonged post-mortem interval of several days' duration results in decreased growth of bacteria from post-mortem cultures, suggesting that a proportion of bacteria may die when the body is stored at cold temperatures for prolonged periods of time, but this merely implies that early sampling is better than delayed sampling after several days, not necessarily that samples should be collected in A&E at the time of death (Weber et al., 2010). A recent study from the UK also directly compared the results of microbiological investigations taken in A&E to those collected at autopsy; in that study, again, no cases with an infective cause of death would have been missed if samples had not been collected in A&E (Pryce et al., 2011).

For these reasons, based on the currently available evidence, the post-mortem investigation is unlikely to be significantly jeopardized if these samples are not taken, as the majority of samples will be and can be collected at the time of the autopsy. However, until such time that the Kennedy guidelines are amended, current best practice recommends that such samples are routinely collected in A&E; importantly, if samples are taken, this must be clearly documented, they should be sent to the local laboratory for analysis and *not* stored with the body, and the results of the investigations must be made available to the coroner and to the pathologist.

4.3.4 Role of the anatomical pathology technologist (APT)

Before going through a detailed description of a post-mortem examination, it is important to acknowledge that other medical professionals may be involved. Formerly known as a mortuary technician, the anatomical pathology technologist (APT) has the responsibility for managing the day-to-day processes relating to all aspects of the mortuary service and assisting the pathologist during post-mortem examinations. It is the APT who ensures that everything runs smoothly in the mortuary, and that all visitors to the mortuary (including police) abide by the health and safety stipulations.

Examples of specific duties may include:

- Receiving and releasing of bodies to and from the mortuary;
- Preparing bodies for viewings by relatives, if requested;
- Organizing skeletal surveys (X-rays), if indicated, prior to the post-mortem examination;
- Preparing the post-mortem room prior to autopsy;

- Assisting the pathologist during the post-mortem examination, including with photography (if required), evisceration in selected cases (eg removing the brain), weighing of organs, and careful reconstruction of the body afterwards;
- Documentation and dispatch of autopsy samples to other departments or establishments;
- Maintaining appropriate records; including the documentation of the family's wishes regarding the future handling of any tissue samples taken during the coroner's post-mortem examination once the coroner's functions have ceased;
- Ensuring that the mortuary upholds the statutory HTA standards;
- Maintaining a regular audit calendar relating to all post-mortem activity;
- Ensuring good communication with the pathologist and other health care professionals, coroners and coroners' officers, police, chaplaincy, bereavement staff, and the relatives of the deceased;
- Participating in taking post-mortem consent in some centres;
- Assisting with the education and training of service users, including post-mortem consent training in selected centres; and
- Participating in continuing professional development activities.

Many APTs in the UK are now registered with the Voluntary Registration Council and are members of the Association of Anatomical Pathology Technology (AAPT), the recognized professional body for APTs employed in hospital and public mortuaries across the UK (<http://www.aaptuk.org>).

4.3.5 Health and safety in the mortuary

Adapted from the HTA Codes of Practice 3 (<http://www.hta.gov.uk/legislation-policiesandcodesofpractice/codesofpractice/code3postmortem.cfm>):

Mortuaries vary enormously in size, configuration, age, and condition, but it is an HTA requirement that the premises are 'fit for purpose', ie that the mortuary storage areas and post-mortem examination rooms provide an environment that is both safe for staff and preserves the dignity of the deceased.

Every employee has a duty to take reasonable care for the health and safety of themselves and of others who may be affected by their acts or omissions at work.

General recommendations include that:

- The mortuary should be clean and well maintained and subject to a regular cleaning and disinfection schedule.
- Access to the mortuary is restricted to authorized personnel only.
- There should be clearly separate 'clean' and 'dirty' areas, and equipment should not be moved between these areas.
- Staff should have hydraulic trolleys to ensure that they can access all bodies safely.

- Staff should have access to personal protective equipment (PPE) such as protective clothing, disposable gloves, boots, and goggles or visors.
- Staff should have facilities for changing, washing, and storing their personal effects.
- All staff should be aware of the Control of Substances Hazardous to Health (COSHH) regulations (<http://www.hse.gov.uk/coshh/>). Where chemicals, such as formalin, are used for the preservation of tissue samples, the area should be adequately ventilated to control exposure; the ventilation system should be maintained and regularly checked, and monitoring of formalin levels may be indicated in some cases.
- Disposable gloves should be worn at all time when handling specimens, chemical solutions, and formalin-fixed tissues.
- All equipment should be regularly maintained and any materials used in the post-mortem room should be easy to clean and non-porous.
- If possible, there should be a separate work room for high-risk post-mortem examinations, ie cases that are infected with so-called class three pathogens such as HIV or hepatitis B. If this is not possible, other measures should be in place in order to minimize the risk of contamination, including carrying out the post-mortem examination last, using ventilated visors, etc.

4.4 SUDI/paediatric post-mortems

The types of post-mortem undertaken will be explained and followed by a detailed step-by-step description of what is involved in a SUDI paediatric post-mortem, including information on the various samples taken and their retention. This again emphasizes the highly specialized nature of child death investigations and the detailed and extensive examinations that are undertaken.

4.4.1 Types of post-mortem

There are three types of post-mortem examinations:

- Forensic post-mortem examination ('special' post-mortem examination);
- Coroner's post-mortem examination;
- Consented ('hospital') post-mortem examination.

The first two are medico-legal autopsies; the consented autopsy, as the name suggests, requires consent by one or both parents since the likely immediate cause of death will be known.

In general, a paediatric post-mortem examination may:

- Determine a medical explanation for the death/cause of death;
- Identify any other diseases that may have contributed to the death;

- Identify conditions, such as genetic disorders, which may be important for the family to be aware of; and
- Provide knowledge that may help other families in the future (ie contribute to research, education, and audit; note that tissue samples cannot be used for research, education, or audit unless the family consents to this).

KEY POINT

In some cases, the post-mortem examination may not find a cause of death and it is interesting to note that, in around two thirds of SUDI, the cause of death will remain unexplained after the post-mortem examination (see below).

4.4.2 Step-by-step post-mortem procedure for SUDI, samples taken, retention of samples

When performing a SUDI post-mortem examination, paediatric pathologists in the UK broadly follow the Kennedy autopsy protocol (see Appendix F).

4.4.3 Radiology

Most post-mortem examinations of sudden unexpected deaths, particularly for children under three years of age, are preceded by a so-called skeletal survey—a series of X-rays of the entire body—to rule out the presence of fractures. The presence of a fracture may not necessarily be indicative of inflicted injury and must be interpreted in the appropriate clinical context. Other imaging modalities include post-mortem computed tomography (CT) and magnetic resonance imaging (MRI), the latter of which has been shown to be useful in examining the brain of infants with suspected brain abnormalities and intracranial haemorrhage, but these are not routinely performed in most centres.

4.4.4 External and macroscopic examination

Once the clinical details have been reviewed by the pathologist, and the body correctly identified, a careful external examination is carried out. The infant is weighed and basic measurements are taken, including head circumference and body length, which are compared to standard reference tables to ensure that the measurements are appropriate for the age of the infant.

The pathologist will specifically look for any signs of injury, eg suspicious marks or bruises, or a torn upper labial frenulum. The presence of such lesions may result in the autopsy being converted from a 'non-suspicious' standard paediatric coroner's post-mortem examination to a forensic paediatric post-mortem examination (see above). The presence of small pinpoint haemorrhages on the face or chest, including on the conjunctivae, may raise the possibility of asphyxia but are not specific.

The infant is assessed for pallor (a non-specific finding that may suggest anae-mia), jaundice, and generalized oedema (swelling of the soft tissues due to fluid retention), as well as for treatment-related lesions, including needle-puncture marks relating to resuscitation. The presence of dysmorphic features (abnormal facial or other external appearances which may suggest an underlying chromo-somal disorder) is carefully documented, and photographs may be taken. The latter are usually stored as part of the infant's medical record and may prove invaluable for review by clinical geneticists to enable direct assessment of pos-sible dysmorphic features rather than having to rely on the pathologist's description.

The external examination is followed by a detailed macroscopic (naked eye) investigation of the body. Access to the thoracic and abdominal viscera is gained via a midline incision through the anterior thorax (chest) and abdomen. A care-ful inspection of the internal organs is carried out; these are then removed, weighed and dissected. All abnormalities are described and may be documented photographically, after which small samples are routinely taken for histological examination (see below). The organs are then returned to the body, which is reconstructed prior to release. All organs are routinely weighed, and the weights are compared to reference tables against the expected weight for the age of the infant.

For examination of the brain, the scalp is incised posteriorly, either by means of a coronal incision (from ear to ear) or vertical midline incision from the vertex (top of the head) to the occiput (lower part of the back of the head). In small babies, the skull may be opened by following the non-fused cranial suture lines, although in older infants and children an electric saw will usually be used. The brain can either be examined immediately ('fresh') or following a period of formalin fixation (see below), which may be several weeks for com-plex brain anomalies.

4.4.5 Microscopic examination

The standard post-mortem examination involves taking small tissue samples of organs for microscopic (histological) examination to confirm or exclude the presence of disease. It is well recognized that many conditions will only be apparent on histological examination, and that in a significant proportion of cases, an organ may be normal on macroscopic examination despite significant pathology on histological examination, eg the heart in myocarditis (inflamma-tion of the heart) or the lungs in pneumonia. Histological examination is the single most useful investigation in the determination of a cause of death in SUDI.

The tissue samples taken for microscopic examination are processed into small paraffin wax blocks and glass microscope slides. The average size of these tissue samples is that of a standard postage stamp and they are around 3–5 mm in thickness. The tissue section on the glass slide, which measures around

3–5 microns in thickness, is stained with a special dye called haematoxylin and eosin (H&E), as well as a range of histochemical and immunohistochemical stains in selected cases, to allow for detailed characterization of the underlying disease process; other options include in-situ hybridization techniques and, occasionally, electron microscopy.

4.4.6 Other ancillary investigations

Samples for bacteriology (bacteria)

These include *cerebrospinal fluid* (CSF, the fluid around the brain and spinal cord, which can be collected from the lumbar region via a lumbar puncture during life, or from the nape of the neck, and which might be expected to be positive in bacterial meningitis; the CSF sample is usually collected at the beginning of the post-mortem examination); blood (often collected from the heart) for *blood culture* (to look for the presence of 'septicaemia'); and *lung* (swab or small tissue sample, which might be expected to be positive in pneumonia). In some centres, the spleen may also be sampled (swab or small tissue sample), and other samples may be taken in selected cases (tracheal swab, bronchial swab, meningeal swab, bowel contents, urine, etc).

Samples for virology (viruses)

These may include nasopharyngeal aspirate or swab, lung (swab or small tissue sample), heart (small tissue sample), or bowel contents. Other samples may be taken in selected cases.

4.4.7 Metabolic studies

These include so-called *frozen sections* of tiny tissue samples of heart, skeletal muscle, liver, and kidney, which are then stained with a special dye called oil-red-O to look for fat, which will be increased in some metabolic disorders; blood (and in some centres bile) on *Guthrie cards* for acylcarnitine profiling by tandem mass spectrometry; and a small skin sample for *fibroblast culture* (this involves growing cells called fibroblasts in the skin, which can then be used for various enzyme tests). The latter is very expensive and may not be carried out in all centres but should be considered in very young infants (less than one month of age) and in cases in which an underlying metabolic disorder is considered clinically.

4.4.8 Toxicology

Many centres do not routinely collect and process samples for toxicology as the tests are expensive and the yield low. Toxicology should, however, be considered if there is a history of recreational drug use, or the parent(s) or child is using prescribed medication (which could have led to an accidental or deliberate overdose). Samples include *femoral blood* (which is almost impossible to sample in small infants, in which case cardiac blood may be used, provided this is indicated on the request form), liver tissue, urine, vitreous humour (from the eye), stomach contents, and others.

4.4.9 **Other samples**

These may include vitreous humour for chemistry or samples for cytogenetics (chromosomes); many centres may also routinely *freeze small tissue samples* (eg tiny tissue samples of heart, skeletal muscle, liver, and kidney) under the authority of the coroner, which can be used for additional diagnostic tests, if required, or for subsequent DNA analysis, provided appropriate authority has been obtained by the coroner or parents.

4.4.10 **Retention of organs**

Occasionally it may be beneficial to retain an organ temporarily for further examination. This usually involves fixing the organ in formalin prior to examination, which hardens the tissues by cross-linking intracellular enzymes and other proteins, thus facilitating a more detailed macroscopic examination and allowing better-quality histological sections to be obtained. Temporary retention of an organ for formalin fixation prior to examination is especially useful for the brain, which is very friable and soft, and prone to disintegrate on handling, thus limiting the extent of the examination. Formalin fixation is also recommended for detailed examination of the heart in cases with suspected structural cardiac malformations. It is, however, worth emphasizing that the retention of an organ for formalin fixation and further examination does not mean that the organ has to be retained indefinitely; in the majority of cases at Great Ormond Street Hospital for Children, the organ is reunited with the body after fixation and examination, prior to release of the body; this may delay the funeral by up to one to two weeks to allow for adequate fixation of the brain, but other organs, such as the heart and lungs, can usually be examined after a mere 24 hours of formalin fixation.

In a coronial post-mortem examination, organs may only be retained for further examination with the express authority of the coroner. The Kennedy guidelines recommend that in SUDI cases with no clinical features or macroscopic autopsy findings to explain the death, the brain should only be examined after adequate formalin fixation for one to two weeks. There is, however, little published evidence that examination of the brain following formalin fixation is better than examination and histological sampling of the unfixed brain during the initial post-mortem examination *for the purposes of establishing a cause of death for the coroner* in cases with no past neurological history, and no features suspicious of abuse, and in Great Ormond Street Hospital for Children, in such cases, the brain is routinely examined 'fresh' and samples obtained for further investigation.

If an organ is retained and the parents wish not to delay the funeral, the retained organs can be returned to the parents at a later stage, usually via their designated undertakers, for subsequent burial or cremation, provided the coroner agrees to this. Alternatively, parents have the option of requesting the hospital to dispose of the organ on their behalf in a lawful way (incineration, burial, or cremation, depending on local protocols) or to donate the organ to the hospital for research, audit, and training purposes.

4.4.11 Disposal of retained tissue samples, including blocks and slides

As outlined above, tissue samples taken during a coronial autopsy are done so under the authority of the coroner. According to the Coroners (Amendment) Rules 2005, only samples that have a bearing on the cause of death, or help to establish the identity of the deceased, may be taken during a coronial autopsy; these samples remain under the coroner's jurisdiction until they have concluded their investigation, after which the tissue samples are subject to the Human Tissue Act 2004 and require parental consent for further handling.

It is recommended that all tissue samples taken as part of the coroner's post-mortem examination (ie blocks and slides, Guthrie cards, frozen tissue samples) be kept indefinitely by the hospital as part of the infant's permanent medical record, but this can only be done with appropriate parental consent. This will ensure that the samples can be reviewed in the future, either in the light of further medical information or new diagnostic tests; these tissue samples may also be valuable for medical education, audit, quality control, and research. Parents have the option to consent to the use of tissue for research which may help other families in the future, and surveys of bereaved parents have shown that the majority of parents are keen to participate in research.

Alternatively, parents may prefer all samples to be disposed of; this can either be done by the hospital on their behalf, or parents may wish to make their own arrangements, usually via their designated undertaker. If parents choose either of these options, it is important that they understand that subsequent review and further diagnosis will not be possible. If parents choose to give permission for the hospital to retain the blocks and slides, parents must be made aware that they can always change their minds in the future.

It is noteworthy that, if no communication has been received by the family within three months of the coroner's function having ceased, the tissue samples, including all blocks and slides, must be disposed of by the hospital according to current legislation in the UK.

4.5 Providing a cause of death in non-suspicious SUDI and pathologist's report

In the majority of paediatric post-mortem examinations performed on behalf of the coroner, a cause of death will not be discernible on naked-eye (macroscopic) examination at the time of autopsy; this particularly applies to SUDI.

The Kennedy guidelines recommend that in such instances the provisional cause of death is formulated as 'Unexplained Pending Further Investigation'. The preliminary cause of death, together with a list of all tissue samples retained under the coroner's authority, is communicated to the coroner's officer as soon as possible after the post-mortem examination.

A final report which incorporates the histological findings and results of all further investigations is usually submitted within four to six weeks but may take several weeks, or sometimes even months, to complete. The post-mortem report must document macroscopic and microscopic findings, as well as the results of all ancillary investigations performed. Importantly, the salient (positive and negative) findings should be summarized, followed by a detailed, directed, and appropriate clinicopathological correlation. Parents and clinicians are entitled to a copy of the report at the discretion of the coroner; it is recommended that the contents of the report be discussed with the family by their lead clinician, as some parents may find the technical jargon used in such reports insensitive and distressing.

As the coroner's post-mortem examination is a medico legal autopsy performed under the authority of the coroner, the final report cannot be made available to anyone else without the appropriate authority of the coroner. Any interested persons wishing to receive a copy of the post-mortem report should contact the coroner's officer and not the pathologist.

When explaining and categorizing the cause of death, a number of terms are used, which, as stated above, may be confusing or even considered distressing and insensitive if taken out of the context in which they appear, eg a factual medical report. However, with the benefit of a greater understanding of the definitions, terms, and their intended usage, some of these very real concerns may be allayed. The following is an explanation of the key areas.

4.5.1 Definitions of SIDS, SUDI, and unascertained

Sudden Infant Death Syndrome (SIDS)

The term Sudden Infant Death Syndrome (SIDS) is broadly synonymous with cot death, but the latter term is potentially misleading as it implies that death invariably occurs in the cot.

Various definitions of SIDS have been formulated over the years; the term was first proposed in 1969, at the Second International Conference on the Causes of Sudden Death in Infants in Seattle, by Bruce Beckwith (1970) and then defined as:

> The sudden death of an infant or young child, which is unexpected by history, and in which a thorough post-mortem examination fails to demonstrate an adequate cause of death.

In 1971 SIDS became a registrable cause of death in England and Wales. In 1989, the National Institute of Child Health and Human Development (NICHD) convened a panel of 12 experts who proposed a modified version of the 1969 SIDS definition (Willinger et al., 1991), namely:

> The sudden death of an infant under one year of age, which remains unexplained after a thorough case investigation, including performance of a complete autopsy, examination of the death scene, and review of the clinical history.

This definition (the '1989 definition') was further modified slightly over the years (for example, substituting 'death scene' with 'circumstances of death', but in essence remains the preferred definition of SIDS, and it is this definition that is also used in the Kennedy guidelines.

In 2004 the definition was again modified; this is the latest revision of the definition and is now widely referred to as the 'San Diego definition', which broadly defines SIDS (Krous et al., 2004) as:

> The sudden unexpected death of an infant less than 1 year of age, with onset of the fatal episode apparently occurring during sleep, that remains unexplained after a thorough investigation, including performance of a complete autopsy and review of the circumstances of death and the clinical history.

This definition was predominantly intended for research and statistical purposes and, for the first time, limits SIDS to *deaths occurring during sleep*; it is, however, *not* widely used in the UK.

Some pathologists object to the term SIDS in view of its inclusion of the term 'syndrome', implying a single underlying cause of death; furthermore, it is argued that SIDS merely represents a 'catch-all diagnosis' for any sudden infant death which remains otherwise unexplained. However, SIDS should *not* be understood as constituting a single cause of death; it is thought to represent a heterogeneous group of sudden infant deaths which share a number of epidemiological risk factors (see below) with a common mechanism(s) of death. Also, whilst the term essentially means that the underlying cause of death is not known, it implies a natural cause of death.

Sudden Unexpected Death in Infancy (SUDI)

It is unclear as to when the term SUDI was first introduced, but the acronym was formally adopted by the CESDI SUDI studies in 1993 (Fleming et al., 2000) and is now the preferred term in the UK for all sudden infant deaths in the first year of life, although usually limited to infants that died suddenly and unexpectedly aged 7–365 days, thus excluding all sudden unexpected deaths in the early neonatal period (first week of life).

As such, the term SUDI is not a pathological diagnosis; it does not correspond to SIDS and is not used in the *International Classification of Diseases* (10th Revision, ICD-10; <http://www.who.int/classifications/icd/en/>). Strictly speaking, the term SUDI denotes the *presentation of death*, regardless of whether a cause of death is identified at autopsy or not. In other words, it is:

That part of infant mortality where the clinical presentation of death occurs more or less suddenly and unexpectedly. The post-mortem examination, which ideally should include a history of the gestation, delivery and postnatal development, a death scene investigation, a family psychosocial history, a complete autopsy, and a confidential case conference:

- May reveal changes that alone—or in combination—constitute a sufficient cause of death ('non-SIDS' or 'explained SUDI'); or
- May reveal changes that even when clearly present are not sufficient to explain death; or
- May fail to demonstrate any abnormalities. (Huber, 1995; adapted from Byard & Krous, 2001, and Bajanowski et al., 2007.)

The last two categories are collectively also referred to as 'unexplained SUDI' which is broadly synonymous with SIDS using the 1989 definition outlined above.

SUDI is, therefore, a much more heterogeneous group of infant deaths, also including those cases in which a cause of death will be identified following detailed investigations ('explained SUDI'), including deaths due to accidents and inflicted injury. Gould (2001) divides SUDI deaths into four main subcategories, ie those with:

1. Fully explained, natural causes of death;
2. Covert unnatural causes of death, including deaths due to accidents (for example accidental asphyxia) and deaths due to inflicted injury (for example, due to trauma or due to intentional suffocation);
3. Unexplained but natural cause of death, ie SIDS; and
4. Unascertained, the latter representing those deaths than cannot be categorized into one of the first three categories with any degree of confidence.

As the distinction between 'explained SUDI' and 'unexplained SUDI' is usually not apparent until after the autopsy (which usually includes histology and other ancillary investigations which may take several weeks), all such deaths should (at least initially) be investigated in the same standardized manner; it is for this reason that the Kennedy guidelines use the broader term SUDI rather than SIDS.

Terminology: practical considerations

In terms of formulating the cause of death, the terms SIDS, SUDI, unascertained, undetermined, and unexplained all broadly mean the same thing, ie that the cause of death is unknown; however, given the many terms, it is perhaps not surprising that there is enormous variation in how these terms are understood. One study has shown that in the UK, around 40 per cent of pathologists surveyed felt that the term SIDS no longer served a useful purpose (Limerick & Bacon, 2004).

Prior to the introduction of the Kennedy guidelines in 2004, when asked to formulate a cause of death of an infant who died suddenly whilst co-sleeping with an adult, with no specific pathological findings at autopsy, 38 pathologists stated 'unascertained', 25 stated 'SIDS', six said 'SUDI', and one said asphyxia, although many respondents suggested that their assignment of a cause of death would depend on the exact circumstances surrounding death, with more than half claiming that they usually did not receive sufficient information at the time of the post-mortem examination to be able to make a firm diagnosis of the cause of death (Limerick & Bacon, 2004).

The Kennedy report encourages pathologists and coroners to certify the death as SIDS if the death meets the diagnostic criteria (which, in the report, are defined as the unexpected death of an infant that 'remains unexplained after a careful review of the history, examination of the circumstances of death and the conduct of a full post-mortem examination to an agreed protocol' (Kennedy, 2004:44, para. 9.6, ie based on the 1989 definition of SIDS), and that 'in all other cases he or she should enter the death as SUDI' (p. 10).

The term 'unascertained' seems to be popular among some pathologists, especially when the pathologist identifies features in the clinical history or at autopsy that raise the suspicion, however subtle, of possible inflicted injury, although some pathologists prefer the term 'unascertained' over 'SIDS' even in the absence of any suspicious features. According to the Kennedy guidelines, the term 'unascertained' should be avoided, if possible: unlike 'SIDS', which implies a natural cause of death, it is argued that the term 'unascertained' includes both natural and non-natural deaths, and that, as a consequence, affected families might be stigmatized by designating a death as 'unascertained', although elsewhere it concedes that, 'where no sufficient cause of death has been established but there are gaps in the documentation, or for other reasons the death, whilst not shown to be due to abuse or neglect, does not meet the definition of SIDS, a designation as "unascertained" may be unavoidable' (p. 44, para. 9.7).

Even following the publication of the Kennedy guidelines, there is much variation in how paediatric pathologists use these terms. A recent study of UK paediatric pathologists, using the Delphi method to investigate their views on the use of these terms in order to determine areas of consensus, showed that there remains a significant lack of agreement. There was consensus that 'SIDS' be used for unexplained sudden unexpected infant deaths that occurred during sleep. There was consensus that 'infancy' was defined as up to one year of age, but there was *no consensus* regarding the lower age limit for SIDS. There was agreement that 'SUDI' be used for unexplained sudden infant deaths with a history of preceding illness, deaths with minor histological abnormalities of uncertain significance, and co-sleeping-associated deaths. Most paediatric pathologists used 'unascertained' for findings suspicious of a non-natural cause of death, and there was consensus that co-sleeping-associated deaths should be classified

99

as 'unascertained' if parents had consumed alcohol or used drugs in the preceding 24 hours.

Many pathologists use the term SUDI as a final cause of death if the death remains unexplained and non-suspicious following the post-mortem examination, but in which, in their opinion, the criteria for SIDS are not met. This is a little confusing, as strictly speaking 'SUDI' is a mode of presentation of death that includes both explained and unexplained deaths, as outlined above.

Finally, therefore, as a rough guide if given as cause of death in the post-mortem report following the autopsy (bearing in mind the enormous variation in their usage outlined above):

- 'SIDS' means that the death remains unexplained but is likely due to natural causes;
- 'SUDI' more or less means the same as 'SIDS' in this context (ie unexplained) and usually also implies a natural cause of death; it may simply be the preferred term for that pathologist, or is being used because the death did not occur during sleep or because this was a co-sleeping-associated death (both of which, according to the 1989 definition of SIDS, would strictly still fulfil the criteria for SIDS provided the latter shows no evidence of asphyxia);
- 'Unascertained' usually means that a non-natural (be it accidental or inflicted) cause of death cannot be excluded.

4.5.2 SIDS research

As the majority of child deaths that the police will invariably deal with may fall into the SIDs category, a brief understanding of the current research will be of great value when examining the circumstances of the death. There is an enormous volume of SIDS research: almost 10,000 publications on PubMed to date. Therefore, the information below is just a brief summary of the main epidemiological risk factors and current hypotheses.

Risk factors for SIDS

- Sleeping position and environment
    - Prone sleeping (drastic decline in SIDS following back to sleep campaigns)
    - Side sleeping
    - Co-sleeping in the presence of smoking, or if the parent(s) have consumed alcohol or drugs; likely also a risk factor in very young infants; mechanism unknown but in some (minority) may be due to overlaying (ie accidental asphyxia)
    - Co-sleeping on sofa (very unsafe; large increased risk)
    - Soft sleep surfaces and/or soft bedding, especially if prone sleeping
    - High ambient room temperatures, as well as excessive clothing and/or bedding
    - Head covering

- Smoking (around two-fold increased risk with dose effect, ie the more cigarettes, the higher the risk); includes smoking during pregnancy and household smoking
- Pregnancy-related factors (other than maternal smoking)
    - Low birth weight: intrauterine growth restriction and preterm birth
    - Young mothers
    - High parity (number of children)
    - Multiple pregnancy (twins and triplets)
    - Antepartum or intrapartum haemorrhage
- Lower socioeconomic status
- Parental alcohol and drug use
- Male gender
- Racial differences (higher incidence in black infants and infants of Native Americans in the US; likewise for Maoris in New Zealand and Aboriginal Australians; low incidence in Asian community in the UK)

The triple risk model for SIDS

The triple risk hypothesis (Filiano & Kinney, 1994; Guntheroth & Spiers, 2002) proposes that SIDS occurs as a consequence of the concurrent interaction of three factors, namely:

1. An intrinsically vulnerable infant;
2. A critical developmental period; and
3. Exposure to exogenous stressors (Figure 4.1, below).

On their own, these factors would not prove fatal: the infant would die only if all three factors intersected, and then only if the stressor(s) matched that infant's specific vulnerability (Byard & Krous, 2001). The model proposes that SIDS infants are not normal but have an underlying biological or genetic predisposition that makes them vulnerable to specific environmental stressors (such as prone sleeping, co-sleeping, cigarette smoke exposure, infections, etc). The critical developmental period is said to be between one and six months of age, which is based on the typical age distribution of SIDS, rather than strong evidence of physiological (cardiovascular, respiratory, immunological, etc) instability during this time of development. Nevertheless, the model serves as a useful 'conceptual framework' (Byard & Krous, 2001) to accommodate potential interactions between the various established epidemiological risk factors (see above), and the diverse biological, genetic, and infective associations (very briefly summarized below) in the pathogenesis of death. Importantly, the model suggests that death in SIDS may be the result of different causes and risk factors that share a final common pathway, rather than there being a single common cause to all SIDS (Fleming et al., 2006).

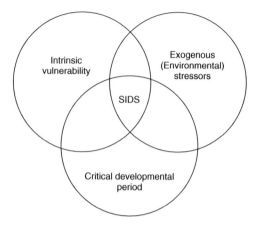

Figure 4.1 The triple risk hypothesis for SIDS
(adapted from Byard & Krous, 2001:131).

Hypotheses for SIDS
- Infection
    - Higher incidence of SIDS in winter months
    - Bacterial toxins (lots of supportive evidence)
    - Single nucleotide polymorphisms (SNPs; ie tiny mutations) involving various immunoregulatory genes (genes that regulate the immune system) that either up- or down-regulate circulating levels of cytokines (mediators of inflammatory reactions in the body)
- Immunological causes: atopy (allergic reactions) and anaphylaxis
- Impaired autonomic regulation (of breathing, heart rate, etc) and arousal responses
- Conduction system abnormalities in the heart (causing abnormal heart rhythms): so-called cardiac ion channelopathies, including long QT syndrome (genetic mutations found in around 10 per cent of SIDS in some studies)
- Abnormalities in areas of the brain involving serotonergic pathways (ie processes that use the chemical substance serotonin), and other developmental brain abnormalities

4.5.3 Natural causes of SUDI (explained SUDI)

For many parents the question of 'Why did my child die?' is answered by establishing a specific cause of death. Explained causes of SUDI are summarized in Table 4.1 below. In a large single-centre study of over 500 SUDI cases, the majority of explained SUDI were due to bacterial infections, principally pneumonia (Weber et al., 2008).

Table 4.1 Causes of explained SUDI

Infective Natural Causes of Death	
Bacterial Infections	• Pneumonia • Meningitis • Septicaemia • Acute epiglottitis • Pyelonephritis • Osteomyelitis • Myocarditis • Bronchiolitis • Encephalitis
Viral Infections	• Gastroenteritis • Disseminated viral infections (eg herpes simplex virus, adenovirus) • Acute laryngotracheobronchitis
Other Infections	• Pneumocystis jirovecii (carinii) infection
Non-Infective Natural Causes of Death	
Cardiovascular Causes	• Structural congenital malformations (including anomalous coronary arteries) • Cardiomyopathy • Tumours • Idiopathic arterial calcification of infancy • Coronary arteritis (Kawasaki disease)
Respiratory Causes	• Pulmonary hypertension (including persistent pulmonary hypertension of the newborn) • Chronic lung disease • Pulmonary veno-occlusive disease • Massive pulmonary haemorrhage • Upper airway obstruction (eg due to structural airway defects, such as laryngeal/tracheal stenosis, and tracheo- and bronchomalacia)
Neurological Causes	• Intracranial haemorrhage (eg due to vascular malformations, arterial aneurysms, fibromuscular dysplasia, or bleeding diathesis) • Structural malformations/defects (eg hydrocephalus, Chiari type II malformation)
Gastrointestinal Causes	• Bowel obstruction (intussusception, volvulus) • Gastro-oesophageal reflux with massive aspiration
Haematological Causes	• Leukaemias • Lymphomas • Langerhans cell histiocytosis • Haemophagocytic lymphohistiocytosis
Endocrine Causes	• Adrenal hypoplasia

(Continued)

Table 4.1 *(Cont'd)*

Immunological Causes	• Anaphylaxis
Metabolic Causes	• Disorders of fatty acid oxidation • (MCAD, VLCAD, carnitine-acylcarnitine translocase deficiency, carnitine palmitoyl-transferase II deficiency) • Mitochondrial disorders • 'Reye syndrome' • Other

Non-Natural Causes of Death

Deaths due to Accidents	• Trauma (eg road traffic accidents, falls) • Accidental asphyxia (eg overlaying, choking, strangulation, wedging) • Drowning • Fire • Poisoning
Non-Accidental/ Intentional Injuries	• Trauma • Thermal injuries • Deliberate asphyxia (smothering, mechanical suffocation due to splinting of chest) • Drowning • Poisoning • Starvation • Factitious illness by proxy (Münchausen syndrome by proxy) (fabricated or induced illness)

(adapted from Weber et al, 2008; Byard, 2004; Byard & Krous, 2003; Fleming et al, 2000; Vargas et al, 1999).

The list is not exhaustive. (MCAD = medium chain acyl-CoA dehydrogenase deficiency; VLCAD = very long chain acyl-CoA dehydrogenase deficiency)

4.6 **The parents' perspective**

Although the right of the deceased child to be the central focus of an investigation, along with any siblings, has been emphasized; clearly of great importance will be the parents and carers of the deceased child, who should always be an integral part of any investigation. The following diagram may be a useful way of considering the relative importance of the various parties to the focus of the process.

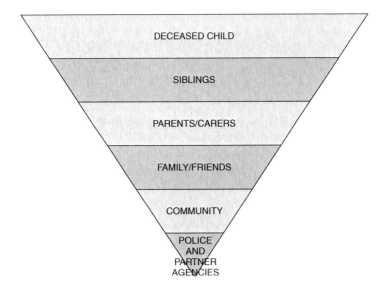

Figure 4.2 Priority in investigative focus

The following true story from a parent whose child died suddenly and unexpectedly illustrates in a very powerful way how life changes forever but also how the perceptions, fear, and understanding develop throughout the process. It requires no commentary—it speaks for itself.

Case study—Neave Sophie Bissmire (23/8/99–24/11/99)

My beautiful second daughter Neave was born one day overdue weighing a healthy 9 lbs.

When my first child Jorgina was born, although I had **heard** about 'cot death' I always assumed that it was something that happened to somebody else. I didn't smoke; I wasn't a young single mum!

On the day Neave died, we had a lovely day together; my husband John had given Neave a bath, we had both sat on the floor with her and were very proud that she had learnt how to shake her rattle on her own for the first time. When Jorgina (7 years old) got home from school, we sat round the table together with Neave on my lap helping Jorgi design her Christmas plate. We had roast chicken and I gave Neave a breastfeed before rushing out of the door to go and do a shift at the pub where I was assistant manager. I had only returned to work the week before and spent my night talking to the customers about Neave! I called John at 8pm and asked how the girls were; Jorgi was in bed and Neave was looking round the room quite happily, John said.

I got home at 9.15pm. Neave had fallen asleep and John placed her on her bean bag at his feet. I stood over her just chatting to John about my night. I kept glancing down at Neave desperate to give her a feed and a cuddle, and just as I was about to pick her up I noticed she was a very strange colour—as I picked her up her little head fell back and I knew immediately that she had died. I literally threw Neave to John, screaming that she was dead and, although I don't remember this, John said I ran to the front door opened it and then called '999'.

I was hysterical and screaming; my poor elderly neighbour came in and took one look at Neave, with John trying to resuscitate her and had to go away. The ambulance took about ten minutes and, when it arrived, the crew grabbed Neave and ran to the ambulance; I followed falling in the mud across the grass. My poor John, realizing he had to stay for Jorgina, just shouted, asking where they were taking her.

In the ambulance, I was begging the paramedic not to give me false hope, just to tell me that yes, she had died, but all she said was to keep talking to Neave and stroking her feet.

Once at Whipps Cross, they whisked Neave into resus and me into a side room, I begged to be with her but they said I couldn't and they would come and see me soon. I will never forget the look of hope on John's face when he arrived at the door; I just shook my head, crying. The doctors and nurses came into see us at 10.10pm, less than an hour after I arrived home, to tell us that Neave had not been breathing on arrival and they had been unable to revive her, and that she had been pronounced dead.

My life, my happy carefree life, had just ended as we knew it. I have never and will never be the same person again. They took Neave's foot and hand prints, cut a lock of her hair, and took some photos. These are invaluable to me and I have often woken up over the years crying and full of fear at the thought of losing them.

When we had to leave the hospital that night, at about 1am, it was traumatic, having to leave my baby there, and there was no one who explained what might happen next, eg in relation to a police visit, other professionals who might be involved, but I didn't take note of that fact for many years and I am glad that now there are protocols and procedures in place so that parents are better informed and supported.

We had been home for about half an hour when the police pulled up. There were a couple of uniform and CID and child protection officers; it wasn't a total shock but at the same time I did wonder what they thought we had done! We were lucky in that I have heard of parents being separated and spoken to whilst apart, or the house being sealed off with tape as a crime scene. We had none of that; the police that came to us had a job to do and asked us if they could do anything to help. My husband was worried that he had his milk round books so the police drove them to the yard in Poplar and broke the news to John's boss as well. They asked us not to touch anything, took some photos of the living room, and said they needed to take Neave's beanbag away.

When they went, they didn't give us a name of a contact in case we had any questions and, again, it wasn't until some years later and by talking to other bereaved parents did I realize that there wasn't a set way of dealing with these sudden deaths.

I am very happy to learn that the police have worked very hard in improving the way things are handled.

The feelings of guilt we had that Neave had died were unbearable. We would lie awake at night full of 'if only' and 'what if's'. Some solace was given nearly a week after she died when we were contacted by the coroner's office. Some tests they had been waiting for had come back and it showed Neave had Overwhelming Staphylococcal Aureus infection present in many of her organs. This would have contributed to her death and, even if we had found Neave in an unconscious state, she would have died in hospital as they wouldn't have tested for it. We knew deep down we hadn't done anything or missed anything but to get some confirmation from professionals definitely helped us.

Just two days before the funeral, her plaque had been put on the coffin and they made her older than she had actually lived for, which was devastating. I said there was no way she was being buried in a coffin with the wrong age on it!—she had never reached that age.

Also, when we received a letter from the hospital offering us a meeting with the paediatrician they said they were sorry to hear about the death of our son! All babies/children are precious, but when they die it's only memories you are left with and they are crystal clear in your mind. There is not a single day apart from the day Neave died that I can remember so vividly from 12 years ago, and it's vital that the details about your baby are correct.

Neave's funeral was very important to us, and for me any thoughts of suicide or falling apart were soon put straight out of my mind as I had a seven year-old daughter who needed me, and I had an overwhelming thought that I didn't want to let Neave down by falling apart. Her funeral was just how we wanted it, not overly religious, and I am very grateful to the minister Martin Coe for sticking by me even after the first words I barked at him were that, if I didn't like him, we wouldn't be using him!

I still say goodnight to Neave every night; we often talk about her and feel she is still part of the family, just not physically.

We went on to have a son, Johnny, just over a year after Neave died and he really is special; obviously we love all our children the same, but with Johnny we understand just how precious our children are and how easily they can be taken away from you.

I could never say I have got over Neave's death; I have simply adjusted to life the way it is now.

I have been a volunteer on the helpline and befriender for the Foundation for Study of Infant Death (FSID) for the past ten years. FSID is the charity which supports bereaved families, informs professionals and new parents, and funds research into trying to find an answer as to why there are still 300 babies dying suddenly and unexpectedly each year. I have been lucky enough to work full time for them since January 2011.

FSID currently provides the following preventative advice for parents and prospective parents.

Advice for parents to reduce the risk of cot death:

- Cut smoking in pregnancy—fathers too! And don't let anyone smoke in the same room as your baby.
- Place your baby on the back to sleep (and not on the front or side).
- Do not let your baby get too hot, and keep your baby's head uncovered.
- Place your baby with their feet to the foot of the cot, to prevent them wriggling down under the covers, or use a baby sleep bag
- Never sleep with your baby on a sofa or armchair.
- The safest place for your baby to sleep is in a crib or cot in a room with you for the first six months.
- It's especially dangerous for your baby to sleep in your bed if you (or your partner):
  - are a smoker, even if you never smoke in bed or at home
  - have been drinking alcohol
  - take medication or drugs that make you drowsy
  - feel very tired;
- or if your baby:
  - was born before 37 weeks
  - weighed less than 2.5kg or 5½ lbs at birth
  - is less than 4 months old.
- Don't forget, accidents can happen: you might roll over in your sleep and suffocate your baby; or your baby could get caught between the wall and the bed, or could roll out of an adult bed and be injured.
- Settling your baby to sleep (day and night) with a dummy can reduce the risk of cot death, even if the dummy falls out while your baby is asleep.
- Breastfeed your baby. Establish breastfeeding before starting to use a dummy.

KEY POINTS FOR POLICE AND PARTNERS

(from a parent's perspective)

- **Do** take the time to get the details right about the baby who has died.
- **Do** provide a point of contact whenever possible—the parents are not in a frame of mind to have to think for themselves or to be proactive.
- **Do** explain why you might need to remove something from the house. It might seem obvious to you—it's your job—but for bereaved parents this may be their very first encounter with the police/other agencies and they have just been thrown into this turmoil.
- **Don't** assume anything—always ASK. For example, it may seem normal to you to want your parents or friends with you at such a traumatic time but for some it might be the last thing they want.
- **Don't** say you understand if you really don't.

4.6.1 **Support agencies**

There are a number of very useful support agencies who can provide advice, publications, and support for those affected by child death including:

The Foundation for the Study of Infant Deaths (FSID)

The Foundation for the Study of Infant Deaths is the UK's leading baby charity working to prevent sudden deaths and promote infant health. FSID funds research (nearly £10 million to date), supports bereaved families, promotes baby care advice, and works to improve investigations when a baby dies.

FSID has a Free Phone helpline: 0808 802 6868. for parents and professionals seeking advice on safe baby care. The helpline also supports bereaved families. Advice for parents and professionals can also be found at <http://www.fsid.org.uk>.

Publications include:

When a baby dies suddenly and unexpectedly
Bereavement support
The child death review—A guide for parents and carers

All are available via their web site.

The Child Bereavement Charity—supporting bereaved families and the professionals who support them: <http://www.childbereavement.org.uk/> and Information and Support Line: 01494 568900.

Child Death Helpline—for anyone affected by the death of a child of any age from any cause: <http://www.childdeathhelpline.org.uk/> and Free Phone 0800 282986 or 0808 800 6019 for all mobiles.

4.7 **The police perspective**

The police have a specific professional role in relation to child death of investigating the circumstances with the coroner and, if any criminal offences are disclosed or suspected, leading the investigation in relation to those.

KEY POINT

The police have a specific role and area of professional responsibility but they must not work in isolation; instead, they must work together with their multi-agency partners so that their contributions will complement each other.

Central to every police investigation, regardless of the incident or criminal offence being considered, should be a search for the truth to very simply establish 'What has happened?'. This is invariably linked to related information comprising six question areas:

- **What**—has happened? Has been done? Needs to be done?
- **Who**—is involved?
- **Where**—did the respective constituent elements of the circumstances occur?
- **When**—did these elements occur?
- **How**—did these elements occur and how are they related? and
- **Why**—did they occur?

Information relevant to all these six areas is crucial. A useful analogy is a jigsaw puzzle with the pieces of information in each of these areas being jigsaw puzzle pieces which, when all put together correctly, produce a complete picture with everything in context. A missing piece or a piece in the wrong position can give a distorted and incorrect picture. In real life, it may not always be possible to answer all the questions, and so sometimes we are left with an incomplete picture. However, every opportunity to try to obtain as many pieces of information as possible should be explored. Forcing pieces into the wrong position or deliberately leaving them out, because they do not fit into the picture we had envisaged, is a betrayal of the true circumstances, and in the area of criminal investigation could lead to miscarriages of justice. Crucially, it could lead to missed opportunities that could have produced a clearer image of the true picture. Continuing the analogy, a jigsaw puzzle is just a 'puzzle' that requires careful consideration, patience, methodology (eg sorting out all the corner pieces and straight sides), co-operation from others, time, sufficient space, and resources. Unlike a jigsaw puzzle that invariably has an image of the final picture, in real life the process is not as straightforward and, at times, can be like completing a jigsaw puzzle face down, with no picture and complicated still further by missing pieces. Possible pictures (hypotheses) may be considered that may assist in assembling the pieces, but the final picture will await the correct positioning of all the pieces and, sadly, sometimes only part of the picture will ever be constructed, still leaving many unanswered questions.

In developing this analogy for the area of child death, the more information that can be ascertained, the more complete the picture will be. The most important point is that no one has all the pieces of information, thus emphasizing the need to obtain information from all those impacted by the death, whether in a personal or professional capacity. Finally, before leaving this analogy, it must be stressed that no picture or puzzle will be identical; they will all be unique and have to be considered on an individual basis. To ensure a comprehensive and consistent and yet flexible approach to investigating childhood death, strategies or methodology incorporating the questions in those six question areas (above) within a multi-agency context is essential.

The police approach utilizes a flexible method of managing investigations based on the 'Five Building Blocks'.

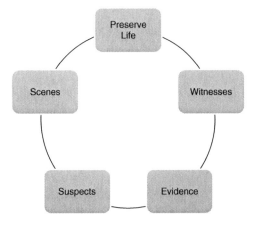

Figure 4.3 'Five Building Blocks'

The terminology utilizes generic terms for areas to consider in all investigations, but which will have varying relevance depending on the specific circumstances. The standard model has an 'ID Victim' block, but for this context this has been replaced with 'Witnesses', which in the standard model would be included under evidence. Each building block will always be considered in a mindset of trying to establish the truth whilst maintaining an open mind. After the initial consideration and subsequent review (if appropriate), as further information becomes available, the building block may not feature further in the case. For example, if a child dies at home, there are no concerning features, and a medical cause of death is ascertained, the 'Suspects' building block will be considered with an open mind in the early stages but, when set in the context of the other information, will subsequently be discarded.

This building block structure of investigation management will feature to some extent in all child death cases, whether 'non-suspicious', 'suspicious', or 'homicide'. There will be considerable differences in the constituent parts of each respective block that will be dependent on the category of death, eg the 'Suspects' block will receive very limited consideration in the 'non-suspicious' cases, whilst there will be considerable time spent in examining the aspects it covers in a homicide enquiry.

As these five building blocks will be such an integral part of the police approach and function in their response to child deaths, this model will be utilized to structure the examination of the issues that impact on all childhood death investigations from a police perspective. There can be a crossover of factors between 'building blocks', and each of the five building block areas can themselves be subdivided further in relation to who, what, where, when, how, and why. The multi-agency partnership approach will also feature in many of the aspects within these investigative areas.

4.7.1 **Preserve life**

This is very important in relation to several different persons.

1. **The child who appears to have died**—it is important to establish that this is actually the case, and never to assume this until a medically qualified person has certified life extinct. This is part of the rationale for children being taken to the hospital A&E department to ensure that everything possible has been done to preserve life.
2. **The siblings of the deceased child and any other children immediately affected by the death**—is there any risk to them from: (a) a medical cause, eg an infection, or (b) a human risk, eg a parent with mental health issues who had been responsible for the deceased child's death.
3. **Anyone else at risk from the unfolding scenario**— for example:
    (a) Murder suicide—an aggrieved and mentally disturbed partner who kills their children and then seeks to kill their partner before committing suicide themselves.
    (b) A mother who has given birth and abandoned her newborn child, who then subsequently dies from exposure. The mother may be in need of urgent medical attention herself.

These examples illustrate just how broad this 'preserve life' building block can be, emphasizing that all life is important and should not be limited to consideration of preserving the life of the deceased child. Background information in relation to the family is clearly an important aspect of this assessment.

4.7.2 **Scenes**

Whilst the term 'scene' can have negative connotations in child deaths, in this particualr context it is used as a generic term for police purposes. How the police would refer to the various scenes in practice, and in particular when speaking to non-police personnel, would be dictated by the individual circumstances, eg 'home visit' not 'scene visit' in relation to a SUDI.

The term 'scene' is a generic term used to describe the location of 'where' something relevant to the investigation has occurred and potential evidence or useful information may be discovered. To illustrate how wide this term is, all the following could, in certain circumstances (depending on the nature of the death), be described as a 'scene':

*   The deceased child themselves—their body;
*   The location where the deceased child was discovered;
*   The location where the deceased child suffered their fatal injuries;
*   An ambulance or other vehicle used to convey the child to hospital;
*   The hospital areas where treatment was given or medical procedures were performed;

- Locations visited before, during, or after the death by the deceased person, a person suspected of committing a criminal act in relation to the death, or a witness to an event linked to the death.

With scenes it is important that they are:

- Identified;
- Designated as scenes;
- Prioritized;
- Secured;
- Preserved in relation to forensic considerations.

As the various locations identified may incorporate public or private places, it is important to have obtained the requisite consent, permission, or legal authority to control them as a scene and so prevent the destruction, loss, or contamination of any potential evidence. If a criminal offence is suspected, then the following powers under the Police and Criminal Evidence Act 1984 may be appropriate:

Section 8—warrant issued by a Justice of the Peace to search for material that is likely to be relevant evidence in relation to an indictable offence.

Section 17—power of entry to search premises to arrest person(s), save life, or prevent damage to property.

Section 18—power to search premises owned or controlled by person arrested for an indictable offence if there are reasonable grounds for suspecting that there is evidence relating to that offence or connected with that or a similar offence.

Section 32—power to search premises where a person arrested for an indictable offence was at the time of arrest or immediately before their arrest, for evidence relating to the offence, providing there are reasonable grounds to believe that evidence is on the premises.

Section 19—general power for a police officer (or designated civilian investigating officer) lawfully on the premises to seize anything which is on the premises if there are reasonable grounds for believing it is either the proceeds of an offence or evidence of an offence, and it is necessary to seize it in order to prevent the evidence being concealed, lost, altered, or destroyed.

Voluntary consent—appropriate parties my be able to consent to a police course of action in relation to a scene, eg lawful occupier.

Routine scene of crime search (PACE Code B).

Cordoning crime scenes—police do not have a right to restrict movement on private land but may be entitled to assume consent to protect a crime scene (*DPP v Morrison* [2003] EWHC 683, HC).

Police have a common law power to prevent and protect items that may be evidence of an offence. Lord Denning stated: 'The police should be able to do whatever is necessary and reasonable to preserve the evidence of the crime' (*Ghani and others v Jones* [1969] 3 All ER 1700).

(document reference 15008) identifies three key conclusions:

The amalgamation of case decisions over the years has arrived at the following conclusions:

a) It should be identified under what guise the scene is being treated;
b) The cordoning of crime scenes on private property to assist in the investigation of crime is acceptable;
c) The length of time that scenes can be retained, is that which can be seen to be necessary and reasonable, and to balance the privacy and possessions of the individual against the interests of society, and the investigation and detection of crime.

The issue of police powers to control a scene may arise when no criminal offence is suspected but the police have a duty to investigate, eg a non-suspicious sudden and unexpected death when directed to do so by HM Coroner.

The following extract from *Home Office Circular 68/1955 to Coroners* sought to address this question and still appears to be the current position.

Custody of property
16. In 1896, the Law Officers of the Crown (Webster, A. G. and Finlay, S. G.) reported that there was practically no direct authority on certain questions which had arisen with regard to the disposal of property which had come into the custody of a coroner in connection with an inquest and that they had to be determined to a great extent by general principles of law. **On these principles they advised that a coroner or his officer is justified in searching, not only the body, but the effects of the deceased, and the premises where the body is found, if there is reason to think that the search is likely to lead to the discovery of evidence bearing on the cause of death.** As a rule, the search should be with reference to questions likely to arise at the inquest, and not a roving investigation. Possession should not be taken of property, other than that which is likely to be required for the purposes of the investigation, unless there is no trustworthy person in whose charge it can be left, but if no such person is available, it is a convenient course for the coroner's officer to take possession of the property, though this is not strictly any part of his duty.

Important additional considerations in relation to scenes include:

• Recording details of the scene—photographs/sketch/images/plan/video;
• Recording controlled access to the scene—scene log;
• Resources required to maintain as a controlled scene—controlled access to keys, police staff (properly briefed as to their role and responsibilities) to maintain a cordon or discreet presence.

This highlights a conundrum for the police in achieving the balance between an effective, thorough, and professional examination of the circumstances, alongside the requirement for a supportive, sensitive, and discreet investigation in line with the family's and other professionals' expectations.

Police operational activity may fall into two categories of either 'overt' or 'discreet' actions ('action'—used to describe a recorded task in relation to an investigation).

(a) 'Overt' actions are those which the family and other professionals involved in the case will be aware of, eg conducting a home visit, talking to siblings and other family members,

whilst

(b) 'Discreet' actions will be carried out in the background: essential legitimate enquiries or actions but conducted in a sensitive and as unobtrusive way to prevent unnecessary concern, eg checking police databases in relation to parents regarding relevant convictions, domestic violence, CCTV coverage to confirm relevant parties' accounts, financial profile, etc.

The proportion of 'Overt' against 'Discreet' actions will obviously depend on the nature of the investigation. It will be determined on a case-by-case basis, endeavouring always to be as professional, sensitive, open, and transparent with family and fellow professionals as legal operational necessities and effectiveness permit. This should also be seen in the context of police recognizing that, not only is communication essential, but it is also a two-way process.

Home visit

The home visit described in Chapter 7 of *Working Together* is a key feature of any child death investigation, but how it is managed may depend on the initial level of suspicion regarding the death. As repeatedly emphasized, the majority of child deaths are non-suspicious and result from natural or medical causes. However, as a home visit should occur in the initial stages of the investigation when some of the essential information is absent, eg the result of the post-mortem, careful and sensitive consideration has to be given to balancing what is currently known against that which is still to be established. A professional judgement needs to be made in relation to securing the integrity of the home environment in such a way as to preserve any potential evidence, should the death subsequently become suspicious. Likewise, a death initially considered suspicious may subsequently on investigation transpire to be a natural death, so equally how the home is managed will have a bearing on the future perception of the parents, family, and other professionals. Maintaining the concept of any child death investigation having the deceased child at the forefront, together with the need for clear communication between the relevant professionals and deceased parents and family, should help allay potential concerns.

The home visit was mentioned in the section on the paediatrician's perspective and, as explained, can provide valuable information in relation to the child's death. The home visit should be conducted jointly by the designated paediatrician and the police with the assistance of a CSI. In some areas, the role of the designated paediatrician is undertaken by a suitably qualified medical professional, eg nurse, under local protocols. It is an assessment of the location of the child's death to establish if there is anything present that may have contributed to or help explain the cause of death—it is a key component of the investigative picture. The respective perspectives of the paeditrician and the police help support a balanced and professional approach. In SUDI cases, the child's sleeping environment including bedding, furniture positioning, room layout and aspect, ventilation, heating, temperature, general upkeep, and provison of food may be of relevance, depending on the individual circumstances. As also explained in the paeditrician's perspective, having a parent(s) present to explain the chronology of events in the home context again can be invaluable. Explanations that may have been difficult to understand, when set within the home could become far clearer. Having a medical professional present to explain the significance of any medication or drugs at the home can also save a considerable amount of time for police who will have a limited medical knowledge.

Having established the rationale for the home visit and explained the sensitivities, the following points need to be taken into account.

- At this early stage where all the facts are not known and where no cause of death has been established, the integrity of the death location needs to be preserved and maintained.
- This will invariably necessitate discreetly maintaining control of the home (being aware of the impact on overt police activity with neighbours, etc) until certain routine but essential tasks have been completed.
- An initial death location **assessment** should be performed by a non-uniformed police officer, specially trained in responding to child death. In some circumstances, the initial **response** to the death, if at home rather than at a hospital, may be by a uniformed officer, but ideally uniformed presence should be kept to a minimum. Detective officers under the direction of a detective inspector responsible for investigating the circumstances of the death should be deployed as soon as possible to undertake the assessment.
- Details should be obtained of all those present at the home, and any useful information in relation to the death.
- Arrangements should be made for the home to be vacated and suitable alternative arrangements made for any occupants pending an assessment and home visit. This should include consideration of temporarily relocating any pets, eg dogs, who if left may adversly affect the environment.
- Recording information in relation to the home in photographic images, video/DVD, sketch, or plan. These will assist the pathologist and other professionals in understanding the circumstances of the death with regards to their respective roles in trying to identify its cause.
- Securing the home to protect its integrity and assist in supporting the accounts of parents and others. This could be achieved by locking the premises, with a non-uniformed officer maintaining a discreet view of the premises.

- Explaining to the parents why these actions are required within the process to establish why their child died.

An open and sensitive approach is clearly required in supporting those whose child has died, but equally these investigative safeguards should ultimately ensure a clearer picture of the circumstances and uphold the rights of the deceased child in establishing the cause of their tragic death.

KEY POINT

If parents realize that many of these actions are routinely undertaken in all similar child deaths and not because the police consider them personally responsible in some way for their child's death, this may help alleviate any concerns in relation to police and other professionals' activities in their home.

4.7.3 **Witnesses**

In the standard model this block is 'identify victim' but for this context, where the victim is known, it has been amended to deal with witnesses. As has been emphasized throughout, communication and information are at the centre of any sucessful investigation. The more information there is, the more detailed the picture of what has happened. The more effective the communication, the greater the flow of information to complete the picture. It, therefore, follows that witnesses to any event related to the death, whether before, during, or after the death, are an essential element of the investigation.

Witnesses will be in many categories, including parents, carers, siblings, family, friends, neighbours, members of the public, professionals in health, education, Social Services, and the police. In some cases where a serious criminal offence is suspected, certain people may be designated as 'significant witnesses'.

Definition of 'significant witness'

Significant witnesses, sometimes referred to as 'key' witnesses, are those who:

Have or claim to have witnessed, visually or otherwise, an indictable offence, part of such an offence or events closely connected with it (including any incriminating comments made by the suspected offender either before or after the offence); and/or

Have a particular relationship to the victim or have a central position in an investigation into an indictable offence.

While significant witnesses are usually defined with reference to indictable-only offences, investigating officers may consider designating witnesses as significant in any other serious case where it might be helpful.

(Ministry of Justice, *Achieving Best Evidence in Criminal Proceedings*, 2011:8)

In child death cases where a criminal offence is suspected, key witnesses may include a parent or carer, sibling, neighbour, or paramedic.

Again, the nature of the child death investigation will invariably determine the number of witnesses identified and those from whom formal witness statements are taken, eg non-suspicious deaths resulting in a report for the coroner and sometimes an inquest will usually have fewer statements taken than where the death is suspicious or a suspected homicide that results in criminal court proceedings.

In childhood death investigations, preparation prior to speaking to witnesses should include considering the following:

- establishing the child's name, the correct pronunciation, and spelling;
- appropriate language and any need for an interpreter;
- any cultural considerations, eg expectation of release of body for burial that will not be met if a post-mortem is required;
- appropriate support in relation to bereavement counselling.

One of the most important aspects of any child death investigation, that can determine the future course of the investigation, is the 'Initial Account' including the 'history' from the parents and/or carers. As previously outlined in non-suspicious cases, it is envisaged that this will be taken jointly by the paediatrician and a police officer utilizing a template to obtain as much relevant information as possible (examples of two templates are included in the Appendices—GM (Appendix A) and Indigo (Appendix B)).

Information is paramount, and particularly information regarding the circumstances of the actual death or events that led up to it—so speaking to the last person to see the child alive is clearly a priority. As explained in the section on the paediatrician's perspective, the parents' intial account and the home visit are often considered to be key elements when assessing the nature of the death and its place on the child death continuum.

There are different views on how this initial account is taken, but each case should be considered by the professionals involved and a judgement made on the specific circumstances. Points to think about include:

1. Speaking to the parents together

Advantages

- support each other;
- prompt each other to remember details with trigger points;
- quicker as one not two history-taking sessions.

Disadvantages

- stronger personality may dominate conversation;
- person may feel intimidated and unable to provide crucial information, eg domestic abuse;

- harder to corroborate accounts independently;
- confusion over who provided which piece of information;
- a composite account rather than individual.

2. Speaking to parents separately

Advantages

- both feel contributed to process;
- speak openly in their own time;
- accounts can be corroborated by each other—establishing their reliability and perhaps removing/lowering possible suspicion if that is a factor.

Disadvantages

- partner unable to support them through very difficult process, especially as so close to the death, although this option does not preclude another family member or person supporting them during the process;
- parents may feel that they are 'under suspicion', feel threatened, and less willing to co-operate or contribute to the process;
- take more time as undertake process twice.

The main determining factor as to which approach is adopted will be the parents' level of interaction and the presence of concerning features within the information already established. This is an initial account at a very early stage of the process that can have an impact on the future character of the ensuing investigation. It is not always an easy decision to make and requires professional agreement on a case-by-case basis. It will assist to keep the deceased child as the central focus in any assessment of the most appropriate course of action if there is any uncertainty.

GOOD PRACTICE

It will help all those involved in the investigation of child deaths if the police and other agencies provide consistent messages for parents/carers—it can be very troubling for them if they are provided with conflicting information from the professionals involved. Four key messages are:

1. We carry out an investigation on behalf of the coroner into every case of sudden and unexplained death.
2. When any child/young person dies unexpectedly, an in-depth investigation by all agencies is carried out—all having the same aim: to find out why the child died.
3. We conduct our investigations in the knowledge that the majority of deaths in children transpire to be from natural causes.
4. Valuable lessons may be learned during our investigations that may help save the lives of other children in the future.

4.7.4 **Suspects**

The generic 'Suspects' building block becomes relevant when answering the investigative question 'Are any criminal offences disclosed?', and the follow-on question 'If so—who was/were responsible for those offences?'.

If the circumstances suggest that there are reasonable grounds to suspect that a criminal offence may have been committed and it is relevant to the death, then those suspected of committing that offence will fall into the category of 'suspect'. It must be emphasized that the level of information and evidence to categorize a person as a suspect can be lower than that to justify a criminal charge, leading to criminal proceedings. Importantly, it is a particular threshold of suspicion that the law dictates requires legal safeguards for those falling into the 'suspect' category. This would include being cautioned before relevant questions were put in relation to the suspected offence, certain procedures to be followed if interviewed, the requirement to arrest in some circumstances, and the right to legal advice.

In the majority of cases, as repeatedly emphasized, there will not be any suspects after the question of criminal offences has been considered with an open mind. In some circumstances, particularly when a child has died and parents are grieving and in a state of shock, they may say or do unusual things and react in a way that raises concern. Great care has to be taken before categorizing a person as a 'suspect' based purely on these observations as there may be a simple explanation for them. In such circumstances a straightforward question of 'what do you mean by that?' or 'why did you do that?' may clarify the position and negate cautioning and/or arrest.

Case study

Police and emergency services were called to an address where a distressed mother who did not speak English was screaming and shouting words in her own language. A sibling explained that her mother was saying 'I have killed my baby, I've killed my baby!' The baby was located and had sadly died, but had no apparent injuries. Subsequently the baby was found to have died from natural causes. The mother had not actually 'killed her baby' but felt, because she was looking after the child at the time, that she was responsible in some way for the death and so had 'killed' her baby. A clarification of what she actually meant by 'I have killed my baby' together with an examination of the known circumstances, eg no apparent injuries, negated any need to arrest. This also highlights the need for great care when presented with a translation of what has been said, as words can have varying contexts and meanings depending on the language.

Factors that may raise suspicion and elevate a person to the category of 'suspect' will be considered in detail in the next chapter which examines 'suspicious deaths'.

4.7.5 **Evidence**

The 'Evidence' building block, like the other four, does not sit in isolation, with its associated considerations impacting on all of the other areas. Evidence is simply information or material in its various forms, that are considered to be in an acceptable format to utilize when considering related events in a legal setting. This legal setting would encompass the Coroner's Court, Criminal Courts, and Family Courts. Evidence may include physical items, documents, verbal accounts, electronic records, forensic samples, and expert medical opinion in child death cases.

Because of the legal requirements in relation to obtaining and adducing evidence, the police and partner agencies have to operate within legal constraints that can impact on the way an investigation is managed. For example, in a case that was considered a suspected homicide, where there were reasonable grounds to suspect a parent of killing their child, it would be inappropriate to sit down with them and the paediatrician to take the medical history from them. This would be contrary to their legal rights which will often come into operation when they are arrested for an offence. They would include being 'cautioned', ie 'You do not have to say anything. But it may harm your defence if you do not mention when questioned something which you later rely on in Court. Anything you do say may be given in evidence', informed of their right to legal advice, and the requirement for interviews to be recorded at a police station. On arrest, certain other powers also come into effect, such as the power to request and take certain samples from arrested persons. Further considerations in relation to the requirement to arrest persons and the implications will be considered in more detail in the next chapter covering suspicious deaths.

Evidence can be lost, destroyed, or contaminated if certain measures are not adhered to in order to protect it and preserve its integrity. Sometimes evidence can be lost forever if action is not taken quickly to secure and preserve it, with often the first 24 hours or 'golden hour' being seen as a critical period. The way evidence is obtained is important so as to retain its integrity and prevent it being discredited at a future date, re-emphasizing the need to comply with legal and practical requirements.

In respect of the initial response the 'Evidence' building block will receive consideration in the following areas:

- The body of the deceased child will be visually examined by the paediatrician and police noting any injuries or unusual features—photographs and other visual representations, eg an annotated diagram, may be taken.
- A full skeletal survey, CT, and MRI scans may be taken depending on the circumstances.
- Eyes may be examined by an ophthalmologist.
- If a SUDI, in some hospitals certain standard samples will be taken with the authority of the coroner under a standing protocol.
- If a post-mortem is required, a number of samples will be taken.

- During the home visit, items that may be relevant to the death can be taken, eg (a) clothing or bedding but only if of forensic value—blood, vomit residue, (b) bottles and containers from child's last feed, (c) last nappy, (d) The personal child health development record sometimes referred to as the 'red book', and (e) medication.
- Photographic and video images of the home—if the parents allow a video of the home visit, including their visual demonstration of how the child was in bed, can be useful in better understanding the circumstances in which the child sadly died.
- If appropriate in deaths where a child may have died as a result of being overlaid by a carer, then a sample of blood or urine may be requested from the carer to confirm or exclude the presence of alcohol or other drugs as a factor in the death. This is more relevant to 'suspicious deaths' and will be covered in detail in that chapter.
- In child deaths, parents are often given the opportunity to have mementos of their child—a photograph, lock of hair, foot or hand print. These can present issues in relation to forensic considerations if taken before the post-mortem but these are easily addressed if arrangements are made for them to be taken at the conclusion of the post-mortem.
- Any location considered as a 'scene' clearly by its designation as such, suggests there may be evidence related to it.

Potential difficulties that the requirements of the police response could generate can be ameliorated by effective communication between the police (including the crime scene investigator/crime scene manager), other professionals, and, most importantly, with the parents and family. It is important to explain why certain potential evidence is required.

The use of the term 'evidence' should **not** be seen solely as referring to material supporting a case of some form of wrongdoing, but seen as essential material or information that helps establish why a child died. As well as suggesting that someone may have acted inappropriately, it can equally corroborate parent's accounts, eliminate possibilities, eg carer was or was not intoxicated whilst asleep with child on a sofa, and provide a clearer, more legally robust picture of events surrounding a child death. It is, like the other four building blocks, a generic categorization of 'jigsaw' pieces of information that help build together a picture of why a child died.

GOOD PRACTICE

It is important and very useful to begin completing a police Policy Book from the outset of any child death investigation. The decisions and their rationale are essential information that should be recorded for future reference, and their usefulness is not limited solely to suspicious or homicide cases. As highlighted previously, it is not always apparent from the outset which path any child death investigation may follow.

4.8 **Conclusion**

This chapter has hopefully provided a detailed overview of the issues that come into play with child deaths and emphasized the need for a multi-agency and professional approach. The impact of a child death on the family has been powerfully illustrated but also considered within the context of an investigation which remains focused on the deceased child. No child death is straightforward, and these themes will remain constant but be developed in certain areas as the investigation progresses across the continuum into suspicious child deaths and onto child homicides in the following chapters.

Further reading and information

Oxford Concise Colour Medical Dictionary (2010), (5th edn, Oxford: OUP).
Medical Glossary—Appendix G.

NOTES

NOTES

5

Suspicious Child Deaths and Related Child Death Offences

5.1 **Introduction**

It is those deaths that fall mid-way along the child death continuum that present real challenges in managing the expectations of the deceased child's family and the other professionals involved. These are not 'straightforward' cases that fit easily within the Rapid Response Process, although they do obviously benefit from it with a continuing multi-agency response, albeit now invariably police led. These types of case require the utmost sensitivities in dealing with parents and carers considered as 'suspects' on occasions, but who, after a protracted investigation, may be:

(a) completely exonerated from any wrong doing in relation to the death; or
(b) found to have deliberately harmed their child; or
(c) left in that very difficult position of unknown culpability where the cause of death may not be established and remain 'unascertained'.

The four key questions to answer in relation in any child death remain:

1. Why did this child die?
2. What was the cause of the death and the circumstances?
3. Are any criminal offences disclosed?
4. If so—who was/were responsible for committing those offences?

but the emphasis of focus on the first two for a non-suspicious death is now extended to encompass: 'Are any criminal offences disclosed?'. If that is established, then the final question will come into play: 'Who was/were responsible for committing those offences?'.

These types of case, in many ways, are some of the hardest to investigate, particularly when balancing the overt and discreet police responses explained in the previous chapter. Again, perhaps the most appropriate way of gauging the level and nature of response, is to always consider the deceased child to be the ultimate focus of every investigation, with their interests paramount. They are no longer alive but they still have their right to a professional and thorough investigation into their death. It may be useful to consider the police as representing the voice of the deceased. The other term 'a compassionate cynic' may also help try and explain the position the police need to adopt whilst walking

Figure 5.1 Investigative mindset line between non-suspicious and suspicious.

the investigative mindset line between a death being considered either suspicious or non-suspicious and balancing the investigative response accordingly.

The term 'suspicious' would suggest that the death may not be from natural causes and, therefore, merit a more detailed examination of the circumstances. The following more comprehensive definition may assist in understanding what is intended by the term in this context.

Definition of 'suspicious death'

Although there is no direct evidence or grounds to suspect a specific criminal act there are, however, factors that raise the possibility that a criminal act may have contributed to the death and thereby merit a more detailed investigation of the circumstances of the death.

(It would NOT include Sudden Unexpected Death in Infancy (SUDI), where there is no apparent medical explanation for the death but equally no grounds to suspect that a criminal act contributed to the death).

KEY POINT

The most important word in the 'suspicious death' definition is the word 'MAY'. Although factors may be present which, based on data from previous cases, raise the level of concern, their presence is NOT conclusive proof of a criminal offence being related to the death. They may, however, when seen in the context of a particular set of circumstances, provide grounds to justify a more detailed and thorough investigation. That investigation may uncover criminal wrongdoing but equally may provide evidence of a natural cause of death.

When considering any child death, but particularly in relation to suspicious deaths, the following model illustrating the investigative process may be useful.

The current knowledge, derived from answering the 'who, what, where, when, why, and how?' questions, enables hypotheses or possible explanations to be considered. These are developed through generating enquiries (actions) to gather further information to ascertain the validity of the hypotheses. Comparisons can then be made between what is known, against what is unknown, together with the conflicts and consistencies in the information. This in turn updates our knowledge and the cycle continues.

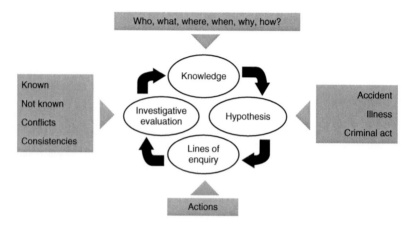

Figure 5.2 Investigative evaluation process
(Boxer, 2011)

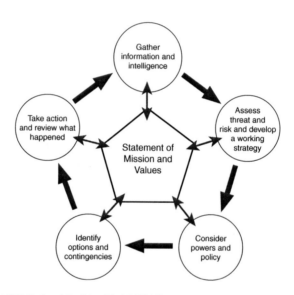

Figure 5.3 ACPO National Decision Model (2011)

The National Decision Model is an additional useful tool to utilize when considering child death investigation, together within the context of the 'Risk Principles' linked with it.

1. As police, we accept that we have a duty to confront risks and to make decisions in uncertain conditions on behalf of the communities we serve.
2. Protecting life is a primary consideration.
3. Even with good decision-making, some harm may still occur.

4. We expect our decisions to be judged by the quality of the decision-making, not by the outcome.
5. While perfect decisions are not expected, they should be consistent with those that a body of officers of similar rank or grade, specialism, or experience would have taken in the same circumstances.
6. We will take a positive, not an aversive, approach to risk.
7. We will learn from both our failures and our successes.

The 'five building blocks' model for the police investigation will still be adopted to manage the different aspects of the investigation but, if it is considered that there is a possibility of a criminal offence having a bearing on the death, then the focus may shift in some of those areas and the respective response be more detailed. The objective, however, remains the same for all child death investigations, ie to establish 'Why did this child die?'. One key area that may shed some light on the factors causing concern or 'suspicion', and even allay those initial concerns, is a post-mortem examination. This is a priority, but depending on the area may take some time to arrange. Other enquiries can continue in the intervening period, but many may not achieve their true relevance until the post-mortem has been conducted. Even then, as previously explained, it may take some weeks for results to be known, but the sooner the process is commenced the better for all concerned.

A suspicious child death is one that occurs, usually suddenly and unexpectedly, in the absence of any known natural disease or of a plausible accidental cause. There may be unexplained injuries or evidence of inflicted trauma. The object of the forensic post-mortem is either to allay suspicion by eliciting evidence of natural disease, to support the possibility of accidental death or, alternatively, to provide evidence of homicide by a third party, and if possible to gain information to identify the perpetrator.

5.2 Factors that may raise 'suspicion'

Recent research (Mayes et al., 2010) has identified a number of social factors and physical findings which are seen significantly more commonly in suspicious than in non-suspicious deaths. The former include the following:

1. A history of domestic abuse, including violence towards children.
2. Accounts by those caring for the dead child are inconsistent with the physical findings, and may vary on questioning.
3. The carer suffers from mental health problems.
4. A history of hospital or GP visits when symptoms ascribed to the child cannot be verified by independent observation or investigation. Numerous visits to different hospitals and/or medical practices may occur.
5. A history of alcohol or drug abuse, or a criminal record for the carer.

6. Deaths over the age of one year are more commonly suspicious than those less than a year.
7. The child or the family is known to Social Services and children in the family may be on a child protection plan.

The occurrence of a previous child death within the family was *not* associated with increased risk of suspicious death.

Suspicious physical findings include:

1. The presence of bruising in a baby too young to be independently mobile, multiple bruises, bruising in unusual sites (eg behind the ears, or on the trunk and abdomen), or bruises of obviously different ages, without a clear and plausible explanation of how they occurred.
2. The child has been dead longer than stated, from the evidence of significant lowering of core temperature, or the presence of established *rigor mortis* inconsistent with the reported time interval since death.
3. Fractures identified on a radiological skeletal survey prior to autopsy. Multiple rib fractures, particularly of different ages, and metaphyseal fractures in limb bones are particularly relevant.
4. Evidence of subdural haemorrhage (ie bleeding over the surface of the brain, between two of the membranes that surround the brain, the *arachnoid mater* on the inside and the *dura mater* on the outside; as the name suggests, in subdural haemorrhage the blood collects underneath the dura, outside of the arachnoid), extensive retinal haemorrhage (ie bleeding into the inside surface of the back of the eye), and brain swelling identified by diagnostic imaging before autopsy.
5. The identification of prescription or recreational drugs, other than those used in attempted resuscitation, in samples taken for toxicological analysis, either in hospital or at autopsy.

The presence of blood on the face, often quoted as a suspicious finding, was found more commonly in non-suspicious than in suspicious deaths in the study quoted. This pink frothy mucous-type blood is often found, whilst thicker blood would merit further examination.

A list of risk factors associated with suspicious deaths is included in Appendix H.

5.3 **The forensic post-mortem**

An invaluable source of information in 'suspicious' child deaths is obtained from an enhanced post-mortem examination. In circumstances where a death may be considered 'suspicious', the coroner will invariably authorize a 'special' or forensic post-mortem. This will require a paediatric pathologist and a Home Office forensic pathologist working together in tandem combining their respective areas of expertise—one in child deaths and the other in homicides. The other option is for a Home Office forensic paediatric pathologist to undertake the post-mortem, but currently there is only one such individual qualified to this standard.

5.3.1 Pathologist's briefing

As repeatedly emphasized, communication between professionals and the pooling of information is essential for an effective investigation. No professional works in isolation, and the link between the police and pathologist has an increased importance when a death is considered potentially suspicious. One of the ways information is shared is in a briefing to the pathologist preceding the post-mortem examination. When a 'special' forensic post-mortem is requested by the police, further information will be required by the pathologist.

1. The precise reason for asking for the post-mortem needs to be clearly identified. This may be for a variety of reasons, such as the following:
   (a) There may be evidence of injury or injuries noticed by clinicians or by police when the body is examined.
   (b) The history of the circumstances surrounding the death may be questionable, the story may change on questioning, there may have been an undue delay in seeking medical assistance, etc. This sort of detail needs to be communicated to the pathologist.
   (c) There may have been past episodes where injury has occurred and there has been doubt about the explanation, or episodes of apparent illness may have occurred where investigation failed to provide a reasonable explanation. When there are a number of such episodes, it is not uncommon for carers to seek medical advice from a different source on each occasion.
   (d) For various reasons, the dead child or a sibling may be known to Social Services and be subject to a child protection plan.
   (e) A post-mortem by a paediatric pathologist may have been requested because there was no clinical suspicion, but a skeletal survey might show evidence of bony injury, or some other injury might have been discovered during an earlier autopsy. Sometimes a case is considered straightforward with no initial concerns, but a paediatric post-mortem may reveal previously unknown injuries or findings that raise concern. In these cases the post-mortem is usually suspended, the coroner consulted, and the post-mortem resumed under the auspices of a 'special' post-mortem that will be more detailed and conducted with a Home Office forensic pathologist present.
   (f) Another child in the family may have died under unusual circumstances or have been the subject of non-accidental injury.
2. The police briefing for the pathologist should include a detailed account of the circumstances surrounding the death and a description of the site and position where the body was found.

3. Photographs taken at the scene, any video that has been made, and any sketches drawn should be made available to the pathologist.

4. Usually, the dead child will have been admitted to hospital, sometimes severely ill and died after unsuccessful resuscitation, either in the A&E department or in Intensive Care, or be dead on arrival. Once the attention of the police has been drawn to the occurrence of a suspicious, unexplained, or violent death, it is very important that any hospital staff involved are identified. They should be interviewed as soon as possible regarding the findings when the child was admitted. The results of any investigations performed, including X-rays, should be assembled together with copies of any clinical photographs, radiographs (X-rays), CT, or MRI scans for the pathologist.

5. Any clinical samples, such as blood, urine, or cerebrospinal fluid (the fluid that surrounds the brain and spinal cord, usually collected by means of a so-called lumbar puncture) taken from the child, particularly samples taken before blood or fluid infusions, should be seized, receipted, and appropriately preserved, as these may prove to be important evidentially.

6. Where sudden deaths have occurred, A&E protocols may indicate that samples as recommended by Kennedy for SUDIs should be taken in the Emergency department. Many forensic pathologists would prefer there to be no interference with the body. Where a post-mortem examination is to be performed rapidly, the possible deterioration of samples for microbiological culture is probably exaggerated, but if such samples are taken it should be requested that only one attempt should be made, particularly if needle puncture is needed to obtain the specimen,. If this is unsuccessful, further attempts should be abandoned, recognizing that the same samples will be obtained at the post-mortem examination. If samples are examined locally, it is very important that the results are communicated to the pathologist who will undertake the autopsy.

7. In a suspicious death the clinicians may request a full, detailed, radiological skeletal survey of the type undertaken in living children as part of the investigation of possible non-accidental injury. This comprises a series of X-rays of all bones of the body to look for fractures. A survey of this nature will be part of the post-mortem protocol, but if it has been done locally, a copy of the full radiological investigation should be obtained, since it is very important that the films are examined by a paediatric radiologist expert in non-accidental bony injuries before the autopsy commences.

8. When an inflicted head injury is suspected, the victim is often admitted in a moribund state but may survive for a variable time on life support. Clinicians will be focused on the possibility of successful resuscitation but, if possible, samples for blood clotting studies and an examination of the fundi (the interior of the eyes, to observe the retinae—the interior lining of the back of the eyes—for possible haemorrhage) by an expert ophthalmologist should be requested as these studies performed as soon as possible after injury may be of vital evidential importance.

9. In a suspicious death where the child is admitted to hospital, it is very important that the scene where death has occurred should be secured and submitted to full forensic investigation.
10. When a 'special' forensic post-mortem is requested, it is usual for the investigating police officers (SIO/IO), the Crime Scene Manager (CSM), Crime Scene Investigator (CSI), a police photographer, Exhibits Officer, and sometimes the Coroner's Officer to attend the examination and briefing beforehand.

GOOD PRACTICE

The police should provide a written briefing for the pathologist from the police perspective to accompany the medical records and other material, eg X-rays/MRI/CT scans collated for the pathologist. Ideally, the briefing document should be sent to the pathologist before the formal briefing but should be the basis of the police briefing and further discussion. A copy should be retained for future reference, as it may be relevant in relation to when certain facts were known and revealed to the pathologist.

The Project Indigo Form 90 would provide a suitable template for this purpose (see Appendix B).

5.3.2 Scene visit by the pathologist

The emergence of fully trained and experienced CSMs, together with logistical problems in getting a forensic pathologist to a scene with sufficient dispatch, means that this function is, perhaps, seen as less vital than formally. However, whilst the actual management of the scene is now very much the responsibility of the CSM, the pathologist should always be given appropriate access. Sometimes the police investigators will make a specific request for the pathologist to visit the scene and to help in the reconstruction of events that might have led to the death. At the very least, there needs to be an opportunity to see a very detailed photographic and video record, and to see any diagrams made.

Where blunt trauma has been inflicted there needs to be a consideration of possible sites or mechanisms. Where inflicted trauma is suspected but accidental alternatives are proposed, such as short distance falls or falls down stairs in fatal head injuries, the various hypotheses may need to be tested at the scene. Occasionally, carers for the child may give a very complicated account of what happened to precipitate the injuries observed at post-mortem.

A useful test of the plausibility of the account may be for the police to ask for the witness(es) to reconstruct what they claim to have happened. This can be done at the actual scene to make it as realistic as possible, using a doll to represent the child. The re-enactment should be videoed and viewed by the pathologist and correlated with the post-mortem findings. This should be regarded as a constituent of the 'search for the truth', that can as equally corroborate a parent/carer's account as cast doubt on its credibility. If corroborated, it can save considerable time and prevent a carer being unnecessarily considered a 'suspect' or being arrested if there were reasonable grounds to doubt their account's validity.

5.3.3 Role of the police at the post-mortem

This refers specifically to the role of the police with regard to the post-mortem, but it is recognized that the forensic evidence obtained from this examination, and the various ancillary investigations that the autopsy generates, may form a crucially important part of the police investigations.

The details of the police investigation of the circumstances surrounding the suspicious death of a child, the results of relevant interviews, the examination of the crime scene, interviews with clinical staff when hospital admission has occurred, and the results of any laboratory tests or diagnostic imaging should be gathered and prepared as a briefing note for the pathologist before the autopsy commences.

Representatives of the investigating police team, as well as the photographer, CSM, etc, who have a more direct role in the examination, should attend the autopsy to establish a dialogue with the pathologist. At the end of the examination it may be useful for the SIO to summarize their understanding of the findings and their possible significance for the pathologist to agree. This will, of necessity, be very preliminary, and the information may be modified by subsequent investigation. **It is important to record this information and ask the pathologist to endorse the record.**

5.4 Account of the forensic post-mortem

5.4.1 Preliminaries

At the commencement of the examination a list should be compiled of the names of the pathologist(s) conducting the post-mortem and all other persons present (police officers, CSM, photographer, Coroner's Officer, etc), together with their rank and contact details. The start and finish times of the examination should be recorded.

5.4.2 External examination

General

As with all forensic autopsies, the external examination is of paramount importance.

- The identification should be confirmed and the name of the identifying officer recorded. The body should be photographed clothed and then unclothed, full length and back and front. Any attached medical equipment used in resuscitation (endotracheal tubes ('breathing tubes'), intravenous catheters ('drip sites'), etc) should be photographed *in situ* before removal.

- The race and sex is noted.
- Swabs from the body surface for DNA analysis may identify third parties who have been in contact with the deceased. Ultra-violet light sourcing may identify bruises not apparent to the naked eye.
- A sample of head hair for toxicological analysis should be taken before the body is opened to avoid contamination. Ideally, a hank of hair about the diameter of a pencil is separated, tied firmly close to the scalp, and cut off below the ligature. Analysis may not only identify a drug, but also give an estimate of the time scale over which it was given. In young babies it may not be technically feasible to obtain an adequate specimen.

5.4.3 Radiological skeletal survey

A full radiological skeletal survey (see above) should be conducted before the autopsy, using the same protocol of views that would be applied in clinical practice in a suspected case of child abuse. This survey should take place in a hospital diagnostic imaging department and not using portable equipment. Ideally, the images should be examined by a paediatric radiologist experienced in the diagnosis of non-accidental injury, and reported to the pathologist before the autopsy starts.

5.4.4 Weights and measurements

The body is accurately weighed on paediatric weight scales and the crown-heel, crown-rump, foot length, and head circumference measured in cm. By comparison with standard tables, the child's centiles are established and, coupled with the general examination, the nutritional status is assessed.

The state of cleanliness (examination of the ears, skin creases, finger and toe nails, evidence and severity of any nappy rash) is commented on.

- In addition, the anteroposterior diameter of the head, the bitemporal and mastoid-vertex-mastoid measurements, the lengths of the palpebral fissures, and the interocular distance is recorded.
- The anterior fontanelle is palpated, measured, and assessed.

5.4.5 Eyes and mouth

- The eyes are examined after fully everting the lids for evidence of injury or the presence of petechial (pin-point) haemorrhages.
- Erupted teeth are assessed against the child's age and any injuries identified. The mouth and gums are carefully examined for evidence of injury and the

buccal mucosa on the insides of the cheeks is examined for injury caused by impact involving the teeth.

- The upper labial frenulum (the fold of tissue in the centre between the gum and the upper lip) is examined for recent or old tears.

5.4.6 Skin

The general skin colour is noted and the pattern and distribution of hypostasis, as well as signs of decomposition, are recorded. An assessment of how the body has been orientated since death by the pattern of hypostasis (the gravitational pooling of blood in the soft tissues after death) is considered. Congestion (engorgement of blood vessels), cyanosis (bluish discolouration of skin), and skin rash, particularly the presence and distribution of a petechial (pin-point haemorrhages) rash is noted.

Any obvious congenital abnormalities and naevi (birthmarks) are recorded. Acquired external marks such as old scars are identified and recorded.

5.4.7 Injuries

Meticulous and detailed examinations and description of all recent injuries are made. Ideally, these should be marked on printed body diagrams to be preserved as part of the examination record. The injuries are numbered, the numbers corresponding to numbered items in the text description in the report. The production of these records may be required later in court. All injuries need to be photographed separately, with and without an accompanying cm scale. Traumatic lesions are identified as abrasions (scratches or grazes), bruises, lacerations (tears), incised wounds, burns, etc. The shape and margins of each lesion is defined and its dimensions recorded (length, breadth, orientation to the body axis, and position with reference to defined body landmarks). The position of the lesions is also described in terms of their height above the heel.

Without a clear and plausible reason for their presence, bruises in young babies who are not independently mobile are always suspicious. In toddlers there may be bruises, for example, on shins and knees, and collision with furniture may produce bruises or superficial abrasions on the forehead. Indications of abuse include bruises under the jaw or behind the ears; bruises or abrasions on the cheeks or buttocks; crescent-shaped bruises indicative of pinching; grip-mark bruises on the arms; bruising of the upper lip, especially if associated with damage to the frenulum.

5.4.8 Bites

Bite marks, which may occur on any part of the child's body, are of special significance since their particular characteristics may allow identification of the perpetrator. Classically, they consist of two opposing semicircles, either in the form of bruises or abrasions, and individual tooth marks may be discernible. Confluent petechiae caused by suction may be present at the centre. Examination of these marks should be undertaken in conjunction with an experienced forensic odontologist (forensic dentist) who will advise on the special requirements in recording and photographing these lesions. A swab for saliva identification is taken.

5.4.9 **Head injuries**

The scalp is examined, photographed, and any trace evidence collected. Clotted blood and other debris, which may obscure injuries, is carefully removed with a sponge and water, after which further descriptions are made and photographs taken. It is often necessary to go further, shaving hair from around the margins of a lesion before it is further described and photographed.

5.4.10 **External genitalia**

The external genitalia and perineum (area around the genitals and anus) are carefully examined. The vulva and anus are inspected for laceration, bruising, discharge, or swelling. Any suspected semen stains not only around the genitalia, but also anywhere on the body or clothing, should be sampled and swabbed. The vulval labia (the external part of the female genitalia) and anal margin are examined with particular care.

Caution is exercised in interpreting apparent dilatation of the anal sphincter as evidence of penetration, since it may become patulous and open as a normal post-mortem change, especially in children. Unless there are additional findings, such as abrasion, bruising, or semen staining, an 'open' anus is unlikely to be significant.

In the presence of suspicious findings, samples are taken for semen and microbiological culture. Plain cotton wool swabs on sticks are used to take samples from:

- The interior of the vulval labia and around the vaginal orifice.
- The margins and interior of the anus.
- The mid-vagina, using an instrument to part the lower vagina and prevent contamination.
- The upper vagina and posterior fornix, again using instrumentation to avoid contamination.

5.4.11 **Investigations prior to internal examination**

A sample of cerebrospinal fluid (CSF, see above) is taken for microscopy and bacterial culture. After sterilizing the skin over the upper cervical spine and occiput with a Steriswab, a sample of CSF is taken by cisternal puncture with a sterile needle and syringe.

A small sample of skin is taken for fibroblast cell culture. After sterilizing the skin over the sternum, a small ellipse of skin is removed with a sterile scalpel blade in the line of the incision planned to open the thorax and abdomen. The skin sample is placed in tissue culture medium.

5.4.12 Internal examination

The basic techniques follow those of a conventional paediatric post-mortem examination (outlined in Chapter 4) with some modifications depending on the circumstances in an individual examination. The order in which systems are examined may be modified in the presence of obvious injuries, which are dealt with first. All notes, diagrams, etc, made during the examination are preserved. The external description is dictated before the internal examination is made, and the internal description should be completed as soon as the examination is complete. The photographs taken are numbered and the views taken are given a short identifying description. After processing, copies of all the photographs are presented to the pathologist.

5.4.13 Thoracic (chest) organs

As a routine, the thoracic pluck (comprising all chest organs together, ie lungs, heart, and thymus) is removed, together with the liver, stomach, spleen, and pancreas. This approach is necessary if some varieties of congenital heart disease are not to be missed or misinterpreted.

5.4.14 Neck

In a death where asphyxia is a possible cause, a careful examination of the neck structures is required. The thoracic pluck is transected at the level of the thoracic inlet and the neck structures are left in situ (inside the body) until the brain has been removed.

The neck sternomastoid muscles are individually dissected and reflected upwards. The sternohyoids, sternothyroids, and omohyoid muscles are then dissected and reflected upwards. Any haemorrhage or bruising is noted. The carotid sheathes (the connective tissue surrounding the neck vessels) on both sides are opened with fine scissors and any intimal damage is noted, with a magnifying glass if necessary. The upper neck suprahyoid muscles are then dissected and reflected downwards, again noting any haemorrhage or bruising.

The tongue and neck structures are then released and removed; the larynx (voice box) is examined for damage to the laryngeal cartilages or fracture or displacement of the four horns (an extremely rare finding in young subjects, even following manual strangulation). The muscles surrounding the larynx, as well as the base of the tongue, are examined and sliced to exclude bruising or haemorrhage.

5.4.15 **Chest wall and ribs**

The muscles of the chest wall are examined for evidence of bruising. The pleural membranes covering the ribs are carefully stripped and each rib is examined visually and by palpation to exclude fractures. This is important since fresh rib fractures may not be visible on radiographs if the view taken is unfavourable.

Any fractures identified at post-mortem, in the ribs or any other bones, either in the radiological survey or by the pathologist during dissection, need further examination. Initially, this requires removal of the fracture site, further high-resolution radiography, followed by decalcification (to remove the calcium, so that it can be processed), processing, and paraffin embedding for histological sectioning and microscopical examination. This whole process can take up to a month.

5.4.16 **Abdominal visceral injuries**

After reflection of the skin over the anterior abdominal wall, the peritoneal cavity is carefully opened in the midline. Visceral intra-abdominal injuries are almost always accompanied by blood or gut content release into the peritoneal cavity. If the injury is other than acute, there may be evidence of peritonitis with exudate into the cavity. Any of these will be apparent on first opening the peritoneum, but even in their absence a careful and complete visual inspection of all the abdominal organs is made with them in situ before their removal. Any injuries are photographed in situ and after removal. The injuries are meticulously described, and their spatial relationships recorded so that the mechanism(s) of infliction can be deduced. Tissue blocks from the injuries are taken for histological evaluation.

5.4.17 **Head injuries**

Head injury is a common cause of death in non-accidental injury (NAI). When a head injury is anticipated from the clinical history, from the external examination, or from investigation before post-mortem, a photographic record is made of each stage of the dissection.

If there is suspicion of a rotational, acceleration/deceleration injury (RADI; previously described as shaking or shaking/impact injury), a dissection of the cervical (neck) region is made before the head is opened. The muscles are dissected and reflected to identify any haematoma (blood clot) or bruising. The neural arches (posterior part of the vertebrae) are exposed, and, if there is evidence of injury, the cervical spinal cord is exposed and removed by the posterior approach.

The scalp and its under-surface are examined for haemorrhage or bruising. After reflecting the scalp, the anterior fontanelle (the soft spot at the top front of the head in small babies, where the skull bones have not yet closed) is examined for evidence of bulging under increased intracranial (inside the head) pressure or blood beneath the dura or meninges (the membranes that surround the brain).

Fractures of the vault of the skull will be apparent at this stage, and, where there is marked brain swelling, the edges of the fracture may be separated. Even in the absence of fracture, if the brain is markedly swollen, there may be separation of the sutures. The shapes, dimensions, and distribution of any fractures of the skull vault, or the less common basal fractures, are recorded, using diagrams as well as photographs.

The technique for opening the skull depends on the age of the child. In very young children the suture lines can be followed and the skull opened like a flower, but in older children a conventional circumferential cut is used. Using the former technique, it may be possible to identify delicate connecting veins between the dura and the surface of the brain, but this is not feasible in the presence of significant subdural haemorrhage. In children, the dura is more firmly fixed to the skull vault than in the adult, and it may be technically difficult to remove the skull cap without lifting or damaging the dura. Too much manipulation may distort the underlying brain, particularly if the brain is very soft as happens when the child has spent time on a ventilator. It may be necessary to keep the skull cap in place whilst the basal connections are released, and only remove the skull cap to expose the surface of the brain after it has been in fixative for a short time. Sometimes the brain can be exposed and then released under fixative to preserve it intact.

In RADIs, subdural haemorrhage (see above) is usually in the form of a thin layer of blood over the upper surface of the cerebral hemispheres (the two halves that make up the main part of the brain), maximal near the sagittal sinus (a large vein that goes over the top of the brain on the underside of the skull), but sometimes extending to the base of the brain and into the interhemispheric fissure (the gap between the two cerebral hemispheres). In impact injuries, subdural haemorrhage tends to be more localized, and may form a recognizable space-occupying lesion (subdural haematoma), the content of which is measured.

The spinal cord and its coverings may be removed by the anterior approach by sawing through the vertebral arches on either side of the vertebral bodies to expose the cord. This is examined for haemorrhage in the coverings and photographed.

After removal of the brain and cord, they are fixed in 20 per cent formalin, the brain suspended by a thread beneath the blood vessels at the base of the brain. They are submitted to a neuropathologist (pathologist who specializes in diseases of the brain), expert in the evaluation of paediatric brain injuries, for specialist description, photography, and interpretation of the neuropathology. The dura should be stripped from the vault and base of the skull, together with any adherent blood, and kept with the brain for histological examination.

5.4.18 **Eyes**

In any case where there is significant head injury, and particularly in RADIs, the eyes are carefully removed through the superior orbital plates (the bony plates on top of the eyes), conserving as much of the optic nerve as possible. The optic nerves (the big nerves that run from the eye to the brain) are examined for evidence of haemorrhage in their coverings and photographed. They are fixed and submitted for expert ophthalmological pathological examination.

5.4.19 **Additional investigations**

In any paediatric post-mortem in a child dying suddenly and unexpectedly, a possible natural cause must be excluded as far as this is possible. In addition, evidence is sought of possible subtle homicide, where pathology visible to the naked eye may not be apparent. The same samples as outlined in Chapter 4 should be taken routinely at autopsy, even though some samples may have been taken by clinicians following the Kennedy guidelines for SUDI.

Blocks of tissue are removed from all major organs for histological evaluation. Special stains may be required in the elucidation of histological changes. Sections of the lung, for example, should be stained by Perls' method to identify haemosiderin-laden macrophages that may indicate previous bleeding into the lung. (Haemosiderin-laden macrophages are scavenger cells that have ingested red blood cells and converted the iron that is present in the haemoglobin into a substance called haemosiderin; this can be stained for with special dyes —such as Perls' which stains the haemosiderin blue. Haemosiderin-laden macrophages in the lungs can be detected around three days after the initial bleed. It is uncertain as to how long haemosiderin-laden macrophages can remain detectable in the lungs, but it is likely to be at least several weeks or even months. The presence of haemosiderin-laden macrophages in the lungs thus indicates that previous pulmonary haemorrhage is likely to have occurred at least three days prior to death, but possibly longer before that. Pulmonary haemorrhage has many causes, including episodes of asphyxia; whilst pulmonary haemosiderin-laden macrophages are more commonly seen in deaths due to inflicted injury; it is recognized that they are also seen in a small proportion of SIDS deaths.)

When examining bone fractures, the fracture site is excised and the tissue fixed in formalin. High resolution radiographs (X-rays) of the specimen(s) are made and reassessed by a paediatric radiologist. The pathologist then submits the tissue to further fixation, followed by decalcification, the preparation of tissue blocks, and histological sectioning. The radiological and histological appearances may help to classify the type of fracture and give an estimate of the time since infliction.

Samples for microbiology, viral studies, and metabolic investigations are taken exactly as described for the SUDI paediatric autopsy. Increasingly, samples for microbiology can be examined for significant pathogens by molecular biological techniques that recognize specific viral and bacterial DNA markers.

For toxicology, samples of blood, urine, and stomach contents are taken and appropriately preserved. Heart blood is the most easily obtained from babies, but blood from this source is not favoured by toxicologists, so there should be an attempt to obtain a sample from the femoral veins. Any urine present can be removed from the bladder with a syringe. Vitreous humour (the fluid inside the eye) is an alternative source when there is difficulty in obtaining a sample, but this is clearly not appropriate when a head injury is present. Head hair is increasingly used for toxicological analysis (see above), but it may be difficult or impossible to obtain a suitable sample from a baby with scanty, short head hair. Samples of liver tissue can be used for toxicological analysis, particularly in a decomposed body.

Samples of plucked hair, muscle, and liver may be retained for DNA analysis in case there are issues of identification, paternity, etc.

5.4.20 Exhibits

All specimens retained from the post-mortem must be given an identifying exhibit number by the attending CSI/exhibits officer. The record should include an exact description of each specimen which is bagged separately, with its identification and a signature from the pathologist to ensure accurate continuity.

Specimens taken from a forensic autopsy are held under the Police and Criminal Evidence Act 1984 (PACE), so that restrictions under Human Tissue Authority regulations associated with retention of specimens from routine autopsies for the coroner are suspended during a criminal investigation.

5.4.21 Continued contact between pathologist and police

Following the examination, it is important that the dialogue is continued, and important new findings in the police investigation and any relevant findings from the further pathological investigations should be communicated immediately.

5.5 Deaths arising from accidents

One category of child deaths that can include concerning factors includes those arising from various forms of accident. In some cases, neglect by the carer contributing directly or indirectly to the death may be an issue for consideration. The principal accidental causes of death in children are accidental airway obstruction or suspension, falls and playground injuries, drowning, electrocution, accidental poisoning, and road traffic injuries.

5.5.1 Airway obstruction

Young babies, particularly those under the age of one month, may suffer from airway obstruction from bed-clothing or even lying prone (on their fronts), particularly on soft bedding. Babies sleeping on adult beds or in other makeshift arrangements may slip into a position, eg between a mattress and a wall, where breathing may be compromised. Airway obstruction may also occur with a deliberate third party involvement, where a hand or a pillow is placed over the baby's face. One form of fabricated or induced illness involves a carer deliberately obstructing a baby's breathing until they become unconscious. Medical attention is then sought to explain the sudden 'collapse'. This type of abuse can lead to permanent brain damage or death.

Death in a young baby where the airway becomes compromised may not be just a simple process, but may involve the capacity of an individual baby to be roused when subjected to this type of adverse stress. Some children may respond very positively and change position to allow them to breathe, whilst others may just gradually lapse under the influence of hypoxia (lack of oxygen) to the point of unconsciousness or death. Rousability, particularly in the very young when homeostatic (internal; control) mechanisms and reflexes are developing, may be a very individual characteristic, and differences between individuals may well have a familial or genetic component. In any event, the removal of the environmental trigger, particularly any reason to cause partial or complete airway obstruction, is an obvious opportunity for prevention. Almost certainly, the success of modifying the sleeping environment, and particularly the drive to sleep babies on their backs ('back to sleep'), in a purpose-made cot, appropriately clothed, indicates the importance of this approach, both from the point of possible accidental airway obstruction, but also from possible overheating, etc.

From a forensic standpoint, the huge problem is the distinction of accidental from deliberately-imposed airway obstruction. Whilst compromise of the airway may lead to asphyxial changes at autopsy, this is by no means universal, particularly in the very young who are most likely to be affected. The changes include pin-point haemorrhages in the skin, conjunctivae, and serosal surfaces of internal organs. There may be microhaemorrhages (small haemorrhages) in the lungs, sometimes associated with blood appearing in the airways or in the nose and mouth. When partial airway obstruction occurs on a number of occasions, lung haemorrhages may be inferred by the presence of a blood breakdown product (haemosiderin) taken up by scavenger cells (macrophages) in tiny terminal airways deep in the lungs. Haemosiderin can be demonstrated in histological sections of the lung using a Prussian blue reaction (Perls' stain). The difficulty is that none of these changes are specific to asphyxia, and, whilst they may be seen in children who have been asphyxiated, they are by no means universal. Equally, some of these features may be seen in babies who have clearly not died asphyxial deaths. Furthermore, these changes in no way distinguish between accidental and deliberately-imposed airway obstruction. In an individual case, even when there is considerable circumstantial evidence to suggest that an asphyxial death is not accidental, acquiring evidence to the legal criterion of 'beyond reasonable doubt' can be virtually impossible. Occasionally, there may be marks on the body suggesting the application of an object or a hand to the face or even evidence of manual strangulation, but this is rare. Both this type of evidence, and the more florid suggestions of asphyxia, such as petechiae on the face and in the conjunctivae, are more likely to be seen in an older child capable of struggling.

In view of the often minimal or absent relevant forensic evidence at post-mortem, and the well-publicized findings of the Court of Appeal, but ultimately failed prosecutions of mothers accused of smothering their children, very few new prosecutions in the criminal court have been judged to be viable.

The police investigation requires a meticulous identification of the circumstances surrounding the death and a careful reconstruction of events and examination of the scene. This information needs to be fully covered in the pathologist's briefing. In older children, accidental airway obstruction may occur by suspension from a piece of furniture, some domestic or garden apparatus, a drape cord, etc, or from accidental imprisonment in some confined space where the child's neck is wedged and pressed on. This sort of accident is only going to occur in an independently mobile child capable of getting into a potentially dangerous position. In older children and teenagers, suspension in a domestic setting may be a result of self harming, and autoerotic neck constriction, usually by a self-applied ligature, may be a cause of accidental death in older post-pubertal males.

In older children too, asphyxiation may occur when a child strays into a confined space where the air supply is deficient.

5.5.2 Falls and playground accidents

As in subjects of all ages, long-distance falls, for example from a window in a block of flats, are one cause of fatal accidental injuries in children. The particular issues in childhood deaths of this nature are a meticulous investigation of the scene, with photographic and video recording, etc, and a detailed reconstruction of the exact sequence of events, particularly when the accident is unwitnessed. It is important to establish whether there are potential hazards that might result in others being liable to be injured in a similar fashion, and whether or not there were deficiencies in the standard of supervision from adults responsible for the child's care.

Playground accidents, especially those causing serious or fatal injuries, are rare. There has been enhanced awareness of health and safety issues as well as an increasing possibility of civil action when injuries to children occur in public facilities. This has resulted in better maintenance of playground facilities and sometimes the provision of features such as energy-absorbing mats under slides and swings. Whenever a playground accident is the subject of a police enquiry, it is essential that the same approach to the investigation as outlined above is applied.

Life-threatening or fatal injuries occurring in this context are largely head injuries. The paper by Plunkett (2001) was designed to demonstrate that similar pathological changes at autopsy to those described in non-accidental head injuries (NAHIs) can be the result of short-distance falls. The fatalities studied were few in number (18), they all occurred in children over the age of a year, and they were derived from a huge database of playground accidents. This illustrates the rarity of such fatalities. Additionally, they were not, strictly speaking, simple short-distance falls and the pathological and clinical differences between accidental deaths of this type and putative NAHI are covered in Chapter 6.

5.5.3 **Drowning**

Particularly in the pre-school years, drowning is an important and frequent cause of accidental death. The pathophysiology is complex, but usually involves inhalation of water down into the terminal airspaces, with consequent hypoxaemia (decreased oxygen in the blood) and fatal cerebral hypoxia. Laryngeal (vocal cord) spasm may also be a factor.

Accidental immersion accidents can occur in a wide variety of settings, including domestic bathtubs, privately owned and public swimming pools, ponds, lakes, canals, rivers, and sea water sites. Childhood immersion deaths may also be a result of homicide. Deliberate drowning of an infant in a domestic setting is most commonly enacted by the child's mother. She may have mental health issues, may kill one or all of her children, and may then commit suicide. Drowning of a newly-delivered infant by the mother in a toilet or bath may occur after a concealed pregnancy and delivery.

Because the actual event leading to immersion is seldom witnessed, meticulous investigation of the circumstances, evaluation of the scene, and reconstruction of the accident is mandatory. When accidents occur in a public setting, there may be civil legal proceedings relating to culpability for the accident by deficiencies in the management of the facility, or those persons supervising the child. For the pathologist, a high level of proof for the cause of death is required, and samples to match the water medium associated with drowning should be taken. It is also important to exclude natural deaths that might have occurred coincidentally, such as hitherto undiagnosed cardiac disease.

With regard to the post-mortem examination, a radiological skeletal survey must be performed before the examination to exclude neck injuries, etc. Some immersion deaths may be a complication of seizures in epileptic children. Levels of any prescribed anticonvulsant drugs should be measured and a blood alcohol level should be taken.

Histological examination of all major organs should be undertaken, and blocks of tissue from the heart, to allow a study of the conducting system, are necessary. Where the possibility of deliberate drowning exists, the examination should seek evidence of injuries indicative of restraint or forcing the child's head below the water.

Deaths of children by immersion in bathtubs are not uncommon and the great majority are accidental. Often, a harassed mother is trying to bathe a

145

number of small children who may be in the tub together. An infant in the bath, particularly if with older children, may be overlooked for some minutes, or the mother may be distracted, for example, by a telephone call. The time taken for death to occur is often an issue in considering whether there is some maternal responsibility in leaving a child unsupervised in the bath. There is a considerable individual variation in this, and the events are very seldom independently witnessed.

5.5.4 Electrocution

The forensic pathology of electrical burns and death by electrocution or lightning strike is essentially similar to that in adults. In childhood, electrocutions occur in independently mobile infants or older children. As these accidents are often unwitnessed, the particular concerns are the detailed examination of the scene and the circumstances surrounding the episode. The pathologist performing an autopsy in a child death from electrocution needs to be informed of the details of the police investigation and to see any photographs, videos, or diagrams made.

Most important is to establish how electrocution occurred, whether there is any deficiency in the electric circuitry or equipment involved, and whether there is personal responsibility for any shortcomings identified. When a child is involved, there is an issue of the adequacy of supervision by a responsible adult.

5.5.5 Poisoning

In the first few months of life, poisoning will involve activity, either deliberate or careless, by a parent or carer rather than the child. Once a child is mobile their innate curiosity may lead them into danger from inadequately secured drugs, potentially poisonous household items, and other environmental hazards. In adolescence, they may fall into use of so-called recreational drugs with the inherent dangers and risks involved.

Drug fatalities in babies are usually due to the introduction of inappropriate drugs (including recreational drugs) or sedatives given in overdose by carers, often to prevent a child crying or to promote sleep. Drug deaths can also occur in a clinical setting from therapeutic mishaps.

In preschool poisoning—those children under the age of two years—it is more commonly due to ingestion of household products, which are often stored at ground level where they can be accessed by a curious child. Above two years, poisoning is more commonly due to drugs. The incidence of such accidental ingestion of drugs has fallen in recent years, partly by the use of 'child-proof' containers and manufacturers avoiding attractive colours and sweeteners that make drugs look and taste like sweets.

Non-accidental poisoning may be deliberate homicide, or it may be a feature of fabricated or induced illness where a carer, usually the mother, introduces drugs or other substances such as salt to induce dramatic symptoms in a child as an apparent attention-seeking device. Clearly, this type of behaviour can be very dangerous or even fatal to the child.

5.5.6 Road traffic collisions

Injuries to children in road traffic accidents are common; approximately two-thirds involve children walking or playing, the majority of victims are boys, and the risk of injury in the paediatric age group increases with age.

Injuries to children in vehicles are much less common when they are suitably restrained in appropriately sized and professionally fitted child seats. Fatal injuries to children in cars are reduced if the child's seat is rear-facing. There are particular dangers to children placed in a front seat from the inflation of air bags in a crash.

The investigation of road traffic accidents should be meticulous, irrespective of the age of the victim.

5.5.7 Fetal and perinatal deaths

Fetal (before birth) and perinatal (around the time of birth, strictly up to less than seven days of life, but often loosely applied to slighter newborns in general) deaths may require forensic examination where there is concealment of pregnancy and delivery, unattended delivery, or suspected infanticide.

5.5.8 Concealed pregnancy and delivery

These are usually first pregnancies and the mothers are frequently teenagers of low educational achievement. They generally conceal both pregnancy and delivery for fear of their families' reaction and may abandon the baby's body after delivery. If this is done outside the home, the mother may never be identified. If the body is hidden even in the home, discovery may be delayed, and establishing the cause of death and other forensic details may be compromised by decomposition. Sometimes the mother is identified when she finally seeks help from her family or is admitted to hospital with such complications as retained placenta, postpartum (after birth) haemorrhage, or infection. Both stillbirth and perinatal death is more common after concealed pregnancy.

The forensic issues include the maturity of the infant, the time of death in relation to delivery, whether the child was live born, and whether there are inflicted injuries that might be responsible for death. The post-mortem should seek as far as possible to address these points and to take samples for DNA analysis if parentage of either sex is important.

Distinguishing between live and stillbirth can be difficult when, as is usual in these cases, death has occurred very soon after delivery. This can be further complicated by seeking the legal criterion of having an independent existence. Definite signs of stillbirth include skin maceration and slippage or overriding of skull vault bones. Evidence of live birth such as fully expanded lungs, a vital reaction (inflammation) at the insertion of the umbilical cord, or milk in the stomach will not be seen immediately after delivery. The best evidence comes from independent witnesses present at the time of delivery or, for example, hearing the baby cry. Histological examination, particularly of the lungs, may be very helpful in evaluating lung expansion, or in a premature baby, the demonstration of pathological changes such as hyaline membrane disease will establish that a baby must have lived for a least a few hours. If the issue of still or live birth cannot be resolved, an assumption of stillbirth is the usual default position.

5.5.9 Delivery in toilets or baths

Deliveries into water, particularly in toilets, are not uncommon in concealed births. Spontaneous delivery of a full-term infant in this manner would be unlikely, but death by drowning may be difficult to prove.

5.5.10 Pathologist's report and providing a cause of death

A pathologist's report on the death of a child always requires additional investigations beyond the naked eye examination of the external appearances and the internal organs. Only exceptionally will there be a limited examination, usually because the child has been thoroughly investigated during life, the examination is consented, and there is agreement between the bereaved family and the clinicians who have looked after the child that there are still issues about the child's natural death that require elucidation by autopsy.

In sudden and unexpected child deaths, there will always be a full radiological skeletal survey, histological examination of small samples of internal organs, examination of microbiological material (bacterial and viral studies), samples taken to investigate the possibility of metabolic disease, and often samples for toxicological studies. In many centres, the brain may be retained after formalin fixation for at least a week before even a naked eye examination.

Even in straightforward cases, the examination of histological slides by the pathologist once the tissue has been processed, and the collecting, interpreting, and collating of the various reports on the ancillary investigations described above, mean a minimum of two to three weeks before a formal report can be issued. In more complicated cases, for example, head injuries requiring formal expert detailed neuropathological examination of the brain and ophthalmological examination of the eyes, or bony fractures requiring further detailed radiological study and examination of histological sections of the affected bone samples after decalcification, may take three or more months before all the information can be assembled.

Because of these inevitable delays, it is customary for the pathologist to issue a preliminary report as quickly as possible after the initial examination, and certainly within a few days. In a 'special' examination, police officers investigating the death will attend the autopsy, and some information can be provided at this time. It is important to realize that the investigation is primarily for the coroner, who must be party to any information divulged. The naked eye examination may well be sufficient to allow a 'ball park' cause of death, for example, 'head injury', and it may be possible to indicate whether or not the death is likely to be 'accidental' or 'non-accidental'. The preliminary report will always be hedged in terms of these important issues, but its intent is to aid the coroner or the SIO in a 'special' forensic examination to decide what further investigation of the circumstances surrounding the death may be needed, and also to indicate what other investigations the pathologist may require, and the likely time scale for their completion.

5.6 The police perspective

As has been previously explained, the police objective, regardless of where the particular death features on the child death continuum, is to establish the answers to the four questions in relation to 'Why did this child die?'. The same investigative process will be adopted throughout, but the nature and extent of the enquiries contained within the 'five building blocks' will be enhanced incrementally, as the position of the particular case in question, progresses on the child death continuum in the direction of an 'intentional' and 'non-natural cause'.

That being the case, the easiest way to look at how the police response increases with suspicious child deaths and homicides, is to examine both in the context of the 'five investigative building blocks'.

KEY POINT

The investigation will continue to be a search for the truth irrespective of it subsequently being designated as a suspicious death or suspected homicide. When the thresholds for these designations are reached, additional safeguards come into operation to further protect the legal rights of the suspected person, eg requirement to caution, arrest. These and other actions can provide the basis for a false perception to some not familiar with the legal framework, that 'guilt' is presumed, rather than seeing this as an essential, although largely inflexible, and difficult constituent part of the process. This is particularly pertinent when there are reasonable (but not conclusive) grounds to suggest a parent may have deliberately harmed their child. Managing the expectations of the suspected person, other parent, family members, and other professionals can present substantial challenges for the police and SIO in particular.

Because of the similarity between suspicious child death and homicide investigations, the actions that may be useful, but which should be individually considered on a case-by-case basis, are grouped together under the five building block headings. This list is not exhaustive but provides a sound basis on which to generate and consider actions. All the actions will not necessarily be relevant for all investigations.

5.6.1 **Preserve life**

- If a child is still alive but not expected to live, formulate a contingency plan for action to be taken should the child sadly die. This could include contact details of who is to be informed and when, the action to be taken, and expectations of those professionals concerned, eg medical and police. These should be recorded and include provision, if appropriate, for allowing suspected parent(s) access to their child in a supervised capacity if the child is likely to die whilst they are in custody. Circumstances could occur where there are reasonable grounds to suspect a parent or parents of being responsible for their child's death or injuries, but after a thorough investigation it is established that a single parent was responsible and the other was unaware of the criminal actions. It would be wrong not to consider this and agree a suitable contingency plan to cater for these eventualities.
- Forensic medical examiner to attend death scene and pronounce life extinct if body still in situ. This may have already been completed by the paramedic attending, as some are now qualified to provide a diagnosis of fact of death.
- Arrange for formal identification of the deceased.
- Identify and locate next-of-kin and arrange for them to be informed of the death.
- Conduct an urgent risk assessment in relation to the safety of other persons, encompassing the siblings of the deceased, any other children connected with the family, parents, and other family members.
- Consider police protection in relation to siblings of the deceased child and section 47 strategy meeting.
- Consider medical examination and toxicology for other siblings.
- Conduct a search of relevant scenes to establish whether any other people have been injured or at risk of harm.

5.6.2 **Scenes**

- Identify, prioritize, and secure all scenes including the deceased, the death scene, potential suspects, vehicles, hospital, and other relevant locations.
- Arrange for crime scene log to be maintained at all scenes and officers involved to be briefed regarding their responsibilities, including completing all entries contemporaneously and making a statement to cover their involvement.

- Undertake initial crime scene assessments and initiate contact with a CSM, CSI, and photographer to 'capture' the scene—images and video. Consider recording temperature in rooms (ambient temperature can be obtained by placing a thermometer in a drawer containing clothing in the same room), noting orientation of rooms for sunlight entering the room and generating heat, bedding quantity and type, whether any blood staining or vomit (appearance of coffee-type grains in vomit can suggest internal bleeding), presence of medications, feeding bottles, prepared feeds, soiled nappies, general condition of premises, child's red/blue book, etc.
- Formulate forensic strategy including recovery of the body if still in situ. Consideration to be given on the impact of initial actions on future actions, eg alternative light sources, detailed scale plans, or 3D graphical representations of the scene if key exhibits removed from scene prior to them being completed. Initial and subsequent forensic strategy meetings to be recorded and minutes retained for case management, eg HOLMES MIR.
- Ensure continuity of identification and transfer of body from scene to hospital to mortuary, with scene log for deceased and police escort when appropriate.
- Consider application for section 8 PACE 1984 warrant to search premises.
- Consider specialist scientific support, eg biologist blood pattern analysis.
- Arrange for full forensic examination and search by police search advisor (POLSA)—ideally after the post-mortem as the initial results may help inform the examination, eg head injury may suggest examination of certain surfaces. If post-mortem delayed may need to proceed with forensic examination.
- Consider seizing furniture or key items to allow reconstruction at court or for interview. If considering a reconstruction within the premises, then timing of removal is clearly relevant.

Case study

A man whose young daughter died as a result of internal injuries caused by a punch or kick to the stomach area initially denied knowing how they had been caused. After he was told about them in interview and had seen information from the pathologist's report mentioning fingertip bruising in the area of the sternum, he provided an explanation for how they may have been caused. He stated that he had been lying on a sofa alongside a coffee table whilst his daughter had been standing in front of her play pen a short distance away. His daughter appeared as if she was about to vomit so he stood up quickly to catch the vomit with a cloth but tripped on the coffee table and fell finger first into his daughter, knocking her to the floor with him on top of her. He denied that an instinctive reaction would have been to hold onto the bar of the play pen to prevent his fall and also prevent him falling on to his daughter and injuring her. His explanation was considered implausible so the room was re-constructed at court using tape to mark the relevant section of the room's dimensions on the floor, and the original furniture including the sofa, coffee table, and play pen were positioned according to the scene plans. This process by itself suggested there was probably insufficient room for the account to be plausible but the father, who had been charged with manslaughter, agreed during his cross examination by the prosecution to re-enact the incident for the benefit of the jury. He did this showing how he had fallen into his daughter and **not** tried to hold onto the play pen bar and so prevent injuring his daughter. However, when he finished giving his evidence from the sofa he stood up, tripped on the coffee table, and fell towards the play pen but, apparently instinctively, put out his hands to hold onto the play pen bar and stopped himself falling to the floor! This was not the only evidence—he was convicted of manslaughter and child cruelty.

KEY POINTS

- Ensure there is a detailed plan of the premises, showing position of furniture, dimensions and heights, floor surfaces, and accompanying photographic images to be used in conjunction with them in graphical representations. Layout to be confirmed by witnesses to establish nothing was moved during initial police or paramedics' attendance. Sometimes furniture or injured person is moved to create space to treat them. Sometimes no explanation or account is provided by a suspected person, so important that able to visualize scene at a later date if an explanation is subsequently provided.
- Consider aerial photographs or satellite picture of scene showing it in context of surrounding area.
- Consider appropriate time scales for release of scenes and agree that they will only be released on the authority of the SIO.
- Consider recording details of vehicles parked in area of scene for future reference in relation to potential witnesses or suspects.
- Arrange for locksmith to attend and secure the death scene. Document process for safe keeping of the key and audit trail of its use and secure location.

5.6.3 **Witnesses**

- Identify and designate any 'significant witnesses', eg paramedics, parents, carer at time of incident, siblings. Consider timings of witness interviews and prioritization with witness interview advisor. If siblings are potential witnesses, review issue of consent and if appropriate seek consent of parent.
- Consider, after interview/statement taken, option of witness revisiting the scene to demonstrate their actions explained in their account. Video and record the process.
- Trace and interview ambulance staff who attended to deceased. Secure their logs and notes relating to the incident.

- Identify and interview personnel connected with emergency '999' calls, including '999' operator, ambulance controller, and police controller. Obtain tapes of all calls for evidential use, and produce transcript for close examination of conversation including background noises/comments.
- Identify all police personnel who attended scene(s) and arrange a 'hot debrief' before they go off duty. Obtain original notes and arrange for statements to be provided.
- Ascertain the contact details for all other persons who attended the scene(s) or witnessed any relevant incidents. Prioritize and make arrangements for them to be interviewed.
- Identify the designated single point of contact (SPOC) for each hospital that had any involvement with the deceased, family, or suspects.
- Identify all hospital and medical staff and their respective roles in relation to the deceased, parents, and relatives at the hospital including any who may have witnessed any initial accounts, explanations, or history.
- In liaison with SPOC, secure rota of medical staff who would have had access to the deceased over the relevant time period. From medical notes and in liaison with key medical personnel, prioritize relevant staff to provide statements, including the doctor who pronounced life extinct. In some cases, it may not be necessary to take witness statements from all medical staff in the initial stages, eg if the deceased was treated in an operating theatre before they died, it may suffice to only take statements from the surgeon and other key personnel in relation to the treatment and any injuries they observed. The medical notes will show who was present; the persons present can also be identified in the statements that are taken and statements taken from them in the future, if this subsequently becomes an issue. This is a decision for the SIO to make considering their available resources and impact on medical staff.
- Consider family liaison strategy and appointing Family Liaison Officer(s) (FLOs) including a meeting with them, the family, and SIO and deputy.
- Through FLO, consider support for family including information and details of support organizations.
- Formulate house to house strategy and parameters with house to house co-ordinator. Agree appropriate wording of questionnaire and content of questions, including details and ages of other children in households. (See specimen in Appendix C.)
- Consider identifying and interviewing local service and delivery persons, eg postal, newspaper, catalogue distributor.
- Consider a witness appeal in vicinity of incident for same time period and day of the week to locate potential witnesses. Appeal boards, posters, and leaflets could also be considered if appropriate.

5.6.4 Suspects

- Identify and designate persons as suspects, recording rationale in Policy File.

- Consider Forensic Medical Examiner (FME) to examine suspect for fitness to detain, fitness for interview, presence of any injuries, need for an appropriate adult, and to take samples, eg blood and urine (both preserved and unpreserved).

It may be useful at this juncture to consider the issues raised in relation to samples in child death cases across the continuum.

Requesting samples from parents to assist in establishing cause of death

If there are **no grounds to arrest** a parent/carer but it is considered appropriate to request a sample of blood and urine to test for drugs/alcohol, as the absence or presence of either may have impacted on the death in some way, this would have to be with their consent, the rationale explained, and everything documented.

This situation might arise where a child has died suddenly and unexpectedly at home and a third party (ex-partner) has suggested that the carer was under the influence of drugs or alcohol at the relevant time. The carer does not appear to be currently under the influence of drink or drugs and the police have no additional grounds to suggest drink or drugs was a factor in the death or to consider arresting the carer for a criminal offence, eg neglect. However, as the value of samples deteriorates rapidly with the passing of time and further information may come to light through the ongoing investigation, a voluntary request for samples may negate any future uncertainty regarding the third party comments.

Blood and urine are intimate samples under section 62 PACE 1984, which specifies how they should be obtained from **arrested** persons who are in police detention. There may be occasions where there are grounds for arrest, eg circumstances suggest that a carer was under the influence of drugs or alcohol, had fallen asleep with their child on a sofa or in a bed, the child had died, and one of the possible causes of death is suffocation as a result of the child being overlaid by the carer. This is not an uncommon scenario and grounds to arrest for an offence of neglect could be justified.

However, the following points are relevant in this context:

- reasonable grounds for arrest (as opposed to sufficient evidence for a criminal prosecution) are present, ie neglect;
- the value of blood and urine samples deteriorates over time—this is potential evidence that could be lost;
- intimate samples of blood and urine can only be authorized under section 62 PACE 1984 in these circumstances for a person in police detention;
- they additionally require the appropriate consent of the suspected person for them to be taken with a possible adverse inference being suggested at court if consent is refused;

- a definitive cause of death has not been currently established and death as a result of suffocation is hard to conclusively prove—death may be from another cause;
- samples may show only low levels of alcohol or a negative result;
- the carer may be distraught and considered unfit for interview or even to be in police detention;
- to arrest solely to request the samples under section 62 PACE 1984 in these circumstances could be counter productive;
- discretion, sensitivity, and compassion should feature in these types of investigation.

BUT equally in a **deceased child focused** investigation, consideration also has to be given in relation to the child's right to life and, if a carer went to bed intoxicated with a child who then died as result of suffocation from overlaying, that is a specific criminal offence (section 1(2) of the Children and Young Persons Act 1933).

GOOD PRACTICE

Possible option to consider when requesting samples from a parent(s) for whom there are grounds to arrest:

- Explain that the police have a duty to investigate the circumstances surrounding the unexpected death of the child.
- Explain your grounds for suspecting that the person was under the influence of alcohol or drugs whilst caring for the child/young person at the time of his/her death.
- Explain that you wish to obtain a urine and blood sample from them to establish the amount of alcohol or drug/s in their system.
- Explain (if relevant) that you have grounds to justify arresting the person for ... (specify the offence), whereupon a formal request for the samples could be made but that you are trying to avoid this on compassionate grounds.
- Explain that the samples, whilst voluntary, may still later be used in criminal or civil proceedings.
- Caution the person, and then ask if they will voluntarily provide the samples.

If the suspect refuses to provide the 'voluntary' samples, you should still consider making an arrest and requesting/obtaining formal samples under the provisions of the PACE Act. In these circumstances (and having regard to the direction given to the police in 'Working Together' about showing sensitivity and discretion when dealing with families/carers) a section 78 PACE unfairness argument may not be accepted in any later trial.

(GMP guidance on investigating unexplained and unexpected deaths in childhood, 2008)

These are all considerations for the SIO who will ultimately have to make the decision and document their rationale justifying it.

- Consider seizing clothing—may be limited value for contact trace evidence unless body fluids, eg blood, vomit, that may assist in corroborating account. Clothing may also be useful regarding identification and verification of movements during relevant time period when viewing CCTV.
- Seize mobile telephone—in previous cases important information in text and images, including physical abuse of the deceased child, has been recovered in addition to identifying movements. Smart phones will also include internet access, emails, contacts, and a wealth of other information that may be of value to the investigation.
- Obtain authority to obtain all medical records from hospital and GP.
- Consider extent of suspect profile to include: nominal data, intelligence and criminal records, family and relationships, lifestyle, habits, transport and employment, financial profile.
- Consider a reconstruction at scene of their account—recorded and solicitor given opportunity to attend. Any reconstruction would have to be with consent of the suspect.

5.6.5 **Evidence**

This would cover intelligence, background information, and analytical products to assist with the investigation and may include the following:

- Criminal records, previous calls to relevant premises, intelligence records.
- Information and records from other agencies including social services, children's social care, health, education in relation to the family and deceased child that may be relevant to the death. On occasions, legal procedures may have to be considered but ideally there should be legal justification for sharing information between the various agencies concerned.
- Complete a full genogram (family tree) including extended family.
- Complete a time line/sequence of events by analyst.
- Collection of passive data—999 tapes, CCTV, NHS Direct/Healthcall tapes, phone analysis, computer.

Other evidential considerations including:

- Identification and location of any samples already taken at hospital—advise hospital of police interest in their existence and results—liaise with Coroner's Officer regarding authority to use if required.
- Secure a pre-transfusion blood sample and continuity.
- Consider intelligence led toxicology screening.
- Secure copies of full skeletal survey, CT, MRI scans.
- Establish if an ophthalmology examination has taken place and consider requesting if appropriate.

- Obtain Guthrie Test sample/results—consider its use as a control or reference sample if required.
- Obtain a recent photograph of deceased and secure any other family photographs and videos.
- Liaise ASAP with HM Coroner and establish link with Coroner's Officer—obtain authority for 'special' forensic post-mortem utilizing Home Office pathologist and paediatric pathologist.
- Obtain set of fingerprints from deceased for police use, eg methadone poisoning—had child handled bottle?
- In consultation with pathologist(s) discuss relevant samples for criminal investigation.

KEY POINT

HM Coroner authority is of paramount importance in child death investigations and required to undertake the post-mortem examination. It is essential that contact is made with them or their officer as soon as possible to ascertain their views, instructions, and timing of an inquest. The subject of samples taken for the coroner's purposes and those taken under PACE 1984 if a criminal offence is suspected can also be clarified. The FLO could be designated as the investigating team's liaison officer with the Coroner's Officer as this will facilitate improved communication with the deceased child's parents and family.

5.6.6 Resourcing and other considerations

If a child death reaches the threshold to be considered as 'suspicious', the rapid response emphasis will alter, with the police taking the lead in relation to the investigation. However, until it is established whether or not a criminal offence has been committed, the police will endeavour to maintain a sensitive and discrete presence in the way that they conduct their enquiries. Many of the actions mentioned above may only become relevant when the suspicious death line is crossed and the investigation clearly falls within the criminal offences non-natural cause/intentional death area.

A child death is as important as any other death and will merit the same level of resources to manage the investigation. All child death investigations should be led by a detective inspector, ideally with Child Abuse Investigation Unit (CAIU) experience and, if considered clearly 'suspicious' or a homicide, should be managed by an accredited 'Professionalizing Investigation Programme' (PIP) Level 3 SIO.

Adequate resources would also encompass the use of HOLMES or an alternative enquiry management system and sufficient police officers and staff (including those with CAIU experience) to undertake the necessary actions.

Other aspects of the investigation which are common to other suspected homicide enquiries would include:

- Media strategy including a holding statement.
- Community impact assessment.
- Briefing for the Senior Management Team (SMT) with consideration of a 'Gold Group' if appropriate.
- Briefing and liaison with the CPS.
- Policy File maintained showing a chronological record of key decisions and the rationale for them.

5.7 **Conclusion**

This chapter has further illustrated the complexity and professional sensitivities involved in a child death investigation. Multi-agency working, communication between professionals and the family, specialist training in the areas of pathology, crime scene management, interviewing and investigative management, and adequate resourcing are recurring themes throughout. These areas will be developed in the following chapter on child homicide.

Further reading and resources

Mayes, et al. (2010), 'Risk factors for intra-familial unlawful and suspicious child deaths: A retrospective study of cases in London'. *The Journal of Homicide and Major Incident Investigation* 6(1) Spring 2010, 77–96.

Plunkett, J. (2001), 'Fatal pediatric head injuries caused by short distance falls'. *The American Journal of Forensic Medicine and Pathology* Mar 22(1), 1–12.

Child Accident Prevention Trust website—a national charity committed to reducing the number of young people killed, disabled, and injured as a result of accidents: <http://www.capt.org.uk>.

Appendix H—Risk Factors for Suspicious Deaths.

NOTES

NOTES

NOTES

Homicide

6.1 **Introduction**

In this chapter, the focus will be on investigations where murder, manslaughter, familial homicide, and infanticide are suspected, although the child death related offences may still feature in these types of case as alternative charges. There will be considerable overlap between the management of these cases and those in the previous chapter on suspicious deaths, as the investigative objective of establishing 'Why did this child die?' is still paramount. The clearer it becomes that a child death is potentially a homicide, the more overt the police response. Sensitivity is still very important, but certain aspects can become more straightforward, eg securing scenes, arresting suspected persons, seizing exhibits.

The building block actions outlined in the previous chapter will continue to apply and will form the basis for developing the investigative themes for each block, but their relevance must be considered on a case-by-case basis. The results of those actions will, in turn, generate further actions that hopefully culminate in answers to the four key questions linked to 'Why did this child die?' and help complete that 'jigsaw picture' of the true events.

In this chapter we will examine some very important aspects of child homicide enquiries that can present further significant challenges for the police and the Senior Investigating Officer (SIO). The topics that will be covered are:

- Family liaison.
- Inflicted injuries.
- Fabricated and induced illness.
- Investigative support.
- Stranger homicides where child is killed by a non-family member.
- Murder suicide.
- Attempted murder.

6.2 **A parent's perspective on a homicide investigation**

Based on the personal experience of a parent involved in a homicide investigation, many of the themes examined so far will be highlighted in a very powerful and impactive way, as the honest and personal account of this parent unfolds. It is important that we learn the lessons from this case and endeavour to view investigations from perspectives other than our own.

6.2.1 **Background**

In 2008 I gave birth to twins, a boy and a girl at hospital. This was the happiest day of my life! As a new mum, I was looking forward to taking my family home. Little did I know that within three months my son would be dead and my daughter taken into foster care. I had never been in trouble with the police or had any dealings with social workers or Social Services. It was inconceivable to think I could ever be in this situation. I came from an educated background, had a full time career with the Ambulance Service. I had great friends and family. I had been married for a few years and had two beautiful babies. Whilst that sounds too good to be true, life wasn't always great. I had my fair share of relationship and financial problems with my husband, which added to the daily stresses and strains of life. I had previously experienced multiple family bereavements and this affected me greatly. Overall I thought life was good and maintained a positive outlook.

I had read about other child abuse cases in newspapers and seen high profile cases in the news. I had even dealt with horrific situations through work. However, the perpetrators of such crimes seemed like a different species to me as I imagined 'horrible monsters' almost inhumane and far removed from my world! So when my husband and I were accused of abusing our children and my husband charged with murdering my son I would not accept the authorities' view at all. How could I? My husband wasn't one of those 'horrible monsters'. I'd known him for ten years, lived with him, washed his clothes, cooked his meals, and shared a bed. Surely I would be able to tell if he was a murderer! Everyone had got this wrong including police and Social Services. I would just have to fight back and prove it.

Of course, hindsight is a wonderful thing. I was repeatedly told 'good people do bad things' and 'humans are not born monsters'. There are multiple factors contributing to why people behave in a certain way. This all seemed like common sense to me, only my common sense, along with other things, went out the window the minute my son died!

That evening in 2008 my son was rushed into hospital. He had stopped breathing. He had been in the sole care of my husband that evening. I was already with my daughter on a children's ward at the same hospital after she had been admitted earlier that day with bronchiolitis. I received a phone call from my husband's colleague who told me my son was downstairs in intensive care and he had stopped breathing. That was the moment my whole world collapsed and so did I. From there my son was transferred to another hospital. His ventilator was turned off two days later when medical reports confirmed he was brain dead. My son had multiple injuries and medics concluded he had been violently shaken and abused. A full skeletal survey also identified that my daughter had multiple rib fractures. These events triggered actions by police and Social Services.

We were both arrested on suspicion of GBH and causing or allowing the death of a child and bailed until the middle of 2009. My husband was charged with the murder of my son and two counts of GBH on both children. I was completely cleared.

The trial started in mid-2010, nearly one year later. After an eight-week trial my husband was acquitted of everything except GBH without intent. He was sentenced to three years' imprisonment which was reduced on appeal so that he was released in mid-2011.

My daughter was returned to me after nearly two years of Family Court proceedings. It was only then that I finally felt able to lay my son to rest.

6.2.2 Feedback from a parent

Throughout the past three years it's been hard to take positives from such an awful experience. However they do exist!

What worked for me?

(a) **Initial police contact**

The police officers who first made contact were sensitive and non-judgemental. They were careful in their approach and I became receptive as a result. I found them accommodating. This made it easier to listen to what they had to say and retain the information given to me.

(b) **Initial Social Services contact**

Social services contacted me the moment my daughter was subject to an emergency care order. They rang immediately and arranged for a meeting. They were well organized and clearly explained their situation. The information presented was uncomplicated and easy to understand when under stress.

(c) **Building agency relationships**

These relationships were incredibly important to me as I wanted access to all information possible and needed to rebuild my trust with the authorities. My sense of trust completely diminished, which I found exceptionally difficult. My long term belief system was challenged as I was raised to respect and trust authority. To redress the balance meant spending time with both the police and Social Services. However, this took a long period of time, but it was time well spent. I wanted to know everyone was working as they should be and not out of their depth, a very important consideration when decisions are being made about your own children! I was able to cast aside preconceived ideas about Social Services. They get a bad press, often branded as 'home wreckers'. By spending time with social workers, the door of help and support opened and I really needed it. It was also important to develop a good relationship with the foster family. This was vital to me as they were my daughter's temporary carers for 18 months. I am still in touch with the family to this day.

(d) **An understanding of police enquiries.**

At first I felt their enquiries were unnecessary and intrusive. I felt violated and couldn't understand the need for the police to interview a multitude of people. These included neighbours I barely knew, employees, and ex-partners. However, those witness statements provided a clear picture of my husband before I met him. It gave me an eerie insight into a person I thought

I knew. This was a very real and disturbing wake-up call for me as it revealed acts of violence and sexual violence.

(e) The Witness Service Programme at the Crown Court

This vital service provides palliative care in times of great stress. Giving evidence during the murder trial of my own son was one of the worst things I've had to endure. The staff and volunteers were helpful, caring, and completely understanding. They really helped me through a difficult time.

(f) Displaying photos of the children

The constant referral of the children as evidence dehumanized things for me. I felt it was important for all involved to see photos of my children, and also refer to them by name. Those included were judges, police, social workers, and the jury, amongst others.

(g) The judicially experienced

Firstly, as a suspect it was important to seek solicitors and barristers experienced at dealing with child abuse/murder cases and, in particular, shaken baby syndrome.

Secondly, after building a relationship with the police and becoming a prosecution witness, it was important to know the CPS barrister team were experienced at dealing with the same cases. Lastly, thank God the judges involved also had previous experience of dealing with cases involving complex medical evidence. To feel confident about the 'teams' described above took a lot of research. Overall this instilled confidence and reassurance.

(h) Communicating with other parents

Talking to other parents became one of the most important parts of this journey. I cannot stress enough just how much this helped on several levels. It helped me hold onto my own sanity and allowed me to share experiences. This became more successful than any form of therapy to help me deal with the horror of what had happened. By sharing stories, I was given better advice and support from other parents who were able to tell me what worked for them and what didn't. This invaluable advice far exceeded any from solicitors, police, and Social Services. Without a doubt I would not have been so receptive or able to work with the police and Social Services without this support. They encouraged me after my trust flew out the window. I became increasingly frustrated with those working around me. They hadn't experienced the murder of a family member and, most importantly, a child homicide. This meant I felt they were patronizing and insensitive and often said the wrong thing at the wrong time. I had a lack of respect because they hadn't 'been there'. I can remember thinking on several occasions 'What do you know? You have no idea how I feel'. For this reason alone I wished I'd contacted parents sooner. Talking to others took away the fear, isolation, and sheer enormity of the situation.

I would like to see a service where parents have access to other parents (who've endured the same kind of experiences) during the legal process and not just at its conclusion: an independent group of parents and relatives recommended by the authorities, to help bridge that gap.

(i) Complete control of my son's funeral

When I was able to bury my son it was important for me to regain control and make both big and small decisions about it. I felt my son was 'owned' by everyone else, so my decisions were so very personal and important. In particular I had waited so long to have him dressed for this day and buying a Thumper babygrow for him meant so much. The funeral was the last thing I could do for my son and I had waited so long.

What didn't work for me?

(a) The medics' attitudes

When my son was admitted to hospital I found the doctors' attitudes harsh and critical. I felt they were assuming the role of amateur detective. Kindness and sensitivity were completely lacking and I didn't appreciate this at all. My trust instantly vanished and I became defensive to protect myself against these appalling attitudes. Compared to the police they embarrassed themselves. I would like this issue to be explored during their child protection training. I think language and wording should also be explored as I was traumatized by what was said and that has left a psychological scar. I had a tendency to fixate on every conversation and will clearly remember those forever regardless of who they are.

(b) Information withheld

The police withheld information from me until the trial. However, if someone had just explained there were valid reasons due to disclosure and witnesses, etc, it would have dissipated those feelings of being shut out.

(c) Timescales

The whole process from start to finish takes too long. Both hearings took too long. The Family Court proceedings took nearly three years and I feel this is too long to allow decisions about a child's future. I feel it is unfair on the child who is often in a 'holding' position with foster carers until it goes to court. My daughter was in foster care for 18 months.

I found it unacceptable that I couldn't bury my son for nearly two years. This suspended my grief and that had a devastating effect.

I also couldn't understand why I was locked out of my house for nearly six months. Again, I feel this was far too long.

(d) Agencies sharing information

I understand information sharing is imperative and vital for all agencies investigating. From a parent's viewpoint this is crucial and should always remain so. However, the exchange of information during those dual proceedings meant the secrecy of the Family Courts wasn't so secret after all.

To this day I still don't have the truth about what happened the night my son was killed. The police had access to the evidence from the Family Court case.

This included my husband's lies about my son's death. With the threat of the criminal trial yet to come, and the knowledge that police would have access to these details, this discouraged my husband from telling the truth in the Family Courts. My husband denied killing my son and continued to protest his innocence to defend himself from a lengthy prison sentence. I feel this is a Catch-22 situation. I wanted the truth and my husband didn't want to go to prison.

(e) **Parent's considerations**

Few professionals involved referred to our rights as parents. Overall, I felt people's agendas often pushed aside parental rights. These included blocking access to my son's post-mortem and my daughter's hospital scans. Quite often it seemed others had more rights over my son's body than I did. So when my parental rights were genuinely considered, I felt a sense of balance and control. Do not lose sight of parents' rights, otherwise this makes for a difficult working relationship.

(f) **Expectations of a parent during the early days**

Those first few days after my son's death left me in shock and at times in a state of collapse. I found it difficult to function. I was frightened and traumatized. As a result, I was unable to cope. I often questioned myself about my own reliability during those early days. Did everyone expect too much too soon?

I would like to see structured explanations delivered at a slow pace in a simplistic form during those early days. Too much information too soon may have a devastating effect. So much happens at a fast pace, and this may be unavoidable, but it may be worth looking at.

(g) **The medical evidence and a lack of understanding**

Medical expert witness reports are complex and extremely difficult to understand. The authorities are not medically trained. I once asked a police officer about his training for this and he said 'What training? It's a medical dictionary'. Should those involved in complex medical cases have a substantial guide or training package? Parents are also in the same boat and, through research and questions, I gained a little understanding. I didn't like the fact that decisions about my family were based on medical complexities and I needed to understand it.

What happens next? The domino effect of murder

Having spent nearly three years living in a bubble, everything suddenly stops and everyone walks away. There is a lack of aftercare. I've heard so many times, 'What do we do now?'. Nearly all of us are left with post-traumatic stress disorder (PTSD) symptoms which makes it difficult to reintegrate back into society. I lost my job, home, and my family. My parents and other relatives have also been badly affected. A referral service/package would be helpful when working with families to help finalize a difficult time. Victims and their families are left to put their lives back together and quite often don't know where to go for help. I think it would be helpful to recommend support groups and other agencies.

KEY POINT

Useful support group

SAMM (Support after Murder and Manslaughter) is a national UK charity supporting families bereaved by murder and manslaughter. They also provide advice and training to many agencies on issues relevant to the traumatically bereaved.

Website: <http://www.samm.org.uk>

Hotline: 0845 872 3440

Email: info@samm.org.uk

These observations illustrate in an illuminating way how the varying issues, concerns, and perceptions interact within the multi-agency framework including the judiciary, medics, police, social workers, family, and many others affected by a child death. The complex issues of family liaison and non-accidental head injury are also highlighted in this case, as is the incomplete picture of 'why this young boy died'.

6.3 Family liaison—suspect within the family

The majority of child homicides are intra-familial in nature, with a family member or members being responsible for the death of a child from within their family. This immediately creates a dilemma for the family liaison strategy.

6.3.1 Aims of the Family Liaison Officer (FLO)

The aims of the FLO in every case are to:

Analyse the needs, concerns and expectations of the family in order to identify all the relevant and realistic action that should be taken in the context of their human rights and obligations.

Also to work with the family in order to comply with their right to receive all relevant information connected with the enquiry, subject to the needs of the investigation, while gathering material from them that assists the investigation in a way that is proportionate to their fundamental right to privacy and family life.

(ACPO/NPIA, *Family Liaison Officer Guidance*, 2008:5)

6.3.2 **Features of the investigative environment in relation to FLO deployments**

In the intra-familial child homicide scenario there are extra dimensions to be considered with regards to the suspect for the suspected offence being within the family, coupled also with the nature and complexity of the investigative environment of child death. Many of the often unique features of the investigative environment have already been alluded to, but can include the following:

- High profile cases of child death and controversy in relation to expert medical evidence with the associated media coverage. There is a wealth of information available via the Internet which, if considered in isolation, could be misleading. There will be a natural curiosity and inclination for family members to undertake their own research, particularly if the professionals involved in the investigation for evidential reasons (not wishing to contaminate evidence from witnesses), do not cover certain contentious issues from the outset. This may be overcome to some extent if the FLO explains why they will not always discuss information having a direct bearing on the case.
- In some cases, there is a huge reliance and emphasis placed on expert medical evidence which, as illustrated in the account above, some of the police officers involved do not understand to a sufficient level to be able to properly explain it. In some circumstances, it may be possible for a medical professional to explain information for the parents and family as they would in non-suspicious deaths in the rapid response process.
- A case may be considered very suspicious from the outset and be correctly treated as such, with the parent(s) being designated as suspects, but then during the ensuing investigation the suspected person(s) are exonerated, affecting the dynamics of the family–police/professionals relationship.
- Suspecting a stranger of killing your child as compared with a trusted family member in a special position of responsibility and trust towards the deceased child may be easier to manage psychologically.
- There may also be a reliance on forensic evidence and, with lengthy periods of delay in receiving results, the status of 'suspect' and family concerns may be prolonged and create tensions. This period of uncertainty perpetuates a very challenging environment and huge psychological pressures for the family members. In some cases, a cause of death may never be established and so the unanswered questions remain, so that uncertainty pervades family life.

6.3.3 **Suspect or victim scenarios**

There are a number of permutations regarding the '*suspect v victim*' status that parents can fulfil, and these include five basic scenarios:

1. Which one did it? Both parents present during relevant times and could have both been responsible or a single individual responsible.

2. Readily identifiable suspect. Only one parent had care of the child during relevant time period.
3. Readily identifiable suspect. A third party was the sole carer during relevant time period, eg baby sitter.
4. Numerous suspects or significant witnesses present during relevant time. If the fatal incident occurred during a family gathering, eg a birthday party, there may be a considerable number of potential suspects and equally large number of potential witnesses.
5. A case could initially be considered a SUDI but during the investigation could develop into one of the four other scenarios listed above.

6.3.4 **Initial account**

A fundamental action in any child death enquiry is to obtain an initial account or history from the parents. In suspicious or homicide cases this is still important, but great care has to be taken by the SIO when determining the status of the parents, ie are they to be designated as 'suspects' or 'victims'. The initial account can answer so many unknowns and even remove some suspicions, so it is important to obtain it as soon as possible. In the suspicious or homicide category of investigation, it would be advisable to speak to the parents individually, but this would not prevent a suitable person supporting them. Providing there are insufficient grounds at that time to support an arrest, the best approach would be for them to be treated as 'significant witnesses' so that the integrity of the process is maintained and a complete record is obtained on video/audio for future reference if required. This additional safeguard would have the additional benefit of reducing the risk of anything said being misunderstood or misinterpreted. This significant witness interview process would usually fall to the FLO to complete and assist in building a rapport with the family, and parents in particular.

KEY POINT

It is essential that the SIO clearly explains and documents their rationale for designating parents as either 'significant witnesses' or 'suspects' in their Policy Book. They should also include the information that they were aware of at that stage of the investigation, and time and date their entries.

6.3.5 **Additional environmental factors**

There are additional factors that can influence the environment in which the FLO will engage with the family members and factors to consider when formulating an FLO strategy. These include:

- A disbelief that a partner is responsible or capable of harming their child. This is not an unusual reaction even with apparently overwhelming evidence to the contrary.

- Family dynamics in the emotional cauldron that suspicious child deaths and homicides can generate for the reasons outlined above, together with historical events and their prejudices being resurrected again, creates a very challenging environment for the FLO.
- Issues will arise in relation to a 'suspect's' access and contact with their partner and other siblings in the family. Some of these may be subject to legal constraints, eg bail conditions, child protection proceedings, but that will not always be the case.
- On occasions both parents may be considered as 'suspects' but that would not necessarily pre-empt the deployment of a FLO either to them directly, or indirectly through a solicitor or nominated family member. Some information could be imparted via a written communication, eg letter. The FLO deployment could be in relation to the grandparents. In some cases a new partner may be suspected, in which case the natural father or mother could be expected to merit a FLO deployment.
- Even if both parents were considered to be 'suspects' it may be considered that they were still entitled to the 'right' to certain information regarding their child's death—eg post-mortem, cause of death, inquest, retention of materials from post-mortem. Depending on how the investigation developed and its ultimate conclusion, this could be very relevant in regards to public confidence and perception if the 'suspect(s)' were subsequently exonerated or the outcome of the investigation was inconclusive.
- The FLO is an essential element of any homicide investigation; they should be properly briefed as to their role and parameters, with these being agreed in the FLO strategy formulated with the SIO and their deputy. The deputy SIO may also be well placed to undertake the role of Family Liaison Co-ordinator (FLC) if suitably trained.
- Because of their relationship, role, and position in relation to the family, the FLO is also well placed to act as the liaison officer between the enquiry team and the Coroner's Officer.
- It would be appropriate that all visits to the family were undertaken by two Family Liaison Officers because of the nature of the deployments in this investigative environment. This would ensure corroboration of accounts between the FLOs and family, and provide continuity if one of the FLOs was unavailable.
- It is good practice at an early stage for the SIO and Deputy SIO to meet the deceased family members with the FLO(s). This enables the SIO to explain their role and the role of the FLO, including important information and restrictions stipulated in the FLO strategy, eg contact times, which the family should be aware of. It is important for the family to recognize that the FLO does not operate independently but is a member of the investigation team and responsible to the SIO.

GOOD PRACTICE

Appendix E contains a generic FLO strategy that can be adapted on a case-by-case basis. The bespoke FLO strategy can then be explained and agreed by the SIO and the FLOs in the presence of the Deputy SIO. Two completed copies of the strategy can be signed and a copy inserted into both the FLO log and the SIO Policy File.

6.4 **Inflicted injuries**

In suspected homicide investigations, the reason they are initially classified as such can be the presence of injuries, which in the absence of a plausible explanation are highly indicative of being non-accidental in nature and deliberately inflicted. Although these injuries may be suspected to be the result of a deliberate act, the search for the truth of what caused them continues, examining other possible causes to confirm or exclude them so as to arrive at a differential diagnosis by a process of exclusion. Here, as elsewhere, the police will work with medical professionals to pool their findings to try and establish the true causation.

6.4.1 **Head injuries**

Fatal paediatric head injuries can be accidental or inflicted by a third party. The subject of non-accidental head injury (NAHI) in babies and young children is controversial, particularly when this topic is considered in court.

The majority view of NAHI amongst experts with experience of dealing with child abuse, such as paediatricians, paediatric intensivists, paediatric diagnostic imagers, or forensic pathologists, is presented first. This is followed by alternative views and comments on the alternative explanations for the pathological changes seen in NAHI presented in court by medical witnesses for the defence.

Most cases of apparently unexplained, fatal, paediatric head injury are associated with a combination of pathological abnormalities at autopsy. These are *subdural haemorrhage, retinal haemorrhage,* and *encephalopathy* (brain damage exemplified by brain swelling). These three findings have been called the 'triad'.

KEY POINT

The term 'triad' has been mentioned in this section as it has been frequently utilized in court proceedings and was the preferred term in several Appeal Court judgments and scientific papers that are referred to in this chapter. However, as the CPS guidance recognizes, the presence of the three features of the 'triad' are not a conclusive diagnosis of an inflicted head injury and, on their own, would usually be insufficient to prove a NAHI case. The identification of a NAHI should always be based on a diagnosis of exclusion (a 'differential diagnosis') following a rigorous examination of all the circumstances.

Whilst there are a number of different causes of each of these components in isolation, the combination of all three in an individual child is highly indicative of NAHI. Over half of individual babies with the 'triad' will also have other signs of abuse, such as bony fractures—often multiple and of different ages—unexplained bruises, abdominal visceral injuries, etc. Clinically affected children usually 'collapse' suddenly, having been perfectly well shortly beforehand. Almost always, the collapse occurs when the child is in the sole care of one adult.

The pathological characteristics of each component of the triad are also important. Subdural haemorrhage usually forms only a thin layer over both cerebral hemispheres, sometimes extending to the base of the brain and into the inter-hemispheric fissure. Brain swelling is generally obvious, particularly when, as is often the case, the child has been maintained on life support prior to being pronounced dead. Retinal haemorrhages are almost always bilateral, diffuse, and widespread, extending right round the back of the eye and through all layers of the retina. Whilst no single criterion is absolutely diagnostic of NAHI, most authorities would regard the extensive retinal haemorrhages as the most useful feature. Severe retinal haemorrhages can occur with forceful accidental trauma, such as falls from a height, or a road traffic accident, and may be seen, for example, in severe haemorrhagic disorders. These alternatives are obvious plausible causes of retinal haemorrhage, but are unlikely to cause diagnostic confusion.

The mechanism of injury is open to dispute in that the precipitating event is almost never witnessed and occurs in the sole presence of the presumed perpetrator, who is unlikely to give an incriminating description of what happened. Until recently, this injury was described as the 'shaken baby syndrome', indicating that the injury is produced by violently shaking the baby backwards and forwards, the unsupported head snapping to and fro as the relatively heavy head and insubstantial neck musculature provide little damping effect. The rotation of the head causes the brain to rotate within the skull, and the rapid reversal of forces stretches small veins on the surface of the brain causing rupture and blood loss. The same traction forces between the retina and the jelly-like vitreous humour filling the eye are responsible for the retinal haemorrhage.

Brain swelling may be due to stretching and damage to the long processes between individual nerve cells (axons), but it has also been plausibly suggested that traction on the midbrain, where the vital centres controlling breathing and the heart rate are located, may cause sudden cessation of breathing leading to lack of oxygen to the brain and hypoxic damage. In either event, the brain will swell, and pressure from this may reduce the volume of blood in the subdural space.

From the rare perpetrator confession data, shaking is undoubtedly one cause of the 'triad'. However, in the absence of good data from independent witnesses, this may well not be the only mechanism. Throwing the child onto a soft surface such as a bed can produce the same injury by a similar mechanism of rotating the head followed by an abrupt halt, allowing the brain rotation within the skull to continue. Impact with a soft surface would also not produce a bruise. For these reasons, even the term 'shaking/impact' injury has been superseded by the more accurate if clumsy term 'rotational acceleration/deceleration' injury.

With regard to explanations of the 'triad' other than from non-accidental trauma, the most common are the suggestion that the three pathological elements can be caused by cerebral hypoxia (oxygen starvation to the brain) or by a short-distance accidental fall.

The first suggestion relies on the demonstration that bleeding into the dura (as opposed to beneath it) may occur in babies dying with changes in the brain indicative of hypoxia and who have brain swelling. Brain swelling is the least specific of the 'triad' changes, occurring in many varieties of acute brain damage. The most important change, ie extensive retinal haemorrhages, is not usually looked for other than in clear examples of head injury. Thus no comment is possible in those post-mortem series where it is implied that retinal haemorrhage is related to cerebral hypoxia, but the eyes have not been examined. This suggestion was originally made by Geddes (2004) and has been resurrected more recently by Cohen and Scheimberg (2008). The Geddes paper only mentioned intradural haemorrhage, and neither subdural nor retinal haemorrhage, as an association with cerebral hypoxia. Scheimberg and Cohen record subdural haemorrhage in some of their perinatal and fetal deaths, but give no indication of the total population from which these cases are derived. This age group is much younger than that in which NAHI is seen, and again the eyes were not examined. With regard to deaths in this younger perinatal age, diagnostic imaging studies have demonstrated subdural haemorrhage, probably related to the trauma of the birth process, in a significant proportion of even normal babies with no clinical indication of cerebral hypoxia. Furthermore, in post-mortem studies and diagnostic imaging studies of living babies with cerebral hypoxia from a number of non-traumatic causes within the age range that NAHI cases are seen, none had evidence of subdural haemorrhage.

Thus, there is no good evidence that cerebral hypoxia produces subdural haemorrhage, let alone retinal haemorrhage. Suggested mechanisms have been considered possibly to precipitate sudden cerebral hypoxia, such as paroxysmal whooping cough or gastro-oesophageal reflux. These have never been shown to produce subdural haemorrhage as a complication in cases where such a diagnosis has been established rather than just postulated.

Accidental short-distance falls are another mechanism suggested to produce the 'triad'. Short-distance falls are extremely common in children who have just become independently mobile. Such falls are very unlikely to cause serious head injury, particularly injuries associated with intracranial brain damage and haemorrhage of a type that might be fatal. The children concerned are generally older than one year, and if symptoms are other than trivial, carers should seek medical help promptly. Very occasionally, more serious and even fatal injuries occur in association with accidental short-distance falls, and very occasionally they may involve 'triad' pathology. Nevertheless, in most cases, apart from the different clinical background, there are distinct differences in the detailed characteristics of the triad changes. The head injuries are usually impacts and produce localized brain parenchymal lesions and possibly fractures to the skull vault. Severe neurological deficit or death is due to raised intracranial pressure due to an expanding collection of blood within the confines of the skull. This may be an extradural haemorrhage, due to damage to the middle meningeal artery at the side of the head, or to a subdural haematoma that forms a discrete space-occupying lesion. This occurs when the impact damages a large venous channel within the skull such as a dural sinus. The haematoma is very much an integral part of the head injury rather than a mere marker of forcible brain rotation, as in the rotational acceleration/deceleration injury of NAHI. Retinal haemorrhage is usually minimal, particularly initially when the child is first seen and before significant brain swelling and raised intracranial pressure have developed.

Short-distance falls are extremely common in independently mobile infants and the overwhelming majority of such accidents do not produce serious head injury. In a small proportion there may be a hairline skull fracture, usually of a parietal bone, confined to one skull bone and not associated with serious clinical signs or intracranial injury. In those short-distance falls that do cause more serious damage, the fall is seldom a simple fall from standing or sitting height, but is more complex, such as a fall from playground apparatus or a fall down stairs.

Recognizing the clinical and pathological differences between NAHI and the vanishingly rare fatal short-distance fall, it is seldom difficult to distinguish the two. The fatal short-distance falls, like falls from a height, are generally in children over the age of one year, are usually witnessed, and promptly reported with a plausible account of what occurred.

6.4.2 Visceral injuries

Injuries to abdominal organs are generally a result of impacts or blunt force injuries. Fatal injuries of this nature are usually inflicted by a forceful punch or kick to the abdomen but may be the result of an accident.

Because of the soft and yielding nature of the anterior abdominal wall, it is not uncommon for blunt force to the front of the abdomen to cause serious and even fatal intra-abdominal injury without superficial skin bruising.

The liver is the organ most commonly injured. There may be extensive, and often deep, irregular lacerations usually accompanied by intra-peritoneal and retroperitoneal haemorrhage. Not uncommonly, the delicate peritoneal membrane supporting the intestine (the mesentery) is torn. As this membrane contains numerous blood vessels, tearing can also lead to extensive haemorrhage. Injuries to the intestine or other organs such as the pancreas and kidneys may also feature.

A particularly characteristic injury is partial or complete transection of the duodenum. This section of intestine lies in front of the bony ridge formed by vertebral bodies of the lumbar spine and is held in place by the peritoneal membrane covering the posterior abdominal wall. If blunt force is applied to the front of the abdomen at this point, it acts like a guillotine slicing the duodenum against the spine. The transection may be so clean that the bowel appears to have been cut with a knife.

Fatal non-accidental visceral injuries may be accompanied by other inflicted injuries occurring either at the same time or on a previous occasion.

Some visceral injuries are accidental, and occur in independently mobile children over the age of one year. They may involve a fall on to an object that protrudes into the abdomen, but a classical scenario involves a fall from a bicycle. With the child pedalling hard, the front wheel of the cycle hits a stationary object bringing the cycle to an abrupt halt and forcing a handlebar into the child's abdomen.

6.4.3 Bony injuries

Whilst it is common for fully mobile children, particularly older and adventurous boys, to suffer fractures, especially of long bones, as a result of physical activity, the circumstances surrounding an injury of this nature should be carefully considered, and the plausibility of the clinical history evaluated. This may appear unduly intrusive, but it is recognized that children who subsequently suffer serious or even fatal injuries often have a history of less serious injury that is accepted at the time as being accidental.

In sudden and unexpected childhood deaths, the radiological skeletal survey is probably the single most important screening procedure in distinguishing suspicious from natural deaths. This investigation should be performed before the autopsy commences, and a paediatric radiologist experienced in child abuse should see the films and ideally should communicate with the pathologist before the start of their examination.

The principal features of abusive skeletal injuries are as follows:

- Limb injuries occur mostly around the metaphyses and epiphyses, and may be associated with lifting of the periosteum, under which a thin rim of new bone forms that is easily seen radiologically. This calcified rim may extend round the end of the bone, or between the metaphysis and epiphysis to give a so-called 'bucket handle' appearance. This is considered a particularly characteristic non-accidental injury in babies, caused by forceful pulling or twisting the limb.

- Transverse or spiral fractures may also occur. These would not be likely accidental injuries in a non-ambulant child, but can be seen in toddlers due to falls or other mishaps involving twisting and shearing forces.
- Rib fractures in infants are an important sign of abuse. They are often multiple and involve consecutive ribs in a line. Not uncommonly, rib fractures occur on both sides, and are usually caused by forceful squeezing of the chest by an adult holding the child beneath the arms. Fractures are usually found posteriorly on each side of the spine or laterally.
- A useful indication of abuse is when rib fractures of different ages are present, implying force applied on more than one occasion. Sometimes fractures that are surrounded by callus and appear to have occurred some time ago may, on histological examination, show a new, fresh fracture line within the old healing fracture. This implies a further episode of squeezing near to the time of death.
- An explanation for rib fractures by the responsible carer might be that they are a result of attempted resuscitation. This clearly could not be the case where there is evidence of healing, such as callus formation. There is no reliable report of posterior rib fractures arising from resuscitation and some authorities claim that rib fractures are not a feature in the resuscitation of babies because the flexibility of the ribs in this age group allows for considerable distortion without fracture. Resuscitation fractures do occur in this age group, but there may be little or no displacement so that they may not be seen radiologically. At post-mortem, these fractures may be difficult to see because there is little or no associated haemorrhage. They will be apparent if the ribs are examined after pleural stripping and cutting the intercostal muscles.
- Characteristically, resuscitation fractures occur on the anterior chest wall, one or two centimetres lateral to the costochondral junctions (the joining points between the bony part of the rib and the cartilaginous part that attaches to the breast bone (sternum)).
- Fractures directly at the junction (costochondral fractures) are definitely not due to resuscitation and are usually seen in conjunction with other fractures which have clearly been inflicted.
- Fractures can be aged radiologically by a sequence of changes occurring during the healing process that involve the deposition of new bone that can be distinguished on an X-ray. In the immediate period of about a week after the fracture is inflicted, no new bone is formed and the radiological appearance of the fracture is unchanged. Nevertheless, under the microscope during this time there is an orderly sequence of haemorrhage and inflammatory changes that can give some information.

In fatal non-accidental injuries, the issue may not be whether the injury is inflicted, but more when it occurred and who was the responsible adult present at the time. Thus the timing of the injury, particularly shortly after its infliction, may be very important evidentially, although the precision with which this can be achieved is often not as clear as investigators would like.

The post-mortem examination of the injuries requires a careful naked eye examination and photography. The fracture site is excised, identified as an exhibit, and submitted to high resolution radiography. The specimen is then fixed, decalcified, processed, and sectioned for histology. The maximum evidential information may require the opinion of a practitioner skilled and experienced in osteoarticular pathology.

Skull fractures may be accidental or part of an inflicted injury. Accidental fractures are usually a very rare complication of short-distance falls followed by impact to the head. Such fractures usually occur in the parietal bones. They are simple, linear, and hairline, with unseparated edges and are confined to one bone without the fracture line crossing a suture. They are not associated with significant intracranial injury and have little or no clinical consequence.

Fractures associated with inflicted injuries have evidence of the application of greater force. They often involve the parietal bones and run either downwards from the sagittal suture or backwards from the frontoparietal suture. There is often associated haemorrhage beneath the scalp and further haemorrhage within the cranial cavity. If there has been brain swelling due to intracranial injury, the edges of the fracture may be separated. Direct inflicted impact injuries to the skull may cause depressed stellate complexes of fracture lines. Basal fractures are not common in child abuse.

The distinction drawn between the characteristics of accidental and inflicted skull fractures merely reflect the likely degree of force applied. Clearly, an accidental head injury in a child falling from a height might well have the same features as an inflicted injury. However, the clear differences in the circumstances in which the skull fracture occurred makes confusion unlikely.

6.4.4 NAHI—police response

Many homicides, particularly of young children under one-year-old, are the result of a head injury. At that young age, their head is proportionally larger than the rest of their body, neck muscles are not fully developed, and their skull bones have not completed the process of fusing together. Injuries may be the result of being hit on the head with an implement, eg a hammer; forcibly swung or thrown against an object, eg a wall or floor; or as a result of rotational, acceleration, deceleration, and impact forces, sometimes referred to as 'shaken baby syndrome', with the child's head moving through an arc and coming to an abrupt halt and damaging the brain in the process.

As explained in Chapter 1 and in the section above, these cases have been the subject of much debate between experts in court cases and in the media. This has resulted in several Appeal Court judgments and consequently updated CPS guidance entitled *Non Accidental Head Injury Cases (NAHI), formerly referred to as Shaken*

Baby Syndrome [SBS]—Prosecution Approach (2011) that is available on the CPS website at <http://www.cps.gov.uk/legal/l_to_o/non_accidental_head_injury_cases>.

As with all child death investigations, irrespective of their cause, the investigative mindset should remain constant, with the objective of answering the key question 'Why did this child die?'. This is no different for cases of suspected non-accidental head injury where the working premise will be that:

In the ABSENCE of any other EVIDENCE for an alternative PLAUSIBLE explanation the following features of:

- retinal haemorrhages (bleeding into the linings of the eyes);
- subdural haemorrhages (bleeding beneath the dural membrane);
- encephalopathy (damage to the brain affecting function);

plus supporting evidence of, for example:

- bruises;
- fractures;
- injury to cervical spine;
- blood in cerebrospinal fluid;
- inconsistent accounts;
- confession or admissions to others, eg in text or document;
- witnessed assault;

will provide a PRIMA FACIE suspicion that the injuries are due to MECHANICAL TRAUMA involving ROTATIONAL, ACCELERATION, DECELERATION, and IMPACT forces, potentially including vigorous shaking.

It should be noted that it is common for there to be no external evidence of trauma but that the following signs and symptoms may be observed:

- In the fatal cases—child usually becomes immediately unconscious and suffers rapidly escalating, life threatening central nervous system dysfunction.
- Lethargy, extreme irritability, poor feeding or vomiting for no apparent reason, inability to suck or swallow, no smiling, limp arms or rigidity, difficulty breathing, seizures, head larger than usual, bulging soft spot, inability to lift head, inability of eyes to focus or track movement, or unequal size pupils.

From the medical nature of much of this evidence, there will be great reliance placed on medical experts, which, depending on the features of the specific case may include:

- paediatric pathologist;
- HO forensic pathologist;
- ophthalmic pathologist—in relation to the examination of the eyes;
- neurosurgeon—in relation to the nervous system including brain, spinal cord;
- neuropathologist—specializing in diseases of brain and spinal cord;

- neuroradiologist—specializing in examination of central nervous system;
- histopathologist—study of tissues;
- radiologist—interpretation of X-rays and other imaging techniques including CT, MRI;
- intensivist—specializing in intensive care;
- paediatrician—specializing in childhood healthcare;
- bio-mechanical engineer—mechanics of movement in living beings.

However, there are a number of additional enquiries—some linked to the medical aspects—that the police could consider in these types of cases, including:

- An account from the carers ASAP—'in absence of any other plausible explanation indicative of NAHI'—so this is a valuable opportunity to provide a plausible explanation.
- Paramedics and other medical staff can provide an account of what they have seen and heard at the home, in the ambulance, and at hospital. This information may include important comments or observations in relation to the injured child, carers, or other family members.
- 999 tapes and passive data may provide useful information in relation to the actual comments made, background noise/comments, text and images on mobile phones, computer use at the time of the incident.
- Scene control, recording, and examination—essential to identify and preserve at the earliest opportunity to assess validity of accounts.
- House to house—local enquiries—may provide valuable information into home life, previous incidents, shouting, screaming, crying, comments, noises.
- Background of individuals concerned may provide valuable insights, may identify stressors—domestic, personal, financial.
- Reconstruction of incident/account (video) as previously discussed; this can help establish the credibility of an account—could be at the scene or in interview. Consider using a weighted doll to demonstrate, but care taken in relation to size and weight compared to injured child.
- NAHI is not always fatal. In this homicide context it is important to note that it may not always be immediately fatal and there may be a period on life support. In these circumstances, it is important to consider a contingency plan to cover this period and for when the child dies including:
  - control/access whilst child still alive;
  - access for parents who might be in police detention should condition rapidly deteriorate;
  - evidential opportunities, eg MRI, CT scans;
  - records—hospital, conversations, comments.

Some of the specialized techniques which may be employed include:

- full skeletal survey, including examination of spine (AP/Lateral) and neck, properly interpreted by a paediatric radiologist;

- thorough ophthalmologic examination, including specialized retinal photography, examination of eyes as soon as possible (whilst the child is still in the Emergency Department), as the picture will deteriorate and the timing of when things are observed is very relevant;
- MRI and CT scans—ensuring that the machine is set up appropriately for a child-sized brain;
- ultra violet photography and alternative light sourcing to locate injuries invisible to the naked eye in normal lighting conditions;
- HO forensic 'special' post-mortem including paediatric pathologist;
- full post-mortem ophthalmologic examination—carried out in a specialized laboratory;
- full post-mortem examination of the brain—carried out in a specialized laboratory;
- the services of a forensic analyst to provide a detailed timeline of all significant events in the child's life. This analytical product is very useful in determining who was present at particular locations in key time parameters, eg when fatal injury sustained, and used to direct enquiries to corroborate witness accounts.

This list should by no means be considered exhaustive, with each case being considered on an individual basis and with any other appropriate lines of enquiry or actions.

Case study—admission

'… I shook xxxx a number of times, probably half a dozen or so. During this short period of shaking I recall that all four of his limbs seemed to be flailing about, and his head was going back and forth, but there was still no response from him. I shook xxxx again for a second and short time, but there was still no response. On this occasion I shook him about half a dozen times or so.'

(London case, 2007)

6.5 Fabricated or induced illness (FII)

This topic will be covered briefly here as it can feature in child homicide enquiries. Some examples have already been provided in Chapter 1, with the case of Beverley Allitt in 1991 and a number of others identified by Professor David Southall between 1986 and 1994.

The following information in relation to FII is adapted from *Working Together*, paras. 6.6–6.9, and HM Government's *Safeguarding Children in Whom Illness is Fabricated or Induced* (2008).

FII is a form of serious child abuse, where the health or development of a child is significantly impaired by a parent or carer who has fabricated or induced illness. Concerns may arise when:

- Reported symptoms and signs found on examination are not explained by any medical condition from which the child may be suffering.
- Physical examination and results of medical investigations do not explain reported symptoms and signs.
- There is an inexplicably poor response to prescribed medication and other treatment.
- New symptoms are reported on resolution of previous ones.
- Reported symptoms and found signs are not seen to begin in the absence of the carer.
- Over time, the child is repeatedly presented with a range of signs and symptoms.
- The child's normal, daily life activities are being curtailed, for example school attendance, beyond that which might be expected for any medical disorder from which the child is known to suffer.

The characteristics of FII include:

- lack of the usual corroboration of findings with symptoms or signs, or
- in circumstances of proven organic illness, lack of the usual response to proven effective treatments.

Three main ways have been identified in which FII may be presented:

1. Fabrication of signs and symptoms. May include fabrication of past medical history.
2. Fabrication of signs and symptoms and falsification of hospital charts, records, and specimens of bodily fluids. May also include falsification of letters and documents.
3. Induction of illness by a variety of means.

KEY POINT

Any investigation of suspected FII requires a multi-agency response with a police lead for any criminal investigation.

Offending behaviours of those responsible can include:

1. **Deliberately inducing symptoms** by:
    - administering medication or substance;
    - intentional transient airways obstruction;
    - interfering with child's body to cause physical signs.

2. **Interfering with treatments** by:
   - overdosing with medication;
   - not administering medication;
   - interfering with medical equipment, eg infusion lines.
3. **Claiming the child has symptoms** which are unverifiable unless observed directly such as:
   - pain;
   - frequency of passing urine, vomiting, or fits.

   These claims will result in unnecessary investigations and treatments which may cause secondary physical problems.
4. **Exaggerating symptoms** which are unverifiable unless observed directly, causing professionals to undertake investigations/treatments which may be invasive, unnecessary, harmful, and dangerous.
5. **Obtaining specialist treatments or equipment** for children who do not require them.
6. **Alleging psychological illness** in a child.

KEY POINT

The majority of cases of fabricated or induced illness are confirmed in a hospital setting, because either medical findings or their absence provide evidence of this type of abuse. Medical histories are likely to have started early and may have become extensive by the time suspected abuse is identified.

Motivation of offender

The following have been identified as the possible motivations for this type of behaviour amongst offenders, who are usually a female carer with a history that might include physical health problems including birth/miscarriages or psychiatric history featuring mental health problems.

1. Gain attention.
2. Sympathy.
3. Psychological benefit.
4. Material benefit.

Investigation

Similar to other investigations, this will aim to be sensitive and discrete, but a police-led criminal investigation in a 'search for the truth' with support from their multi-agency partners.

This is particularly important, with the immediate protection of the child and any siblings being of paramount importance together with support for the offender if a psychological or mental health problem is the root cause for their motivation and behaviour.

The guidance recognizes that this area of crime may justify the use of covert surveillance, but stresses that the use of covert surveillance will be undertaken by the POLICE and must be compliant with the Regulation of Investigatory Powers Act 2000 (RIPA) and guidance in paras 6.35–6.40 of *Safeguarding Children in Whom Illness is Fabricated or Induced*.

6.6 Investigative support: National Injuries Database and CATCHEM database

By the very multi-agency approach to child death, a number of professionals with a multitude of skills can be involved in contributing to the investigations. In addition to those already mentioned, the police can obtain further assistance from two support services currently located within the National Police Improvement Agency (NPIA) and very pertinent to child death enquiries. They are the National Injuries Database and the CATCHEM database.

6.6.1 National Injuries Database

The National Injuries Database (NID) can offer a range of services to investigating officers dealing with child death investigations:

1. The NID is held by the NPIA and stores data focused on victims and injuries. This data covers a wide variety of cases, including: non-accidental injuries in children, suspicious child deaths, and child homicides. The database can be searched to provide supporting cases for an investigation team that can assist with identifying the cause of injuries. Search reports produced from the database can support investigative strategies and the medical experts involved in cases.
2. The NID also collates data on behalf of the Association of Chief Police Officers (ACPO) Homicide Working Group—Child Death Subgroup on all child (under the age of 18 years) suspicious deaths and child homicide investigations across England and Wales via the method of Form 76 (see Appendix D). This data is utilized to inform research and best practice in the field of child death investigation, and to identify experts for the NPIA Expert Advisers Database and relevant cases for the NID. For more information contact childdeathinfo@npia.pnn.police.uk.
3. If an injury is patterned in nature, and a particular weapon is suspected to have been used to inflict the injury, the NID can scope the potential for an overlay which might depict the correlation between the injury and the weapon.
4. The NID team have access to the NPIA Expert Advisers Database, which contains, amongst other things, details of medical experts covering a wide range of paediatric specialist disciplines. The staff at the NID are experienced in assisting investigating officers with sourcing the appropriate medical experts to provide expert medical opinion.

5. A member of the NID team holds a portfolio in paediatric cases and keeps up to date with emerging medical research in the field of child deaths. Investigating officers can be provided with updates in relation to recent Court of Appeal judgments, prosecution and defence arguments, and also given references for informative research and guidance, as well as, if required, being provided with contact details for other SIOs who have recently dealt with similar inquiries.

6.6.2 **CATCHEM database**

What is the CATCHEM database?

The data consists of all child murders in England, Scotland, and Wales since 1 January 1960. It also contains details of missing children, where there is potential for them to have been a victim of crime, as well as some attempted murders, child abduction, and attempted abduction cases. The relevant information is recorded on HOLMES.

What does CATCHEM mean?

CATCHEM is an acronym for Centralized Analytical Team Collating Homicide Expertise and Management. This was the name given to the initial project to collate details of child homicide, missing persons, and abduction in 1986. It has since become synonymous with the database that was created as a result.

Why was the database created?

In August 1986, a conference was convened at the Home Office for Senior Police Officers who were involved in investigations into unsolved child murders. It was prompted by West Yorkshire Police during their investigation of the murder of Sarah Jayne Harper, ten years old, who had been abducted from Morley, Leeds on 26 March 1986 and whose dead body was recovered from the River Trent at Ratcliffe-on-Soar near Nottingham, some 81 miles away, on 19 April 1986. The purpose of the conference was to discuss the problems of comparing such a murder to other outstanding similar crimes, due to the lack of any comprehensive records. Specific reference was made to the possibility of connecting this murder to the murders of Susan Claire Maxwell, 11 years old, in 1982, and Caroline Hogg, 5 years old, who was killed in 1983. Maxwell was abducted from Coldstream in the Borders, and her body was found at Loxley, Ashby de la Zouch, 264 miles away. Hogg was taken from Portabello in Edinburgh and she was found a distance of 308 miles away, at Twycross in Leicestershire.

Her Majesty's Inspector of Constabulary (HMI) Sir John Brownlow requested that these three murders be formally linked together, and the result of the conference was to set in motion firstly research into the feasibility of their unification, bearing in mind that they were constructed on different police enquiry systems.

The second recommendation from this conference was to examine all outstanding undetected murders and missing person inquiries, to establish if consideration should be given to linking any others to these three cases. This collation of information was also to ensure that, should they arise, any similar future cases were to be brought to the attention of the combined inquiry. This was extended to include a study of all child murders, all cases of children missing in circumstances where foul play was suspected, and offences of child abduction where details were obtainable.

This was, in effect, a full search of all UK police record systems for a serial killer.

Why wasn't this information readily available to the investigation teams?

Existing methods of obtaining records of child murder were by referring to crime pattern analysis (CPA) central records, but these were found to have too many discretion levels to be useful and were not comprehensive. Personal contact with police forces depended greatly on the memories of those contacted. This process had been carried out by officers involved in the Maxwell case, then repeated by those involved in the Hogg murder, and then, three years later, by those dealing with the Harper enquiries.

Why was information collected for male victims as well as female victims?

Answers were being sought to questions of killers' methods—do they select victims by gender? In the three murders being examined, the victims were all female, but this fact alone could not be used to prove the theory. So both male and female victims were included in the study.

Why were female cases collected for victims up to 21 who were no longer children?

The age of the victims was regarded as important, as the study aimed to look at offenders who killed children. It was thought that, as girls are generally slighter in stature and possibly more easily overcome, age may not necessarily deter an offender. What was important was how old the victim might have appeared to be to the offender; this was more relevant to abduction cases, especially those committed by strangers. It was considered that males were less vulnerable once they reached 17, hence the difference in ages.

Were the three girls killed by the same person?

Yes: Robert Black was arrested in Scotland in 1990 just after he had abducted another young girl. He was convicted later that year of abduction and assault. In 1992, he was charged with the murders of Maxwell, Hogg, and Harper and, in 1994, he received ten life sentences.

Who created the CATCHEM database?

These tasks were undertaken by a team of detectives, drawn from Derbyshire, Staffordshire, and Northumbria, working at Derbyshire Police HQ under the command of Assistant Chief Constable Don Dovaston.

The database and its uses were further developed by Chuck Burton, OBE, who was custodian of the database until its transfer from Derbyshire police to the National Crime Faculty (NCF) in 2003.

Where did all of the information come from to create the database?

During the course of the early research, one of the officers working on the project discovered that the details of all murders committed in the UK were available from the Statistics Department of the Home Office in the shape of a CRIMSEC 7A form submitted by all forces in England, Scotland, and Wales, in respect of all homicides committed since 1 January 1960. The details on these forms was sufficient to identify all the crimes and commence a trawl of all forces for a copy of the prosecution file, where it existed and, a copy of the enquiry closure report, where the offences remained undetected. It was also discovered that a similar system existed in Scotland whereby all Scottish forces notified the Scottish Executive in Edinburgh of their homicides.

Collecting data for missing children was a lot more problematic. The Police National Computer (PNC) was able to provide some useful information, but the research team had to contact every police force in England, Wales, and Scotland; this was a lengthy process as this information was not readily available.

The collection of cases involving abduction was even more problematic, largely due to the way that offences of abduction were recorded. The response from some police forces was very comprehensive, whereas others did not supply any cases at all, despite numerous requests; it was decided to work with the cases that had been supplied and accept that this would never be a complete dataset.

How many cases of homicide are there on the database?

There are over 5000 cases of homicide recorded on the database as well as those for attempted murder, abduction, and attempted abduction, so it is a very comprehensive set of data.

What is the age range for victims on the database?

'Child' is defined for the purpose of this research, as a female victim under the age of 22 years and as a male victim under the age of 17 years at the time of death. Although the initial research project did not include the killings of babies, these have now been added.

What information is recorded for each case of homicide?

The initial data collection focused on the victim, the offender, and the offence.

Details of the victim include: name, sex, and age at the time they were killed.

Details of the offender include: name and sex, and when the homicides were committed.

Details of the offence include: location and police force dealing, date of offence, and the brief circumstances.

Additional information includes: the relationship between the victim and offender, the cause of death, any indication that the homicide was sexually motivated, or that the motivation was unknown.

The victims are sub-divided into children who were killed without apparent sexual motive and those murders where a sexual motivation can be inferred by the presence of crime scene characteristics and criminal characteristics. This subset then creates what is known as the 'relevant dataset', and it is this that is used for the profiling and research into child murders. The sexually motivated crime files have been retrieved for female victims under 18 years old and male victims under 17 years old, and details of the victim, crime scenes, deposition sites, and offender (where detected) recorded.

Why was the age reduced to under 18 for sexually motivated cases?

The age grouping chosen for the study of sexually motivated murders was 16 years and under for male victims, and 17 years and under for female victims, the thought being that these groups would encompass the apparent age of children along with their actual ages. The initial project was time constrained, and reducing the age for female cases allowed for the project to be completed on time. The cases for female victims aged 18 to 21 had been identified, and as such could be analysed at a later date if necessary.

What additional information is collected for the sexually motivated cases?

Areas of analysis in relation to the victim include:

- location of the victim at time of contact or last sighting;
- the nature of the area of contact or last sighting;
- activity of the victim at time of contact or last sighting;
- mode of travel of victim at time of contact or last sighting.

Areas of analysis in relation to the offender include:

- activity of offender at time of contact;
- immediate action of offender at time of contact with victim;
- inducements or deceptions practised by offender;
- weapons used or produced;
- the number of assault locations.

Areas of analysis in relation to the offence include:

- nature of the offence location;
- specific details of major attack scenes and body deposition sites;
- sexual activity of the offender;
- distance travelled from point of contact to abandonment;
- peculiarities of offence;
- period of detention of victim;
- secondary injuries to victim;
- clothing interference;
- details of body deposition;
- offender peculiarities.

Further analysis in relation to the offender includes:

- age of offender at time of murder(s);
- offender's marital status;
- offender's previous criminal record;
- breakdown of sexual and violent convictions;
- offender's links with the area where contact with the victim was made.

How was the data consistently coded and recorded?

The research, which was developed under the acronym CATCHEM, approached each case in a structured and consistent manner, recording what were considered to be the salient features of the murders. Every case was subjected to analysis of its 'salient features' by a standard interrogation pro-forma which comprises 208 questions.

How can this data be used to assist with child homicide?

An early definition stated that 'CATCHEM is a distillation of facts from a comprehensive study of child sexually motivated murders and the persons who have committed them over the past years'. It aims to provide a *Decision Support System* to enable investigating officers to validate enquiry paths to identify the suspect type, based on the percentage probability from statistics.

The database utilizes historical data to analyse current cases. It was the first meaningful approach to 'Artificial Intelligence'. It can be used to identify suspects or prioritize suspects through statistical profiling of the probable characteristics of an unknown offender. The end product of the whole process is 'Statistical Modelling'—the prediction of the probable characteristics of an unknown offender, based on comparative case analysis, which is the analysis of historical crime data against a current crime in an effort to identify the most likely characteristics of the unknown offender based on the percentage probability. Each crime is studied and assessments are made of the victim demographics, the geography of the crime, the method of the killings, the mechanism of injuries, the sexual behaviour, and the full details of the offenders, inclusive of previous offending histories and antecedents.

The aim is to provide advice and, in appropriate cases, an outline profile of the probable characteristics of an unknown offender from the broad data as collected, and to refine it by studying the influence of salient features from within the offence.

More simplistically, it can be a very useful tool to assist SIOs with their decision-making process.

It can also be used for comparative case analysis to identify potential links between offences. This is particularly useful in cases where it is suspected that an offender may have been committing offences against children for a considerable number of years.

With data going back to 1960, it is also an invaluable source of information for police officers looking to identify a particular case when they have limited information available to conduct a search.

What information was collected for missing person cases?

The research team initially identified 1,538 cases for missing females 21 years and under and males 16 years and under, 1960 to 1986 inclusive. These were subject of initial analysis, to separate those where the reason for disappearance could not be explained and had the potential to have been victims of crime. This resulted in 375 cases being entered onto the database and further details of these cases were obtained. These were then subject to further analysis in an attempt to identify those that were to be classified as 'victims of crime'.

Can the CATCHEM database assist with cases of missing children whose disappearance is suspicious?

Where a child has gone missing in suspicious circumstances and there is reason to believe that they have become a victim of homicide, the CATCHEM database can assist with the search strategy utilizing data from previous cases. The database contains details of body deposition, distance from point of contact, evidence of transportation, distance from paths, roads, and any attempt to conceal the body.

How else can CATCHEM assist with missing persons?

The CATCHEM project team devised a methodology to analyse missing person cases. This involves addressing a series of subject areas and answering a variety of questions including:

- What are the significant features of the missing person report?
- Is there a reason to go missing?
- Is the disappearance out of character?
- What are the circumstances of the last sighting?

- Did the missing person prepare for an absence from home?
- Is the subject considered at risk?

This process has been developed since the initial project started and involves hypothesis generation, investigative suggestions, and advice regarding search.

Is the database still being updated?

The database is currently maintained by the Crime Analysis Unit of the NPIA, which means that it is in the same unit as the Serious Crimes Analysis Section (SCAS) and the Missing Persons Bureau (MPB). The database is regularly updated with homicide cases and missing persons who are believed to be the victims of crime, but no further cases are added in respect of attempted murder, child abduction, or attempted child abduction.

The CATCHEM database has now been used to support in excess of 250 homicide and suspicious missing person investigations in the UK and abroad.

6.7 **Stranger homicides**

Although the majority of child homicides or suspicious child deaths occur within the family or carers' setting, there are occasions when these deaths occur outside of this home-type environment, for example the deaths of Milly Dowler, Sarah Payne, Holly Wells, and Jessica Chapman are high profile examples of where this has occurred in the past.

On each of these occasions, the girls were reported as missing from home by their parents. The police initiated missing from home enquiries (MFH). It is essential that an investigating officer of at least an inspector rank reviews the circumstances of a child who has gone missing and makes a decision whether to deem that the circumstances amount to a critical incident. **It is essential that the inquiry adopts a dual approach in relation to: (a) their serious concerns for the child's safety, and (b) investigates as suspicious the fact that they have gone missing.**

Using the example of the Holly Wells and Jessica Chapman high profile murder investigation as a case study will help to examine this investigative approach in this particular suspicious missing child investigation. This case involved the disappearance and subsequent murder of two ten-year-old girls who lived in a small market town in Cambridgeshire. It will be useful to consider which steps were taken together with those that should also have been taken:

- The local safer neighbourhood policing team were informed that the girls hadn't returned to their respective homes and were missing; they went to each respective home to take the MFH reports.
- A dog handler and other staff were called to search.

- The duty inspector and the on call SIO were informed (this was by now the middle of the night).
- A 'critical incident' should be declared as it is clear there is no history or reason why the two girls in this case should have gone missing.
- The SIO should now take charge and will now make use of their training and the guidance highlighted in the Core Investigation Doctrine, the *Murder Investigation Manual* (MIM), and the Major Investigation Room Standard Administration Procedures (MIRSAP).
- Two FLOs are appointed to each of the families; although in this case the children are still classified as MFH, it is important to find out the family background and circumstances as soon as it is felt that children are at high risk of significant harm. In the ACPO guidance for investigating child deaths, it states that this should be FLOs with a background of child protection.
- Similarly, a deputy SIO should have this background experience as well.
- Multi-agency enquiries are important also at an early stage, and in this case study enquiries with both social services and education are important. Also vital to carry out enquiries with friends of the two girls; it is important that suitably trained officers carry this out.
- In high profile cases like this one, the media intrusion will be massive and it is a key line of enquiry to engage them at an early stage, allocating staff to manage this. In the Soham case, the SIO made great use of the media not just for making appeals but in the case management and at the subsequent trial, as a number of them and their footage of interviews with the defendant in this case, Ian Huntley, were used in evidence.
- The community, especially if a very close one like in the small market town of Soham, will be very keen to assist with any search; this must be managed and only be done in an organized way.
- The SIO will set his lines of enquiry and follow the investigative strategies available to them. The SIO will also use hypotheses as to what may have occurred and these lines of enquiry will confirm or disprove theses hypotheses. In the Soham case one of the lines of the enquiry was that the two children were still alive and that they had been abducted.
- The NPIA should be contacted at an early stage for the use of a number of their specialist services; for example, in this case, advice was sought from the staff that manage the CATCHEM database, to help with searching and identifying possible suspects.
- When the girls in this case were found dead, a full forensic body recovery took place and post-mortems with a forensic pathologist were completed. Careful consideration for the use of a paediatric pathologist to assist should also take place.
- There are a large number of different experts that you could use at scenes like a deposition site and it is important that a briefing takes place to ensure that a phased recovery takes place and each of the experts are used at the appropriate stage;

- It is also worth bearing in mind the feelings of the families involved. The recovery of the two girls' bodies was to take place the next day after being discovered. Kevin Wells wrote the following in his book, *Goodbye, Dearest Holly* (Wells, 2005):

  The priority now is to secure as much evidence as possible to convict the person or persons responsible for the murders. That makes sense. But what hurts at this moment is the fact that Holly although dead, is going to be left in a ditch. It seems so demeaning.

- The volume of information in these types of cases is vast; for example, in the Soham case, they received 25,000 calls within a 14-day period. With this comes the huge issue of how you prioritize which information to act on.
- In a number of child death cases, due to the length of time that medical tests take, causing a delay in the release of the body for a funeral, parents consider a memorial service. In this case, albeit the coroner had released the bodies quicker than suspected and it was fully understandable that the parents wanted private family funerals, a memorial service was held at Ely Cathedral. This was a very kind and courageous step by the parents to try and help the huge public outpouring of grief for both these young girls. There were 2000 people present and the service was filmed live across the world.
- In child death cases, welfare of the staff is very important and in this case it was no different, with all staff being offered both individual and team counselling and de-briefing. Multi-agency partners also did this, for example, offering a service to pupils in the girls' school.
- Achieving Best Evidence (ABE) interviews should take place with any possible child witnesses, to ensure their evidence is captured appropriately.
- Case management is crucial in order to secure a conviction, and in the Soham case, a large team were retained in order to make sure all lines of enquiry were completed and thereby enable the prosecution the best chance of success.
- In December 2003, Ian Huntley was convicted of both girls' murders. Although the case was over, the examination of the circumstances surrounding the girls' deaths and Ian Huntley was not finished, as the then Home Secretary David Blunkett ordered a Public Inquiry to be chaired by the now Lord Bichard.
- Public Inquiries into child deaths are very stressful for those investigators and families involved, as they are held in the full glare of the public and, in this case, the world's media. However, it must be remembered that a child, or children in this case, died and that lessons must be learnt from their deaths.

The Bichard Inquiry made the following main recommendations:

1. A registration scheme for everyone working with children or vulnerable adults, which employers can access. This would show if there was a reason why someone should not work with children. (This was brought in as the 'Vetting and Barring Scheme', but found to be too draconian and is the subject of further revision and simplification.)

2. A National IT system for police forces in England and Wales. (This came into full use in 2011, a full seven years after the recommendation was made, albeit an interim solution Impact Nominal Index (INI) came in very quickly. The Police National Database (PND) appears to be an excellent development.)
3. Investment in the PNC system to secure its medium and long-term future.
4. All applications for positions in schools should be subject to a requirement for enhanced disclosure criminal checks.
5. A national code of practice for all police forces on the creation and upkeep of records. (The management of police information (MOPI) grew out of this recommendation.)
6. Training for head teachers and school governors to ensure interview panels are aware of the importance of safeguarding children.
7. Underage sex between 15 year-olds and older people is not always treated seriously enough, so the government should reaffirm its guidance on this. All decisions not to inform the police of underage sex should be subject to review, and guidance is needed on when referrals must be made to the police and when discretion can be exercised in not doing so.
8. The Data Protection Act 1998 is fit for purpose.

The above case study demonstrates that normal homicide investigation procedures should take place in cases of child deaths that take place outside the home environment, but what shouldn't be forgotten is that these homicide investigations are different, and all of the principles involved in investigating child deaths should also be employed in these cases. This mindset and investigative approach is equally applicable to cases where one child kills another child.

6.8 Murder suicides

Another alarming phenomenon in child deaths is the murder suicide. This is usually intra-familial in nature and results in a parent killing the children in the family, possibly their partner in addition, before then committing suicide. The apparent motives for such action could include:

- In a bitter custody battle over children, an estranged partner seeks revenge by killing their own children so that neither parent can have them. Children are seen as property rather than individuals and used as a weapon to seek revenge. The perpetrator may then seek to murder their former partner and then kill themselves.
- A person in a suicidal state as a result of financial, psychological, or emotional pressures considers that life is no longer worth living. They wish to take their own life but have the distorted belief that, if they die, their child/children will suffer so much that life would not be worth living for them either, so they decide to murder them to 'prevent them suffering'.

- A person suffering from a mental illness or with strong distorted beliefs may believe that a child is possessed by an evil spirit and the only way of dealing with the evil spirit is to kill their child. Having killed their own child they then commit suicide.

These are just three possible scenarios with numerous possible variations, including where a perpetrator manages to kill other family members but is unsuccessful in their attempt to kill themselves.

Great care has to be taken when dealing with these cases, and they should be dealt with in a similar way to any other homicide inquiry. There is a real danger that, if assumptions are made and due diligence not given to the investigation, a homicide may potentially go undetected. The scene could have been staged so that it is assumed that a mother has killed her children and then committed suicide, where in reality she was also a victim of homicide at the hands of an estranged partner or acquaintance.

The security of the premises, a suicide note, the cause of death, the absence of defence wounds on the suspected perpetrator, may all assist in establishing the incident as murder suicide but every realistic hypothesis should be explored.

6.9 **Attempted murders**

Sometimes, because of the designation of roles within the police service and the establishment of specialized units with fixed terms of reference, attempted murders may not always receive the same response as for a homicide. The point can be well made that, by very definition, an attempted murder is not as serious as a murder but, from an investigative standpoint, solving an attempted murder can sometimes be far more problematic than some homicides, and can be often harder to prove the offence.

Attempted murders are simply mentioned to underline the importance of allocating sufficient resources and expertise to them, as what distinguishes an attempted murder from a homicide may be the few millimetres a knife blade was away from a vital organ. Children are in a very vulnerable position and, with the additional concern regarding siblings, it is important that attempted murders are identified as such and thoroughly investigated with a police-led multi-agency response.

6.10 **Conclusion**

We have now travelled along the entire length of the child death continuum from the non-suspicious natural cause, through to the suspicious, and then to the extreme end of the continuum of non-natural intentional homicides. At every point on the continuum, there have been issues for the police and their multi-agency partners. The field of child death investigation, as illustrated, is a very specialized, demanding, and often unique investigative area, with numerous challenges for the SIO, in particular. Ultimately, though, the aim has been for everyone to acknowledge that the whole rationale for any child death investigation is to establish 'Why did this child die?', and to keep that child as the central focus throughout the investigative and decision-making processes involved.

Further information and reading

HM Government (2010), *Working Together to Safeguard Children. A guide to inter-agency working to safeguard and promote the welfare of children* (Nottingham: DCSF Publications), Chapter 5.

The National Center on Shaken Baby Syndrome website at <http://www.dontshake.org>.

Inflicted Injuries information leaflets with summaries of current knowledge based on academic systematic reviews in relation to oral injuries, fractures, bruises, thermal injuries, and head and spinal injuries in children.

CORE-INFO website: <http://www.core-info.cardiff.ac.uk> (a collaborative project between DCH, Cardiff University, and the NSPCC).

NOTES

NOTES

NOTES

Case Management
and Reviews

7.1 **Introduction**

Another facet of child death investigations that is different to other deaths is the number of additional related processes and proceedings that can be involved. These can include:

- Rapid Response
- Child Death Overview Panel (CDOP)
- Inquest
- Criminal Court proceedings
- Serious Case Review
- Family Court proceedings in relation to siblings
- Public Inquiry
- General Medical Council (GMC) disciplinary proceedings.

Inquests, Criminal Court proceedings, and Public Inquiries can be relevant for adult cases but the specialist nature of child death investigation is further emphasized by the additional processes and proceedings specifically linked to child death.

Whilst some processes complement each other, eg Rapid Response and CDOP, others can present logistical and disclosure issues with their often perceived conflicting demands. It is important to consider them together rather than in isolation, as actions in relation to one may, if not properly managed, have an adverse impact on investigations and other processes. The following hypothetical but realistic example illustrates some of the issues that might arise.

Scenario

A father is suspected of killing a nine-month-old baby by violently shaking him and hitting him against a wall. This is apparently witnessed by a six-year-old sibling. The mother of the children, who is currently pregnant, has been the victim of domestic abuse from the father and was unhappy with the way the father had recently been acting towards the baby. Both mother and father were arrested on suspicion of causing or allowing the death of a child. They were both interviewed but, on the advice of their legal representative, made 'no comment'. Pending the final results from the post-mortem, other expert evidence, and the outcome of further police enquiries, both parents were released on police bail. The children were taken into the care of the local authority.

In this scenario the following issues could arise in relation to the interaction of processes and proceedings. These will not be examined in detail but hopefully provide a greater appreciation of the issues involved.

1. Rapid Response was initiated but, when the death became a suspected homicide, police assumed the lead for the investigation.

2. HM Coroner authorized a forensic post-mortem of which the preliminary findings supported a non-accidental head injury.
3. HM Coroner opened and adjourned an inquest.
4. The LSCB considered it appropriate to initiate the Serious Case Review process.
5. Children's Social Care and the police were concerned about the safety of the surviving sibling and the unborn child. Care proceedings are initiated at the Family Court.
6. Medical experts (in addition to those providing evidence for criminal proceedings) are instructed for the Family Court proceedings to provide evidence in relation to the injuries.
7. The final report for the post-mortem is completed and the injury being a non-accidental head injury is confirmed. In light of this information, the police want to re-interview both the parents and put this new information to them in a staged disclosure.
8. The Serious Case Review team make known to the police their intention to speak to the parents.
9. Solicitors representing the parents request a copy of the final post-mortem report prior to their interviews.
10. The Family Court request copies of all the police material in relation to the criminal investigation. Police and the CPS consider making an application for Family Court proceeding documents.
11. A medical expert in the case becomes the subject of complaint to the GMC in the way they reported on the post-mortem findings. The GMC request information from the police under s. 35A of the Medical Act 1983—power to require disclosure of information.
12. The mother and father are charged with causing or allowing the death of a child and remanded on bail.
13. The Family Court grant the mother access to her daughter (the deceased baby's six-year-old sibling) but the bail conditions from the Crown Court are that neither parent is to have contact with any prosecution witnesses. The daughter is a prosecution witness.

Hopefully, this hypothetical example illustrates how, in a relatively short period of time, the respective demands of each process or proceedings can become intertwined and complex, clearly requiring very careful management of apparently conflicting demands.

KEY POINT

Without wishing to oversimplify this complex investigative environment there are two principles which, if promoted, may alleviate some of the issues that might otherwise arise.

> 1. Any investigation should be primarily focused on the deceased child and upholding their right to a thorough and professional investigation into the circumstances of their death and justice in relation to any wrong doing.
> 2. Child death investigations are multi-agency in nature and under the Children Acts 1989 and 2004 organizations have a duty to co-operate with each other to safeguard and promote the welfare of children. This duty implies a need for honest communication and a positive obligation towards sharing information.
>
> When a potential problem is identified by those involved, the solution may become evident through pro-active communication between those affected together with serious reflection on these two principles.

7.2 Case management

Child homicides, like any other major crime, will invariably culminate in judicial proceedings at Crown Court. Professional preparation, planning, and presentation with regards to a trial or sentencing is expected from SIOs and their teams tasked with this responsibility. Child homicide trials can present additional challenges in the case management and trial process. The following observations and suggestions may help in addressing these for future cases.

- Early dialogue with the CPS from the outset of any homicide enquiry is essential. Hopefully they will endeavour to allocate the case to a lawyer with experience of child homicide cases and the associated legal issues.
- In relation to non-accidental head injury (NAHI), as with many other areas, there is specific CPS guidance outlining CPS policy regarding prosecutions to ensure a consistent approach. This states that 'Strategy and Policy Directorate must be informed of NAHI cases'.
- When counsel is appointed, the CPS guidance advocates using those with experience of child homicide cases and who are familiar with the legal and medical issues.
- Child homicide is a specialized serious crime area. It is essential that those involved have a good understanding of the legislation, procedures, and issues.
- Medical experts are invariably central to the prosecution case with the main areas of contention in the trial falling within the medical arena. It is important to obtain experts who are eminent in their field and experienced at giving evidence in court. There are a relatively limited number of medical experts who are qualified and willing to take on criminal cases, so there is a huge demand for their services. They can also be costly to employ so it is good practice to have a written agreement detailing the work they are being commissioned to undertake and the respective costs. This agreement should also set out their legal obligations as an expert witness including disclosure.

- Medical experts use complex terminology to describe their subject matter area including many terms which non-experts do not readily understand. This can be alleviated by the medical experts still using the correct medical terms in their statements but including a simple definition alongside in brackets. They should also keep this in mind when giving their evidence in court before a jury so that they can be assisted in understanding some very difficult and technical areas. Another way of assisting in this regard is with the utilization of a medical glossary of the terms the experts will use when giving evidence for the jury to refer to.
- Another aid to understanding expert evidence is through the use of graphics to demonstrate anatomy. If these graphics are combined with carefully selected photographic, CT, MRI, or X-ray images illustrating the nature of injuries in real life, it can be very effective without being too disturbing for the jury. Some experts may prepare Power Point presentations to explain their findings—these need to be agreed with counsel and checked for compatibility with the courtroom technology.
- It is advisable to show the experts the images in advance and for them to agree their anatomical accuracy, correct labelling, and location of injuries or features. Counsel should also be consulted in this process.
- The availability of medical experts to give evidence at court can be very problematic especially if the witness schedule timetable is disrupted in any way. It can be helpful to have a designated Single Point Of Contact (SPOC) for all the medical experts, who can be responsible for checking their availability, dates to avoid, and contacting them if there is a delay in proceedings.
- It is advisable for the exhibits officer to have copies of statements/reports/ photographs and graphics that expert witnesses will refer to.
- If exhibits, eg blocks and slides, are passed to other experts for a second opinion it is important that everyone involved understands the importance of continuity evidence. This is an area that should be covered in the written agreement.
- An important Statutory Instrument—The Criminal Procedure Rules 2011, Part 33—provides instructions for experts regarding definition of expert (rule 33.1); expert's duty to the court (rule 33.2); content of expert's report (rule 33.3); service of expert evidence (rule 33.4); expert to be informed of service of report (rule 33.5); pre-hearing discussion of expert evidence (if more than one party wants to introduce expert evidence then experts may be directed to discuss and prepare a statement for the court of the matters on which they agree and disagree giving their reasons) (rule 33.6); and court's power to direct that evidence is to be given by a single joint expert (rule 33.7). It is important that experts are aware of the requirements of these rules.
- It can be very useful if several experts are giving evidence that is related for permission to be obtained for them to sit in court while the other experts give their evidence. It can also assist counsel if they sit in while the experts providing evidence on behalf of the defence give their evidence. If required,

prosecution counsel are then able to consult the experts to assist in understanding answers which may be very technical in nature.

- It is important for the jury to have a picture of the victim in life so that they can put the victim's name to a face rather than a computer graphic. It may be a good idea to ask the victim's family to help select a suitable photograph.
- The victim's family should be made aware of the limitations that the judge has in protecting the anonymity of the victim and their siblings. It may not be possible to protect the identity of the victim (as they have died and are no longer provided protection) even if it may affect the siblings, eg at school with other children. However, if the siblings are involved in the proceedings, eg as a witness, then the judge can make an order protecting their identity under s. 39 of the Children and Young Persons Act 1933. This is an issue that needs to be discussed in advance with the CPS and counsel.

7.3 Parallel proceedings

A case may be simultaneously subject to criminal investigation/prosecution, family proceedings such as care or wardship, and/or a Serious Case Review (SCR). Where there are parallel proceedings, the timing and extent of disclosure of information between the different proceedings is often extremely important.

One or more of the proceedings may be jeopardized by inappropriate disclosure or non-disclosure. Therefore, if justice is to be done, close liaison and mutual understanding of what each process is trying to achieve are essential. There must be clarity of purpose, awareness of timescales, and an underlying desire to ensure that the integrity of all sets of proceedings is protected. Requests for disclosure should be focused and identify the relevant issues; they should not be fishing trips.

Inappropriate disclosure of information from the criminal proceedings into other proceedings can risk prejudicing the criminal proceedings through, for example, contamination of witness evidence or hindrance of the collection and preservation of evidence. Appropriate disclosure will, however, enable the Family Court or SCR Panel to consider all relevant evidence and to reach a proper conclusion.

Inappropriate disclosure of information from other proceedings into the criminal proceedings can risk damaging the general ethos of the Family Court and SCR Panel (which encourage full and frank disclosure by the parties) and risk breaching the Family Court's strict rules of confidentiality. Appropriate disclosure will, however, enable the prosecution team to judge the strength of its case and to comply with its duties under the Criminal Procedure and Investigations Act 1996.

The prosecution team, Family Court, and SCR Panel are all likely to be interested in documents such as previous consistent or inconsistent statements, admissions, evidence of similar incidents, expert/medical reports, etc.

7.3.1 **Family Court documents**

The disclosure and use of documents is strictly regulated by the Family Procedure Rules and breach may lead to proceedings for contempt of court.

Where documents have already been filed in family proceedings, the local authority (in care proceedings) or the parties' solicitors (in private proceedings) should be contacted to seek general information about what documents exist. A decision can then be made about whether or not to apply to the Family Court for leave to see/use those documents.

Where documents have not yet been filed in family proceedings, information sharing protocols such as the national ACPO/ADSS/CPS *Protocol on the Exchange of Information in the Investigation and Prosecution of Child Abuse Cases* (2003) provides guidance.

Section 98(1) of the Children Act 1989 provides that, in proceedings under Part IV or V of the Act (eg care, supervision, emergency protection orders), no person should be excused from giving evidence in any matter or answering any questions put to him in the course of his giving evidence on the grounds that doing so might incriminate him or his spouse of an offence.

Section 98(2) provides that a statement of admission made in such proceedings shall not be admissible in evidence against the person making it, or his spouse, in proceedings for offences other than perjury.

It should be noted that s. 98(2) refers to '*criminal proceedings*' and does not extend to a police investigation. Matters may, therefore, be put to a suspect in an interview under caution. If adopted, the admissions become admissible in the criminal proceedings in the usual way—subject to the usual provisions of ss. 76 and 78 of the Police and Criminal Evidence Act 1984.

The protection offered by s. 98(2) is just one of the factors to be considered by the Family Court when deciding whether to permit disclosure of documents to the prosecution team. The court also has to consider, for example, confidentiality, the child's best interests (which are not paramount in this context), and the public interest in the effectiveness of both family and criminal proceedings.

7.3.2 **Disclosure of criminal material to the Family Courts/Serious Case Review Panel**

Family Court proceedings and SCRs often start when the criminal investigation is only at an early stage or before the Criminal Court proceedings have been concluded. Case law confirms that, where possible, it is desirable for the criminal proceedings to be concluded first, but the challenging, statutory timescales to which the Family Court and SCR work can create tensions between the different sets of proceedings.

The police and CPS often receive requests for disclosure of material generated during the police investigation. Neither blanket approval nor blanket denial would be appropriate responses. The merits and risks of disclosure (in terms of content and timing) should be considered in respect of each item. Where criminal proceedings have already started, the decision should be made by the CPS. Where criminal proceedings have not yet started, it is usually wise for the police and prosecution to liaise before responding to the request.

The national *ACPO Police/Family Protocol* sets out the mechanisms for appropriate disclosure of police information in family proceedings. Although specifically designed for use with the Family Court, the general principles can be applied to disclosure in the context of SCRs.

The police representative on a SCR Panel should liaise with the criminal case OIC to identify likely areas for disclosure (both into and out of the SCR) so that both can discharge their respective responsibilities. He should also ensure appropriate input when the SCR's Terms of Reference are being drafted.

7.3.3 The Family Procedure Rules 2010

The Family Procedure Rules 2010 (FPR), which came into force on 6 April 2011, provide a single set of rules, supplemented by Practice Directions, for proceedings in the magistrates' court, county court and High Court. The FPR replace existing rules of court for family proceedings, including the Family Proceedings Rules 1991. See the Ministry of Justice website: <http://www.justice.gov.uk/guidance/courts-and-tribunals/courts/procedure-rules/index.htm>.

Matters relating specifically to children (public and private children law) are set out in **Part 12** of the FPR, and should be considered in conjunction with the general matters set out elsewhere in the FPR, for example the overriding objective and the rules on evidence and experts, etc.

Where there are parallel criminal and care proceedings, it is vital that the prosecution team understands the timetables and processes of the Family Court. **Practice Direction 12A** is a key piece of guidance. It sets out the *Public Law Proceedings Guide to Case Management: April 2010*, incorporating the *Public Law Outline 2010* (PLO).

The Practice Direction (PD) sets out the stages (Issue and First Appointment; Advocates' Meeting, and Case Management Conference; Advocates' Meeting and Issues Resolution Meeting; Final Hearing) and the strict timescales involved. The PLO forms to be used include information of relevance to the prosecution team, such as the Local Authority Case Summary, Draft Case Management Order, Timetable for the child/ren, Standard Directions, disclosure, etc.

PD 12A states at para. 3.9:

> Where there are parallel care proceedings and criminal proceedings against a person connected with the child for a serious offence against the child, linked directions hearings should where practicable take place as the case progresses. The timing of the proceedings in a linked care and criminal case should appear in the Timetable for the Child.

PLO Form 4 makes specific reference to parallel criminal proceedings.

Case Management Orders will include orders relating to the disclosure of documents into the proceedings held by third parties, including medical records, police records, and the disclosure of documents and information relating to the proceedings to non-parties.

The Timetable for the Child includes not only legal steps but also social, care, health, and education steps. Due regard is required to be paid to the Timetable to ensure the court remains child-focused throughout the progress of the proceedings and that any procedural steps proposed under the PLO are considered in the context of significant events in the child's life.

The expectations are that the proceedings should be finally determined within the timetable fixed by the court in accordance with the Timetable for the Child—the timescales in the PLO being adhered to and being taken as the *maximum* permissible time for the taking of the step referred to in the Outline, unless the Timetable for the Child demands otherwise.

The prosecution team must bear in mind the Timetable. They will need to contribute information regarding criminal proceedings dates/events and, equally, they should take the contents of the Timetable into account when contributing to the case management procedures in the criminal proceedings. For example, where a trial appears likely, it should not simply be a matter of witness availability, but information should be obtained concerning significant steps in the child's life that are likely to take place during the proceedings (such as exams, revision, special events, Family Court proceedings etc) and efforts should be made to fix the trial date accordingly.

Such an approach should help both the Family Court and the Criminal Court to work together in the interests of justice and the welfare of the child.

Part 21, rules 21.2–21.3 set out the provisions for orders for disclosure and inspection of documents against a person not a party and for claims to withhold inspection or disclosure of a document.

7.3.4 **Communication of information—Practice Direction 12G**

Practice Direction 12G sets out what information can be communicated to third parties—including the police and CPS. The tables from the old rules (Part X, Rules 11.2–11.9 of the Family Proceedings (Amendment) (No. 2) Rules 2009, which amended the Family Proceedings Rules 1991) are restated.

In essence, a party in family proceedings or any person lawfully in receipt of information can give 'the text or summary of the whole or part of a judgment given in the proceedings' to a police officer for the purposes of a criminal investigation or to a member of the CPS 'to enable the Crown Prosecution Service to discharge its functions under any enactment'.

As mentioned above, apart from the judgment, there may also be information contained in Family Court case papers that would be relevant to the criminal case, such as admissions, previous consistent or inconsistent statements of witnesses or defendants, similar incidents, medical reports/medical expert evidence, etc.

Disclosure and use of such documents is restricted. But the information contained may be crucial to the decision to charge, the choice of charge, the setting of bail conditions, the handling of witnesses (including whether special measures may be required), bad character/hearsay applications, etc.

The rules permit the communication of information relating to the proceedings (whether or not contained in a document filed with the court) not only where the court gives permission, but also where communication is to (amongst others) 'a professional acting in furtherance of the protection of children', which is defined as including a police officer who is exercising powers under s. 46 of the Children Act 1989 (removal and accommodation of children in an emergency) or is serving in a child protection unit or a paedophile unit of a police force, or a professional person attending a child protection conference or review in relation to a child who is the subject of the proceedings to which the information relates.

The investigation and prosecution of offences against a child will be part of the protection of children; it is, therefore, permissible to disclose to an officer acting in a child protection function documents relating to proceedings in addition to the information contained within them. However, the police officer or professional receiving the communication is not entitled to make use of the documents (as opposed to the information contained within them) without the permission of the Family Court.

7.3.5 In summary

Where there are parallel proceedings, informal and timely discussions should be held first, to identify what relevant material exists and whether it can be disclosed by agreement. The principles of the Family Procedure Rules, *Working Together*, and the national information sharing protocols should be applied and particular attention paid to timescales. If a formal application needs to be made, parties should assist each other in understanding how this might be done. Whether criminal, family, or SCR proceedings, the shared overriding objective must be to deal with cases fairly and expeditiously.

Further information and reading

CPS/ACPO Homicide Working Group (2011), *Guide for The Police, The CPS, LSCBs to assist with liaison and exchange of information when there are simultaneous Chapter 8 Serious case reviews and Criminal Proceedings*. Available at <http://www.baspcan.org.uk/files/SCR%20Guidance%20Document%20Final-%20John%20Fox.pdf>.

Information presented in section 7.3 is taken from the Crown Prosecution Service's Legal Guidance: <http://www.cps.gov.uk/legal/v_to_z/safeguarding_children_as_victims_and_witnesses/ #a16>

7.4 **Serious case reviews**

The need to complete a serious case review (SCR) comes from the statutory guidance contained in *Working Together* and is found at Chapter 8.

The purpose of an SCR is to:

- Establish what lessons are to be learned from the case about the way in which local professionals and organizations work individually and together to safeguard and promote the welfare of children;
- Identify clearly what those lessons are both within and between agencies, how and within what timescales they will be acted on, and what is expected to change as a result;
- Improve intra- and inter-agency working and better safeguard and promote the welfare of children;
- The prime purpose of an SCR is for agencies and individuals to learn lessons to improve the way in which they work both individually and collectively to safeguard and promote the welfare of children;
- The lessons learned should be disseminated effectively and the recommendations should be implemented in a timely manner so that the changes required results wherever possible, in children being protected from suffering or being likely to suffer harm in the future.

Current guidelines on the process required in order to complete an SCR are contained in *Working Together*. This statutory guidance states that the timescales involved are a maximum of one month to commission the review. This is a decision made by the LSCB's standing SCR panel and agreed by the LSCB chair. There are then six months to complete the review.

The activity that then takes place as an SCR Panel is formed—often a superintendent is the police representative, but in any case there is a senior police representative, as is the case for all agencies that there is a senior representative on this SCR Panel.

An independent panel chair of this SCR Panel and overview report author are employed. The SCR Panel then draw up terms of reference, and Individual Management Reviews (IMR) are commissioned from all agencies based on these terms of reference.

An independent person, not connected with the case, will conduct the police IMR. This is the same process for all the agencies, who will ensure the securing of files in each agency, interviewing staff involved, eg doctors, social workers, and Child Abuse Investigators. A full chronology and IMR report will be completed with critical analysis of agency involvement leading up to the death of the child.

The reports will be submitted to SCR Panel, where they will be either read by the police delegate or presented by the IMR author. A full report by the Independent Author will be written based on the collection of all of the IMRs and will be made public. Either the SCR Panel or the overview author will prepare an executive summary, also publicly available; both reports are anonymized.

It is important that any lessons to be learned arising out of the SCR are actioned by individual agencies and the LSCB as soon as they are identified.

7.4.1 **Learning the lessons from Serious Case Reviews**

In order to learn lessons from SCRs taken collectively there has been a number of research and analysis reviews. The University of East Anglia (UEA) has completed a biennial series of reviews, and Ofsted has produced another series.

The first time the UEA carried out their research and analysis, their researchers commented:

> The findings about the children and their circumstances make powerful and painful reading. Prevention of child death or injury through abuse or neglect is uppermost in the minds of practitioners and managers working with children and families.
>
> However, the complexity of family circumstances means that even if the 'whole picture' of family circumstances had been known, it would not always have been possible to predict an outcome for most of the children.[1]

Some of the key lessons from the years that UEA, on behalf of the Department for Children, Schools and Families, and Ofsted have carried out research are bulletpointed below, but it must be emphasized that it is the same lessons that come out time and time again.[2]

- In many cases parents were hostile to helping agencies, and workers were often frightened to visit family homes. These circumstances could have a paralyzing effect on practitioners, hampering their ability to reflect, make judgments, and act clearly.
- There was hesitancy in challenging the opinion of other professionals which appeared to stem from a lack of confidence, knowledge, experience, or status.
- Supervision helps practitioners to think, to explain, and to understand. It also helps them to cope with the complex emotional demands of work with children and their families.
- Our argument throughout this study has been for the need for practitioners and managers to be curious, to be sceptical; to think critically and systematically but to act compassionately.

---

[1] M Brandon, et al. (2008), *Analysing child deaths and serious injury through abuse and neglect: what can we learn? A biennial analysis of serious case reviews 2003–2005* (Nottingham: DCSF Publications).

[2] M Brandon, et al. (2008), ibid.; M Brandon, et al. (2009), *Understanding serious case reviews and their impact. A biennial analysis of serious case reviews 2005–2007* (Nottingham: DCSF); Ofsted (2008), *Learning lessons, taking action: Ofsted's evaluations of serious case reviews 1 April 2007–31 March 2008* (London: Ofsted); Ofsted (2009), *Learning lessons from serious case reviews year 2 (2008–2009)* (London: Ofsted); Ofsted (2010), *Learning lessons from serious case reviews : interim report 2009–2010* (London: Ofsted).

- High levels of current or past domestic violence and/or parental mental ill health and/or parental substance misuse, often in combination, were apparent throughout and this is a major feature throughout all of the years that SCRs have been analysed.
- The police tended to be the agency most involved with these families, often containing domestic or community conflict or violence. Also with cases of substance misuse.
- There was sometimes a lack of awareness on the part of health staff and some branches of the police force to the link between domestic violence and the risk of harm to the child.
- Half of the parents/carers had criminal convictions. Many families were overwhelmed, with poor or negative family support. Nearly three-quarters of the children lived with past or present domestic violence and/or past or present parental mental ill health, and/or past or present parental substance misuse. These three parental characteristics often co-existed.
- Three-quarters of the 40 families did not co-operate with services. Patterns of hostility and lack of compliance included: deliberate deception, disguised compliance and 'telling workers what they want to hear', selective engagement, and sporadic, passive, or desultory compliance. Reluctant parental co-operation and multiple moves meant that many children went off the radar of professionals.
- While the youngest children are the most vulnerable to death from abuse or neglect, the next most vulnerable group were adolescents.
- Some young people might have been amenable to help if they had been offered the right approach. Some young people were seen as a nuisance and not easy to work with.
- There is less public concern, however, on behalf of the vulnerable adolescents who feature repeatedly in Serious Case Reviews and homicide statistics.
- This suggests a level of 'agency neglect' of this vulnerable group of young people, many of whom are on the cusp of adulthood (Stein et al., 2009). A high proportion of these young people will have had similar damaging early experiences to Baby P.
- The tendency towards 'silo practice' that we found, where professionals preferred to work within the comfort zone of their own specialism, underlines the importance of joint child protection training. This should continue to be offered not just for those working with children but also to the adult workforce and any groups of workers coming into contact with children and families.
- Professionals' working together can be tentative with the perceived responsibilities and priorities of separate agencies overshadowing the safeguarding responsibility.
- This is possibly the single most significant practice failing throughout the majority of the Serious Case Reviews—the failure of all professionals to see the situation from the child's perspective and experience; to see and speak to the children; to listen to what they said; to observe how they were; and to take serious account of their views in supporting their needs.

Ofsted in April 2011 published a further report which was themed looking at the voice of the child. The following key points are highlighted in this report:[3]

There are five main messages with regard to the voice of the child. In too many cases:

- the child was not seen frequently enough by the professionals involved, or was not asked about their views and feelings;
- agencies did not listen to adults who tried to speak on behalf of the child and who had important information to contribute;
- parents and carers prevented professionals from seeing and listening to the child;
- practitioners focused too much on the needs of the parents, especially on vulnerable parents, and overlooked the implications for the child;
- agencies did not interpret their findings well enough to protect the child.

A wider study was carried out by Dr Peter Sidebotham et al., and looked at a four-year period: this research was published in 2011.[4] The researchers found the following were of significance in the Serious Case Reviews they looked at:

Parental mental health issues	24 per cent
Parental substance misuse	19 per cent
Parental alcohol misuse	18 per cent
Domestic violence	28 per cent
Evidence of previous physical abuse	36 per cent
Evidence of previous neglect	40 per cent

Nb The figures total more than 100 per cent as the maltreatments overlap.

The study also highlighted severe physical assault as the commonest form of fatal maltreatment, with non accidental head injuries being the most common mode of death in this group, and a male as the most usual offender; however, it was often the case that both carers were involved.

Serious Case Reviews present a lasting testimony and memorial to children who die in horrific circumstances. This must be remembered in order to learn from these reviews.

7.5 Major crime reviews

7.5.1 Background to reviews

In cases of suspicious child deaths, it is good practice to have regular reviews of the crime investigation. The importance of carrying out reviews of child deaths

---

[3] Ofsted (2011), *The voice of the child: learning lessons from serious case reviews* (London: Ofsted).

[4] P Sidebotham, S Bailey, P Belderson, and M Brandon (2011), 'Fatal child maltreatment in England, 2005–2009', published online at *Child Abuse & Neglect* 35(4) 299–306.

is evident across all agencies. Within policing they came to prominence after the Yorkshire Ripper case. The Byford report into this case recognized that, if regular reviews of that investigation had been carried out, Peter Sutcliffe (The Yorkshire Ripper) may have been caught earlier. Peter Sutcliffe was convicted in 1989 of murdering 13 females and seven further attacks on other women. The *MacPherson Inquiry* after the death of Stephen Lawrence made a recommendation in relation to reviews at recommendation 19 of its 70 recommendations. This recommendation stated that 'ACPO should devise codes of practice to govern reviews of investigations, in order to ensure that such reviews are open and thorough. Such codes should be consistently used by police services' (MacPherson, 1999). ACPO has, over the intervening years from the Byford report and MacPherson report, issued guidance which has been updated on a number of occasions.

In 'Reviewing the Reviewers: The review of Homicides in the United Kingdom' by Dean Jones[5] he states at p. 9: 'A review is defined as "A constructive evaluation of the conduct of an investigation to ensure that an objective and thorough investigation has been conducted to national standards and which seeks to ensure investigative opportunities are not overlooked and that good practice is identified" (Rogers, 2005:3).[6]

Reviews are not re-investigations or to take over the investigation. Both review officers and SIOs must ensure that this doesn't take place. A review has a number of purposes but in particular to assist and support the SIO in their investigation and make sure that any investigative opportunities are not overlooked but highlighted. Other purposes are to ensure that both national and local investigative standards are being complied with, and any lessons, including good practice, that can be learned from an individual investigation are being captured and then appropriately disseminated.

7.5.2 Different types of review

There are various forms of major crime reviews:

- Management intervention;
- 28 day review;
- Thematic reviews;
- Closure review;
- Peer reviews;
- Detected review;
- Cold case review;

---

[5] D Jones, J Grieve, and B Milne (2010), 'Reviewing the Reviewers: The review of Homicides in the United Kingdom' *Investigative Sciences Journal* 2(1).

[6] T Rogers (2005), *Serious Crime Investigation Review Course* (Harrogate: November, 2005).

- Multi-agency reviews, which include Serious Case Reviews for both children and adults, domestic homicide reviews, Multi Agency Public Protection Arrangements (MAPPA) reviews; and
- Hot de-briefs.

The first is a management intervention review: this type of review is normally completed within the first 24 hours or so, but can take place at seven days. Its purpose is often to ensure that nothing has been missed in the first day(s), confirm categorization of the inquiry, and also to assist with staffing requirements. In child death cases this, as per the statutory requirement from Chapter 7 of *Working Together*, will also involve a multi-agency discussion. The next type of review is commonly known as a 28-day review or progress review. This review is often seen as a formal review and invariably involves a full team being utilized. Other forms of review are 'thematic' ones, which could look at a particular part of the investigation; for example, if there are any issues with the family, a review of the family liaison strategy could be appropriate. There is also at the time of the 28 day review a formal multi-agency review that takes place as described in Chapter 7 of Working Together 2010. There will be much to be learnt from this meeting that can be used to assist any formal police review. Then there could be a closure review, to make sure an undetected major crime is suitable to be closed down.

There also needs to be in place a policy to carry out 'cold case' reviews for cases that have been closed down. It is good practice to review all undetected murders every two years. There are a number of different methods and models used around the country in different police forces in order to risk assess and highlight the potential for carrying out a 'cold case' review. The ACPO one is shown below.

HIGH			LOW
A	B	C	D
• Fingerprint identification • DNA identification • New identification witness • Significant actionable intelligence	• New forensic opportunity and/or technologies • Significant outstanding enquiries • Linked incidents or new intelligence that may provide significant lines of enquiry. • Change of allegiance	• Intelligence and/or evidence of limited – no value • Potential linked incidents of value	• No new information and/or evidence • No new intelligence • No new forensic opportunities
1	2	3	4
• Complete original case papers • Significant exhibits • High integrity/continuity	• Limited original case papers • Limited exhibits • Questioned integrity/continuity	• Copies of case papers • Inquest files • DPP files • Non significant exhibits	• No case papers • No exhibits

Figure 7.1 Risk Assessment Matrix

These cold case reviews are particularly important in cases that involve children. It may be an offence that occurred within a family, in which there could be other siblings including newly born ones that need protection, so this also needs to figure in the above matrix as a consideration.

Reviews that are not carried out on a regular basis but have a lot of benefits, are 'peer reviews' and 'detected reviews'. A 'peer review' is one where a number of experienced SIOs are gathered together in order to give the SIO an alternative view; this can be done independently or, as is often the case, at a meeting where the SIO presents their case. In terms of suspicious child deaths, this can be done with a meeting between regional colleagues, ensuring that appropriate medical practitioners are also invited. The ACPO sub-group for investigating child deaths has done this in the past and is very willing to carry out 'peer reviews' whenever requested. Detected reviews can take place at two different stages: one is after charge and before trial, and the other is after conviction. The review before charge is often one that ensures that everything has been considered for the forthcoming trial. The post-conviction review focuses on what has gone well and what others can learn from this particular case.

Hot de-briefs are good practice and can take place at various stages. The first stage is in order to capture initial actions; these can either be completed individually or collectively. The first stage is normally to help develop the investigation. Other 'Hot de-briefs' can take place at any time, including after charge to pick up on good practice, what went well, and what can be improved on for the future.

7.5.3 Makeup of review team

The review should be lead by a senior review officer. This senior review officer should be experienced in the investigation of suspicious child deaths. Dean Jones' research study 'Reviewing the Reviewers' confirmed 'the ACPO stance that reviewing officers need to be experienced in the actual investigation of murder. Having stated this however, the use of the structured tool does enhance the quality of the review both for experienced and inexperienced officers'.[7] The murder review tool he advocates is one that covers each area of an investigation and ensures that appropriate national and local benchmarks/standards are taken into account, for example, the *Murder Investigation Manual* or the Core Investigative Doctrine.

Review officers can be civilian members of staff, and a number of police forces have employed support staff members in this capacity. They and police officers who carry out the role ideally need to have the experience of being involved in a major investigation. However, it is also important that the makeup of the team to assist both the senior review officer and review officer to carry out a review is focused on the technical skills that some of them have, for example Crime Scene Investigator/Manager. It may be appropriate also to bring in people from outside to assist, for example, forensic experts. In the case of suspicious

---

[7] D Jones, J Grieve, and B Milne (2010), 'Reviewing the Reviewers: The review of Homicides in the United Kingdom' *Investigative Sciences Journal* 2(1).

child deaths, in particular if it involves non accidental head injuries in an infant, it is important to enlist the help of specialist medical practitioners to assist the review, for example, a pathologist to provide an overview of all of the medical information provided.

7.5.4 Terms of reference

The setting of the terms of reference for a review is probably the most important decision that is made and, unless the terms are made out in a manner that is focused and specific to an individual enquiry, this will hamper the prospect of having a successful review.

The terms of reference are normally set by the ACC who will have consulted with the Head of Crime, the SIO, and in cases of child death with the Head of Public Protection. It is also important that the senior review officer plays a key role in the setting of the terms of reference and is part of the review process from the beginning.

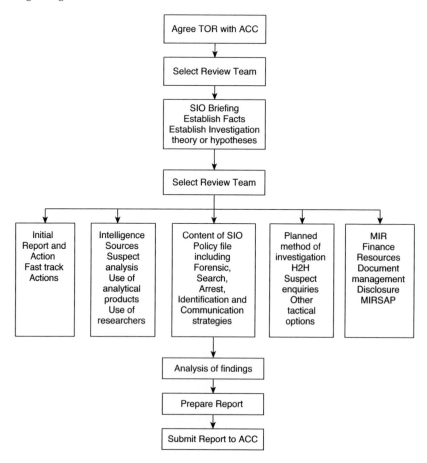

Figure 7.2 Schematic of review

In the review of suspicious child deaths when setting the terms of reference, a key area to think about in their format is to make sure that they are themed appropriately to capture, if necessary, information that any external agencies may have: the very basis of these enquiries is their multi-agency nature.

In every review, it is important that good practice is highlighted and investigations improved by learning from reviews. This should always be highlighted in the terms of reference. The parallel reviews that occur during child death investigations, for example, Serious Case Reviews, will have this as their role, but it should not stop reviews also examining this.

7.5.5 **Methodology**

As discussed earlier, the senior review officer should be appointed at the earliest opportunity so that they can be involved in forming the terms of reference. In keeping with the terms of reference and their purpose, they should appoint their review officer and team at the next earliest opportunity, looking for the particular technical skills required.

The SIO of the investigation must then be given time to prepare a briefing, including the current situation report, log of events, and other important documents, in particular copies of their policy/decision making file. They should also have images of the scenes or scenes available to show at the briefing. The SIO's briefing should be to as many of the review team who can attend as possible, and the team should be prepared to ask questions as appropriate to their part of the review.

Visiting the MIR and having a SPOC appointed from the MIR is essential, in order to ensure the smooth running of the review in relation to collecting information for the inquiry such as investigative strategies. The review should have access and the ability to read the HOLMES account for the investigation.

It is crucial that the senior review officer and all members of the review team visit scenes, in order for them to put into context what they have read and been told. Reviews always involve interviews with key members of the investigation, including SIOs and crime scene managers.

7.5.6 **Report preparation**

It is essential if any fast track recommendations are identified, that the SIO is informed as soon as possible, so that they can consider whether they need to act on them immediately.

The report must be factually accurate, so will need checking by the SIO to ensure there are no inaccuracies. The SIO should then be afforded an opportunity to meet with the review officer so that any further discrepancies can be resolved. The exact format varies, but the following headings are a useful structure:

• Executive summary (if the report is of a size that would benefit from one);
• Introduction, to include the background to the case;

- Methodology;
- Terms of reference;
- Main lines of enquiry;
- SIO policy/decision-making;
- Media;
- House to house;
- Forensic;
- Suspect/Trace, Interview, Eliminate (TIE)/Person of Interest (POI);
- Family liaison;
- MIR structure and action management;
- Other investigative opportunities, eg passive data sources or financial enquiries;
- List of good practice;
- List of recommendations;
- Appendices.

Recommendations in the main should be in three categories: (a) incident specific, (b) policy/procedural, and (c) organizational. Coupled with these recommendations is ensuring that good practice and learning are captured and disseminated both locally and nationally.

Reviewing officers need to be aware that the report—all or parts of it—may be disclosed, and it should be written with that in mind.

7.5.7 Review panel

All forces should have in place a review panel who will sit on either a regular or ad hoc basis, in order to have reviews presented to them, and to agree with recommendations and areas of good practice. They then decide on how best to disseminate and action plan the organizational recommendations.

The panels should be chaired by the ACC crime, and have the head of CID sit on them, often in company with the head of the major investigation team. Other members of the panel can vary and will include individual SIOs when their enquiry is being discussed. Local senior officers will also be involved, for example, the Basic Command Unit (BCU) commander for the area.

Case study

Child A was five months old when he died. The post-mortem revealed no external injuries, but found a sub-dural haematoma, bi-lateral retinal haemorrhages, and brain encephalopathy (swelling to the brain).

All samples were sent off for specialist paediatric examination, for example, the brain to a paediatric neuropathologist. Both parents were interviewed and other enquiries commenced.

After four months very little information had been received from the experts. A review was commissioned by the ACC and terms of reference established.

Recommendations from the review included:

- All experts to see each others' statements;
- Experts meeting to be held after this;
- Overview paediatric expert to be commissioned;
- Analyst to produce a timeline;
- SIO to re-visit parents with FLO to explain course of action;
- Covert consideration;
- All sets of expert statements sent to each parent;
- Independent PACE interviews of each parent to take place after time to analyse statements.

All recommendations took place and the father was subsequently charged and convicted of manslaughter.

7.6 Future considerations and research

As illustrated in Chapter 1 and throughout the subsequent chapters, it can be seen that there have been many advances in childhood death investigation and especially in relation to guidance, procedures, legislation, and medical research. These advances and increased learning can, in turn, prompt further progress, developments, considerations, and research, some examples of which are included below.

7.6.1 The minimally invasive autopsy

As the standard post-mortem examination requires large incisions and, as a result of concerns regarding organ retention, there has been much interest in developing alternative, non- or minimally invasive methods to determine or confirm diagnoses at post-mortem. Post-mortem MRI imaging, particularly when combined with post-mortem CT scanning, can provide very high quality images of both bony and soft-tissue elements, and with acquisition protocols optimized for the specific post-mortem setting, excellent tissue resolution is achievable (Thayyil et al., 2009). Post-mortem MRI imaging is particularly good for central nervous system defects (Thayyil et al., 2010). However, since a significant proportion of causes of death and other significant pathologies at autopsy can only be detected following direct inspection of organs and the use of ancillary investigations, such as histological sampling or microbiological investigations, post-mortem imaging alone is unlikely to replace traditional autopsies, particularly in the setting of a coroner's autopsy.

Nevertheless, post-mortem MRI imaging is likely to significantly contribute to future autopsy practice. Firstly, anatomical detail is excellent with MRI and there is the significant added advantage that, once an original dataset is captured, the anatomical features may be reviewed again at a later date, if required. Secondly, accurate reconstruction of internal organs and skeletal injuries can be carried out by rapid prototyping of three-dimensional MRI and CT datasets, and these may be extremely useful in forensic cases.

Finally, post-mortem imaging techniques, such as MRI, can be used in conjunction with modified tissue examination and sampling techniques, such as endoscopic/laparoscopic (keyhole) examination; the novel combination of these two modalities allows for the acquisition of datasets for review, reconstruction, and determination of accurate anatomical information, whilst maintaining the ability to directly examine organs and tissues, and taking appropriate samples for histological examination or other ancillary investigations (Sebire et al., 2011).

7.6.2 **Future studies/research**

Numerous potentially valuable research studies are in progress regarding the post-mortem examination of SUDI which may impact on the way such deaths are investigated in the future. These include:

- Cardiac gene mutation testing for arrhythmia-associated deaths;
- Genetic polymorphism testing for atypical immune/inflammatory responses;
- Development of novel imaging approaches;
- Development of new targeted tests for better determination of the timing and mode of death;
- Improved methods to interpret the significance of results of post-mortem microbiological cultures.

7.7 **Conclusion**

The journey along the child death continuum and the consideration of the challenges facing all those involved in the investigation into 'why did this child die?' has been completed. Features along the route will continue to be developed as time progresses. Sometimes the police have been perceived as insensitive or professionally lacking in their response to child death, particularly in relation to the deceased child's parents. It is hoped that having contemplated the issues raised in this book that the investigative predicament which the police, and others in this specialized area of investigation, face is now better appreciated. Policies, procedures, and guidance can in the pages of a document appear deceptively straightforward, whereas the operational reality is far more complex—there are no easy answers.

Irrespective of where a child's death features on the investigative continuum the child must remain as the prime focus for the investigation. Key themes complementing this focus should include:

- Child-focused approach including siblings;
- Support for families and all those affected by the death;
- Clear communication between all those involved in the investigative process with consistent messages and explanations of why respective actions are undertaken;
- Effective professional multi-agency working;
- Prevention driven by medical research and dynamic child protection;
- An unbiased and genuine 'search for the truth' wherever it leads.

Guidance helps when negotiating unknown territory providing points to consider, contingencies to employ, procedures to follow, and operationally based advice from those who have gone before. However, each pathway in this area will in some way be unique; there may be similarities, eg legislation, legal boundaries, themes (domestic abuse, drug/alcohol abuse, mental health issues), but ultimately no case is the same. Most importantly in this investigative context, all children who die are, without exception, unique individuals who all deserve special consideration of their individual circumstances to answer the question 'Why did they die?'.

This book has been written to assist those tasked with this demanding, challenging, and very privileged responsibility.

Further information and reading

The Stephen Lawrence Inquiry: Report of an Inquiry by Sir William MacPherson of Cluny (1999) (London: The Stationery Office). Available at <http://www.archive.official-documents.co.uk/document/cm42/4262/4262.htm>.
Louise Casey CB Commissioner for Victims and Witnesses (2011) Review into the Needs of Families Bereaved by Homicide. MOJ.

NOTES

NOTES

Appendix A
Greater Manchester History Template

A number of templates have been developed around the country which are utilized in recording the history and other key details in relation to the death of a child that falls within the Rapid Response Processes. This and the following MPS template in Appendix B are just two examples that illustrate the way this information can be recorded.

1. Rapid Response Checklist

Name:

	Yes/No	Date
Initial case discussion		
Form A		
Home visit		
Report for PM/coroner		
24-hour review discussion		
Summary of discussion to attendees		
PM		
Form B		
Final PM result		
Final case discussion		
Form C/report of final case discussion to coroner/CDOP		
Inquest		
Meeting with parents		
Letter to parents		
Audit form		
Time sheet		

Cc final report/Form C to: Hospital paediatrician   SIO
Coroner   GP(s)
HV/SN   SW
Local Safeguarding
Team   Local SUDC lead
Others present at final
meeting   ED/TC
Local CDOP

2. Child's details

Name of Child (First name and family name plus any other names)	
NHS number	
Date of birth	
Ethnicity	
Sex	
Address 	
Post code	
Date of Death	

Initial telephone call information including brief description of cause of death

Called by

Time/date

3. Documentation of initial discussion following notification of death:

Date

Name/position of those involved in discussion

To attend A&E   Y/N

If so when

To arrange joint home visit   Y/N

If so when

With whom

If A&E is not attended or a home visit is not deemed necessary it should be documented why that decision was made. The points raised on page 25 should be answerable. (13. AUDIT)

4. Contact names/addresses and telephone numbers

GP Name and Address	
Consultant at time of death/name of hospital	
SUDC Consultant	
Police Officer/SIO	
Social Worker	
Coroner/ Coroner's Officer	
HV/SN	
Pathologist	
Other Professionals	

5. Family Details

Mother

Full name (plus any other names)	
Full address (inc postcode)	
NHS number	
Date of birth	
Ethnicity	
First Language	
Phone number (home/mobile or that of close relative/ friend)	
Address/phone no. Mother will be using if different to home	

Father

Full name (plus any other names)	
Full address (inc postcode)	
NHS number	
Date of birth	
Ethnicity	
First Language	
Phone number (home/mobile/ that of close relative/ friend)	
Address/phone no. Father will be using if different to home	

Siblings

Name	Date of birth	Primary address

Other members of household (Present and recent past)

Name	Date of birth	Relationship to child who has died

6. Details of Transport of Child to Hospital:

(information from ambulance crew, if from another source please state)

Place of death: Home address as above/Another location
                                         (specify)/ Hospital (specify)

Time found:

By whom/how:

Who called emergency services:

Time arrived in A&E:

Resuscitation carried out: Y/N

Where?   At scene of death/Ambulance/ A&E

By whom?   carers/GP/ambulance/hospital staff/others

What responses, (if any), were
obtained from the child?

How long did it take for the
emergency services to arrive?
(from ambulance call times)

Confirmation of death   Date   Time   Location

                               By whom?

Any additional information from NWAS :

7. History

Taken in A&E by:

History given by:

Relationship to child:

Events surrounding death

(Include photocopies of all relevant A&E notes)

8. For infant deaths/older children where appropriate
Detailed narrative account of events of the 24-48 hours
prior to the child being found

(This may be taken in a number of locations in more than one episode. Please document when and where the information was obtained and from whom. Document negatives.)

To include details of all activities and carers during last 24-48 hours; whether child was feeding as well as, or less than usual; any changes in routine care or activity levels; any disruptions to normal patterns; any alcohol drugs consumed by child or carers; any emotional upsets.

Final sleep checklist (if relevant)

Nature of surface	
Clothing	
Bedding	
Arrangement of bedding	
Precise sleeping position	
Who was sharing the sleeping surface	
How often the child was checked	
When he/she was seen or heard	
The time at which the child awoke for feeds	
Whether feeds were given	
Whether they were taken well	
What were the activities of others in the room	
Where, when and by whom was the child found	
What was the appearance of the child when they were found	
Where was the bedding	
Were there any covers over the child	
Had the covers and the position of the covers moved	
Were there any other objects adjacent or close to the child (e.g. pillows, teddies)	
Regular use of pacifier, was it used that night	
Was the heating on/what type	
Were the windows and/or doors open or closed	

Detailed narrative account of the baby/child's feeding, sleeping, activity, and health over the 2-week period prior to death

(This may be taken in a number of locations in more than one episode. Please document when and where the information was obtained and from whom. Document negatives.)

Include changes in feeding/sleeping pattern; changes in place of sleep; changes in individuals responsible for providing care to child; social, family or health related changes in routine; any illness, accident or other major event affecting other family members. For older children note whether at school or on holiday; any changes at school/exams etc; change of friends/recreational activities.

Any vomiting; any respiratory difficulty, noisy breathing/in drawing of ribs/ wheeze or stridor; excessive sweating; unusual activity or behaviour; change in level of alertness; difficulty sleeping; difficulty waking; passage of stool (how often and how much); were any health care professionals consulted in the last 2 weeks; if yes who, why, and what advice was given; was the child SEEN and assessed in the last 2 weeks; any self-harming behaviour.

Medical and developmental history of the child:

(This may be taken in a number of locations in more than one episode. Please document when and where the information was obtained and from whom. Document negatives.)

9. Family Medical and Social History: include detailed family tree of relatives and significant others

Details of all family and household members including names; dates of birth; health; any previous or current illnesses including mental health; any medications (prescription and non-prescription); occupation

Maternal parity and obstetric history

Parental relationships

Children, including children by other partners

Household composition (and recent changes in composition, who has come or gone for what reasons)

Any previous childhood deaths in the family (siblings or close relatives of other members of the household)

Detail on smoking (who and where)

Alcohol consumption

Drug use

Pets

Foreign travel

10. **Physical Examination**

Physical examination carried out by:
Others present
Time after death

• Rectal Temp (low reading thermometer) _____
Date/Time _____ and interval from death _____

• Full Growth Measurements   Centile
           Length (cm)   _____   _____
           head circ (cm)   _____   _____
           weight (kg)   _____   _____

• Retinal Examination

• State of nutrition and hygiene

• Marks, Livido, Bruises or evidence of injury—
  To include any medical puncture sites and failed
  attempts, and should also be drawn on body chart overleaf.

Check genitalia and back:

Check mouth: Is the frenum of lips/tongue intact?

• Further details, observations and comments:

• List all drugs given at hospital and any interventions
  carried out at resuscitation

- Document direct observation of position of endotracheal tube prior to removal or name of senior doctor who checked tube position.

Date, Time
Signature(s)

Name _____   D.O.B. _____

Physical Examination

Body Chart

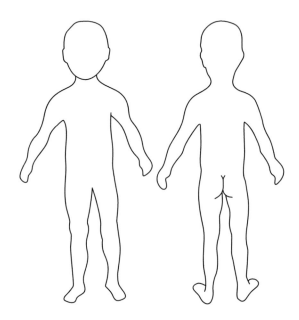

Name _____   D.O.B. _____

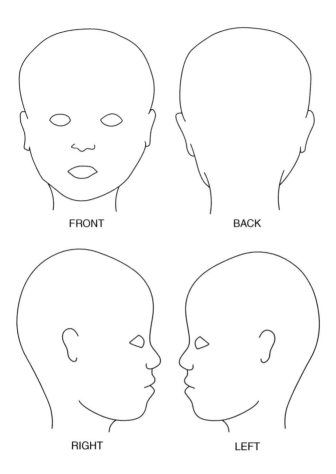

FRONT   BACK

RIGHT   LEFT

Appendix A: Greater Manchester History Template

Name _____   D.O.B. _____

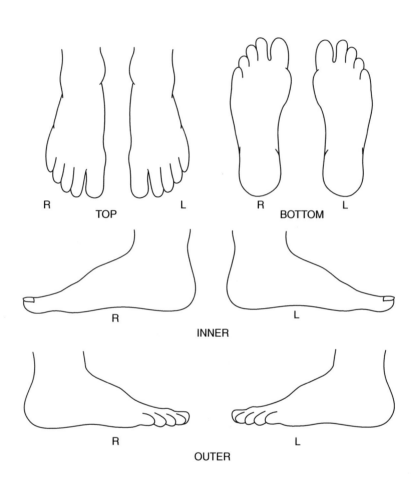

R   L   R   L
   TOP   BOTTOM

R   L
   INNER

R   L
   OUTER

238

11. Scene Examination

Child's Name ....

Date of Birth ....   Date of Death ....

Address ....

Date of scene visit ....

Persons Present ....

....

Room

Note: size; orientation (compass); contents; "clutter"

Ventilation: windows & doors (open or shut)

Heating: (including times switched on/off); measure drawer temperature   °C

Sleep environment

Note: location, position of bed /cot in relation to other objects in room, mattress, bedding, objects

Position of baby

When put down:

When found

- Any evidence of over-wrapping or over-heating?   Yes/No

- Any restriction to ventilation or breathing?   Yes/No

- Any risk of smothering?   Yes/No

- Any potential hazards?   Yes/No

- Any evidence of neglectful care?   Yes/No

Further information from police and social services available at initial assessment

POLICE

SOCIAL SERVICES

Following initial assessment are there thought to be on-going child protection issues for siblings?   Y/N

Name _____   D.O.B. _____

Documentation of discussion with Rapid Response Team following initial information gathering:

(Document decisions taken and reasons why)

Date

Name/position of those involved in discussion

Checklist for issues to be discussed during initial discussion

- Background information/presentation of the sudden unexpected death including details of any explanations given by parents/carers to ambulance, hospital or police staff.
- Background information of the child, family & significant others to check if the child and or siblings are known to children's social care or subject to a child protection plan.
- Consideration of safeguarding issues of surviving children.
- Outstanding/ Immediate child protection issues.
- Nature of suspicions.
- Consider what other records should be reviewed (e.g. adult health records for persons living/visiting the home). Police to obtain consent if individuals refuse.
- Consideration of requesting blood and urine samples from parents/carers to indicate any level of intoxication or drug use.
- Scene Management (including advising on taking items for further examination and imaging requirements).
- Appropriateness of joint home visit by police and SUDC paediatrician and need for interpreter.
- Contact with the coroner.
- Timing of post mortem and briefing of pathologist.
- Restrictions on viewing body.
- Significant police action taken or proposed (e.g. arrest of suspect, obtaining statements).
- Immediate support of the bereaved (e.g. allocation of Family Liaison Officer (FLO) or named point of contact).
- Co-ordination of professional's contact with the family including the paediatrician meeting with the family. This may be appropriately done jointly with police.
- Agreed point of contact with mortuary and bereavement staff/access of family to deceased.
- Status of the enquiry/ investigation (criminal/Section 47).
- Time and date of review case discussion meeting.
- Staff welfare.

The SUDC paediatrician will summarise the discussion and distribute the actions and timescales to the relevant individuals.

Further information from:

Health visitor/School nurse/community records

Hospital records (hospital number)

Further information from:

GP records

(include relevant parental information, siblings and other significant others in household)

Midwife/NHS Direct if relevant

12. Further information from:

Social Services

Police

Review case discussion following completion of information gathering:

Date   Time

Name/position of those involved in discussion

Has a written summary of the review case discussion been completed?

Y/N

Has the coroner agreed to a meeting with the family to explain the outcome of the case discussion?

Y/N

13. Audit for Rapid Response

To be completed for each unexpected child death

1.	Date of Death:	/ /			
	Age of Child:	y m	d	Age not known ☐	
2.	**Who notified the rapid response team of the death?** (Please tick all that apply)				
	Ambulance Control		☐	Hospital Emergency Dept	☐
	Not notified		☐	Not known	☐
		Other (please specify)			
3.	**How soon after discovery of the death was the child notified to the team?**				
	Within 2 hours		☐	Within 24 hours	☐
	Next working day		☐	Not known	☐
		Later (please specify)			
4.	**Was an initial history taken in hospital, if so by whom?** (tick all that apply)				
	Paediatrician		☐	Emergency Dept Doctor	☐
	Police Officer		☐	No history taken	☐
	Not known		☐		
		Other (please specify)			
5.	**Was the child examined in hospital, if so by whom?** (tick all that apply)				
	Paediatrician		☐	Child not examined	☐
	Emergency Dept Doctor		☐	Not known	☐
	Police Officer		☐		
		Other (please specify)			
6.	**Were appropriate laboratory investigations carried out?**				
	All investigations according to local protocol		☐	Not appropriate	☐
	Some investigations		☐	Not known	☐
	No investigations		☐		
7.	**Were the parents offered the following care and support?** (tick all that apply)				
	Allowed to hold their child		☐	Offered written information	☐
	Offered photographs and mementos		☐	Given contact numbers	☐
	Offered bereavement counselling or religious support		☐	Informed about the post-mortem	☐
	Given information about the rapid response process		☐	Not appropriate	☐
	Not known		☐		

8.	**Was an early multi-agency information sharing and planning meeting held, if so when was this held?** (tick all that apply)				
	Yes—telephone discussions	☐	Same day	☐	
	Yes—sit down meeting	☐	Later (please specify)		
	No	☐	Not known	☐	
9.	**Did a joint agency home visit take place?**				
	Yes	☐	Not appropriate	☐	
	No	☐	Not known	☐	
	If so, when did this take place?				
	Same day	☐	Later (please specify)		
	Next working day	☐	Not known	☐	
	Who took part in the home visit? (tick all that apply)				
	General paediatrician	☐	General practitioner	☐	
	SUDI paediatrician	☐	Health visitor/ midwife	☐	
	Police officer (Child Abuse Investigation Unit)	☐	Bereavement support worker	☐	
	Police officer (other)	☐	Social worker	☐	
	Scenes of crime/forensic officer	☐	Not known	☐	
10.	**Was an autopsy carried out? If so by whom?** (tick all that apply)				
	Yes	☐	No	☐	
	General hospital pathologist	☐	Paediatric pathologist	☐	
	Forensic pathologist	☐	Not known	☐	
	Other (please specify)				
	If so, when did this take place?				
	Same day	☐	Later (please specify)		
	Next working day	☐	Not known	☐	
11.	**Was there a final case discussion?**				
	Yes	☐	Not yet, but planned	☐	
	No	☐	Not known	☐	
	How long after the death did this take place?				
	Within 2 months	☐	Later (please specify)		
	2–4 months	☐	Not known	☐	

	If an inquest was held/planned, did the final case discussion precede or follow the inquest?			
	Preceded the inquest	☐	Followed the inquest	☐
	No inquest held	☐	Not known	☐
	Who attended the final case discussion? (tick all that apply)			
	General paediatrician	☐	General practitioner	☐
	SUDI paediatrician	☐	Health visitor/ midwife	☐
	Police officer (Child Abuse Investigation Unit)	☐	Bereavement support worker	☐
	Police officer (other)	☐	Social worker	☐
	Scenes of crime/forensic officer	☐	Not known	☐
	Other (please specify)			
	Were the family informed of the outcome of the final case discussion?			
	Yes – through a home visit	☐	Yes—by letter	☐
	Yes – by telephone	☐	Yes—other	☐
	No	☐	Not known	☐
12.	**What was the final cause of death?**			
	Death from natural causes	☐	SIDS	☐
	Accident	☐	Homicide	☐
	Suicide	☐	Cause of death not established	☐
	Not known	☐		
	Other (please specify)			
13.	**Were any concerns of a child protection nature identified?**			
	Yes	☐	No	☐
	Not known	☐		
14.	**Was the case referred on to the CPS for a criminal investigation?**			
	Yes	☐	No	☐
	Not known	☐		

14. Timesheet for

Completed by

Initial call out

Appendix B
MPS Project Indigo History Template

Within the MPS boroughs all SUDI/SUDC (under 2 years) are dealt with by the respective borough's child abuse investigation teams under the responsibility of a detective inspector. To ensure that there is consistency of approach, and to enable collation and comparison of details to assist in the CDOP-related processes, a single form template (Form 90) is utilized. This is an electronic form with drop down menus; in the copy below the details showing may be option 1 in the respective drop down menu—the other options will only be visible on the electronic version. This form when completed can also be used as a briefing document for the pathologist and as a report for the coroner.

Form 90

Original Notes of	Please Enter Your Name	Exhibit No.	Enter Exhibit Ref
Signature			

Investigation Details			
SIO/OIC	Please Enter Name	Contact No.	Telephone Number
SCD5 SPOC	Please Entre Name	Contact No.	Telephone Number
CRIS No.	CRIS Ref	Classification	CRIS Classification
Merlin No.	Merlin Ref	CAD No.	CAD Number
Form 91 Sent?	No	CDOP Ref No.	CDOP Ref
Location Details			
Date of Death	DD/MM/YYYY	Date of Report	DD/MM/YYYY
Location of child prior to hospital		Location Details	
Hospital child seen at		Hospital Name	
Time of Incident	00:00	Time of Death	00:00
CAIT	CAIT Name or Code	BOCU	ZZ
Professional Details			
Paediatrician	Full Name	Contact Number	Telephone Number
Did Paediatrician attend the home visit?		No	

Coroner's Officer	Full Name		Contact Number	Telephone Number
Coroner's E-Mail	Work E-mail Address		Fax Number	Fax Number
Coroner's Reference Number		Reference Number		

Child's and Home Details				
Child's Forenames				
Child's Family Name				
Date of Birth	DD/MM/YYYY		Gender	Please Enter
Nationality			Ethnicity	A1 Asian—Indian
Place of Birth				
Fostered/Adopted?				
Home Address				
Post Code				
Carer's Details				
Primary Carer's Name			Role	Please Enter
Telephone Number			E-Mail	
Mobile Number				
Preferred Method of Contact?				
Mother's Details				
Mother's Forenames				
Mother's Family Name				
Mother's Maiden Name				
Date of Birth	DD/MM/YYYY		Mother's Age	
Place of Birth			Nationality	
Self Defined Ethnicity	A1 Asian—Indian			
1st Language				
If English is not the first language, do they understand English?			Yes	
Religion/Culture				
Occupation				
Is the Mother a Single Parent?	No		Relationship with Partner	Please Enter
Actively involved in raising the child?	Yes			

Smoking, Alcohol, Drugs Use	Smoking	No
Further details to be provided in 'Issues of Note'	Alcohol	No
	Drugs	No
Contact Number (if different from above)		

Father's/Partner's Details				
Partner's Forenames				
Partner's Family Name				
Partner's Maiden Name				
Date of Birth	DD/MM/YYYY	Partner's Age		
Place of Birth		Nationality		
Self Defined Ethnicity	A1 Asian—Indian			
1st Language:				
If English is not the first language, do they understand English?			Yes	
Religion/Culture				
Occupation				
Actively involved in raising the child?	Yes	Relationship with Partner		Married
Is the Father/Partner a single parent?	No			
Smoking, Alcohol, Drugs Use	Smoking	No		
Further details to be provided in 'Issues of Note'	Alcohol	No		
	Drugs	No		
Contact Number (if different from above)				

Other Substantive Carers Details			
Carer's Forenames			
Carer's Family Name			
Date of Birth	DD/MM/YYYY	Carer's Age	
Place of Birth		Nationality	
Self Defined Ethnicity	A1 Asian - Indian		
1st Language			
If English is not the first language, do they understand English?		Yes	
Religion/Culture			
Occupation			
Actively involved in raising the child?	Yes	Relationship with Parents	

Smoking, Alcohol, Drugs Use	Smoking	No
Further details to be provided in 'Issues of Note'	Alcohol	No
	Drugs	No
Contact Number (if Different from Above)		

Results of Police Checks (PNC)		
Father		
Mother		
Others		
Others		

Previous Deaths of Children in the Family			
Have there been other child deaths in the family?	No	*Further details to be provided in Issues of Note*	
Siblings Details			
Forenames			
Family Name			
Age		Date of Birth	DD/MM/ YYYY
Gender	Please Select	Relationship	Full
Health Issues			
Forenames			
Family Name			
Age		Date of Birth	DD/MM/ YYYY
Gender	Please Select	Relationship	Full
Health Issues			
Forenames			
Family Name			
Age		Date of Birth	DD/MM/ YYYY
Gender	Please Select	Relationship	Full
Health Issues			

Health Details					
Single or Multiple Birth		Single	IVF?	No	
Was child born after full term pregnancy?		Yes	No. of Weeks' Gestation		Weeks (0–43)
A Natural Birth?		Yes	Weight at Birth		
Assisted Birth?	Yes	Assistance Required	None		
Was child discharged with mother?	Yes		If no, after how many days?		
Reason for delay in discharge					
Did the child make good progress?	Yes				
Did child attend clinic?	Yes		Name of Clinic		
Date of last attendance					
Name of GP			GP Surgery		
Red Book seen?	N/A	Up to date?	N/A		

Injections	
2 months—Pneumococcal Infection (PCV)	Yes
3 months—DtaP/IPV/Hib	Yes
3 months—Meningitis C (MenC)	Yes
4 months—DtaP/IPV/Hib	Yes
4 months—MenC	Yes
4 months—PCV	Yes
12 months—Hib/MenC	Yes
13 months—Measles, Mumps & Rubella (MMR)	Yes
13 months—PCV	Yes

Illness	
Major illness from birth	
Minor illness from birth	
Allergies	
Child unwell in the last 24 hours	
Recent illness of household members	
Any recent accidents with child	
Child's Medication	

Other Household Members' Medications	
Mother's Medication	
Father's/Partner's Medication	
Sibling's Medication	
Other	

Feeding Details			
Breast or Bottle Fed?	Breast	If bottle, what formula?	
Time of last feed			
Does the child normally settle afterwards?	Yes	Did they settle after the last feed?	Yes

Sleeping Details		
Where does the child normally sleep ?	Own Bedroom	If Other
What does the child sleep in?	Moses Basket	If Other
How do you normally put the child to sleep?	On Back	
Does the child normally have a dummy?	Yes	
Was last sleep day time or night time?	Day Time	
In what was the child found deceased (bed)?	Moses Basket	
Which room was the child found in?	Own Bedroom	
Was the child co-sleeping?	No	
Reason for Co-Sleeping		
Who was the child co-sleeping with?		
What position was the child in relation to the co-sleeper?		
What position was the child put to sleep in?	On Back	
What position was the child found in?		
Was a pillow present (child's/adult's)?	No	
Age of mattress		
Bed coverings used		
Was a dummy used?	No	
Extreme temperature where the child slept	Recorded Temperature	
Had parent(s) consumed alcohol/drug/smoked prior to last sleep?	No	
Details of consumption		
Additional Sleeping Details		
Who normally puts the child to bed?		
Who put the child to bed for the last sleep?		
What time was the child last checked on?	00:00	
Any change to the sleeping routine?		
Was the child crying more than usual?	No	If Yes, why?
Any significant changes in routine?		
Any potential obstruction of child's airway?		
Other Household Details		
Any household pets?	Yes	
If Yes, please give further details		

Hospital			
Name of examining paediatrician		Contact No.	
Place of examination			
Time of examination	00:00		
General appearance of child			

Visual Examination	
Resuscitation Equipment Used:	
Resuscitation Marks:	
Head/Face Injuries	
Bone Injuries:	
Cuts:	
Bruises:	
Grazes:	
Abnormalities:	

If any marks are found please complete a body chart—This <u>must</u> be signed by the SIO and the paediatrician

Does the child have any signs of NAI or possible neglect?	No
If Yes, details	

Samples taken at Hospital			
Blood	Yes		
Cerebrospinal Fluid	Yes		
Nasopharyngeal Aspirate	Yes		
Swab – Lesions	Yes		
Swab – Throat	Yes		
Urine	Yes		
Other	Yes	Details	

Medication Notes	
Any medication taken from home address?	Yes
Details	
Description of any issued medical equipment at home address	
Equipment left at scene	N/A
Where is the equipment now?	

257

Additional Information and Circumstances
Summary of events and time scale prior to police involvement
Will self expand
Police Action
Issues of Note
Conclusion
Details of previous contact with Social Services/Care

Body Chart Front

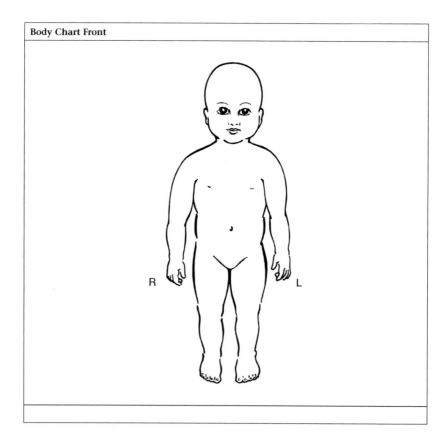

R   L

SIO Name:	
SIO Signature:	
Paediatrician's Name:	
Paediatrician's Signature:	

Body Chart Back

SIO Name:	
SIO Signature:	
Paediatrician's Name:	
Paediatrician's Signature:	

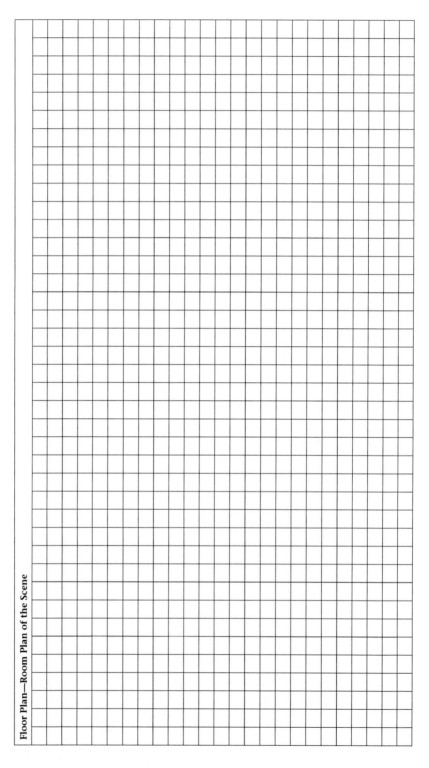

Floor Plan—Room Plan of the Scene

SUDI Daily Bulletin Briefing Note	
CRIS Ref.	
Name of Child	
Name of Child	
Date of Birth	
Is the child on/has been subject of a protection plan? Details if known	
Any relevant previous family history with police/other agencies?	
Brief circumstances of incident	
Any Risks identified?	
CAIT dealing	
Officer(s) in case	
Contact number for OIC	
Name of On call Superintendent informed	

Appendix C
Specimen House to House Questionnaire

Due to the sensitive nature of child deaths and the impact local enquiries may have in the community and in relation to the family of the deceased child great care is required when conducting local enquiries, particularly in the phrasing of questions. This is an example of a questionnaire template used in the MPS.

H......../......../.......

Localized Enquiries Questionnaire

Name .... DOB......./..../......
Place of birth ....

Description: Ethnic App: .... Height .... Occupation ....

Further description: .... (Accent) ....
Address..
....

Home Tel No..
Mobile ....Work...

Date   Time
....

I am a police officer who is part of a team currently investigating the circumstances surrounding the death of a baby. When a child dies suddenly and unexpectedly we have to find out as much as possible about the child to help determine why they died. We routinely speak to people who knew the child and the family, including neighbours to find out if they have any information that may be able to help us. The (incident that is related to the death/or the death) is believed to have happened at (Address of incident/death)

1. Were you aware of any incident at (Address of incident/death) ?
....
....

2. Do you know the people that live there? Do you know their names?

....

....

3. A baby that lived at the address has died. Do you have any information that can assist police?

....

....

4. Do you recall hearing anything from/seeing anything of the residents of this address during the last 2 or 3 weeks (or other relevant time period)?

....

....

5. Did you see or hear anything that gave you cause for concern regarding the child/children at (Address)?

....

....

6. Were you aware that the (lady/man/family) had a young baby and when did you last see that child?

....

....

7. As far as you are aware are there any other people that lived or visited the home?

....

....

8. Have you ever heard or seen anything that gave you cause for concern regarding the family?

....

....

9. How would you describe the (lady/man/family) at (Address) and (her/his/their) relationship towards (her/his/their) child?

....

....

10. Do you have any other information, which you feel may be relevant to our investigation, particularly with regards to (Date) and the (relevant time period eg morning of (Date) however small you may feel it to be?

....

....

Occupancy Details:

This House: Males .... Females .... Children u /14 ....

Either side: Number .... Males .... Females .... Children u/14 ....

        Number .... Males .... Females .... Children u/14.........

Officer Completing: ....Sign ....Date........

Signed (subject)...

Comments..
....

Supervision:
H/H Control.... Action? Yes ☐ No ☐   Signed .... OICharge

Incident Room .... Action No: ....   Checked .... Office Manager

Appendix D
Sample Form 76

These are collated on a national basis for the reasons detailed in the template's heading. This is an electronic form with drop down menus for different options when answering certain questions.

	Form 76

Child Homicide and Suspicious Death* Key Features Summary Sheet to assist analysis and inform future prevention and detection initiatives in relation to the incidence and nature of these deaths

* 'Suspicious Death' – where insufficient evidence for homicide classification but where death accompanied by suspected non-accidental injuries, e.g. fractures or wilful neglect

General Details

Crime Ref.:	Operation Name:	HOLMES Ref.:
SIO:		Force Dealing:
Contact Details:		
Offence charged with (if any):		
Day:	Date:	Time:

Venue Details (location of victim when death reported to police – if at hospital, location immediately prior to admission or location where fatal injury occurred, if known)

Location (e.g. hospital, home address):

OCU/BCU:

Condition of premises (if relevant):

Circumstance of Death

Brief summary of circumstances:

Cause of Death (official C.O.D. as it appears on the death certificate if available):

Any additional injuries:

Victim Details (under 18 years)			
Sex:	Age (in months if <2): yrs mths	Ethnicity Code:	Nationality:

Other victim information (check as appropriate and elaborate in space provided after check boxes):

Subject to Child Protection Plan	Yes ☐ No ☐ Unknown ☐	
Known to Children's Social Care	Yes ☐ No ☐ Unknown ☐	
Victim has disability	Yes ☐ No ☐ Unknown ☐	
Pre-existing medical condition	Yes ☐ No ☐ Unknown ☐	
Death of another sibling (show cause if known)	Yes ☐ No ☐ Unknown ☐	
Atypical hospital visits	Yes ☐ No ☐ Unknown ☐	
Drugs present, e.g. in hair	Yes ☐ No ☐ Unknown ☐	
Dead longer than stated	Yes ☐ No ☐ Unknown ☐	
Atypical bruises or petechiae	Yes ☐ No ☐ Unknown ☐	
Blood on face (not pinkish mucus regularly found)	Yes ☐ No ☐ Unknown ☐	
Foreign body in airway	Yes ☐ No ☐ Unknown ☐	
Fractures	Yes ☐ No ☐ Unknown ☐	
RADI (rotational acceleration deceleration impact injuries)	Yes ☐ No ☐ Unknown ☐	
Sibling subject to child protection plan (current or previous)	Yes ☐ No ☐ Unknown ☐	

Any other relevant information:

Suspect Details

Sex:	Age:	Ethnicity Code:	Nationality:	Place of Birth:
Immigration Status:		PNC/CRO:	Relationship to Victim:	

Other children in case (if any and relationship):

Other information (check as appropriate and elaborate in space provided):

Drug use	Yes ☐ No ☐ Unknown ☐	
Alcohol use	Yes ☐ No ☐ Unknown ☐	
Domestic violence	Yes ☐ No ☐ Unknown ☐	
Mental health issues	Yes ☐ No ☐ Unknown ☐	

Suicide attempt	Yes ☐ No ☐ Unknown ☐	
History of violence to children	Yes ☐ No ☐ Unknown ☐	
Criminal record	Yes ☐ No ☐ Unknown ☐	
Inconsistent account	Yes ☐ No ☐ Unknown ☐	
Suspect admissions/explanations:		
Any other relevant information:		
Court/Coroner's Verdict		
Court Result:		
Coroner's Verdict:		
Any other relevant information:		
Key Issues for Investigation		
Lessons Learned		
All Medical or Other Experts Utilised		
Title:	Name:	
Establishment/Organisation:		
Area of expertise:		
Any other relevant information:		

Appendix E
Generic Family Liaison Strategy

This is a generic Family Liaison Strategy that is adaptable on a case-by-case basis. Some sections may not be applicable to all cases and in some cases additional strategies may have to be included—this is a template that contains a framework which has been found useful in investigations by the Metropolitan Police Service.

Family Liaison Strategy Operation xxxxxxxxxxx

AIM

To facilitate the police investigation into the circumstances leading to the death/ serious potential life threatening injuries sustained by xxxxxxxxxxx.

This will be achieved by:

(i) ensuring that the family are considered as partners in the investigation; and
(ii) establishing and maintaining a sensitive, supportive, and appropriate relationship with the family and extended family.

The Family Liaison Officers will be open and honest with the family within the parameters of this strategy.

OBJECTIVES

- To endeavour to provide care, support, and information in a sensitive and compassionate manner which is appropriate to the needs of the family.
- To gather evidence and information from the family in a manner which contributes to the investigation and preserves its integrity.
- To document any request made by the family. Such requests will be forwarded for consideration by the SIO.
- To act as a conduit between the family and the SIO/IO and investigation team.

THE FAMILY

For the purposes of this strategy the family and extended family are:
    (1) (mother)
    (2) (father)
    (3) (grandfather)
    (4) (grandmother)

(5) (grandfather)

(6) (These are just a sample of persons for whom it may be relevant to include as family for the purposes of the FLO strategy.)

STRATEGY

(1) The FLO will be open and honest at all times with all members of the family. HOWEVER, WHERE THE SIO CONSIDERS THAT THE GIVING OF PARTI-CULAR INFORMATION MAY BE LIKELY TO COMPROMISE THE INTEGRITY OF THE INVESTIGATION, THE FAMILY WILL NOT BE PROVIDED WITH SUCH INFORMATION AT THAT TIME.

(2) Family members will not be given the expectation that any information they provide will be given in confidence. The nature of the FLO role precludes this approach.

(3) The FLO will set and maintain clear boundaries with the family and extended family. Telephone numbers and times of contact will be set by the FLO—usually within office hours and only outside these in extraordinary circumstances.

(4) The IO/FLC will maintain contact with the FLO and ensure regular debriefs and support.

(5) There will be a deputy/second FLO to support the FLO, providing continuity and cover for them when unavailable.

(6) All contact with the family will be recorded in a FLO log that will be regularly supervised by the IO/FLC.

(7) If parent(s) are charged with an offence contact will be through the respective solicitor or grandparent if appropriate. If on bail all contact will be recorded as normal in the FLO log but any meeting will be subject to the appropriate authorities and conditions regarding meeting/contacting persons who are on bail to ensure the integrity of the investigation.

(8) In line with Decision xx (SIO LOG) to comply with integrity/accuracy of any comments made and H & S considerations there will always be 2 officers present for all meetings. Ideally this will be FLO and Deputy/second FLO.

Agreed by SIO and IO

SIO _____

IO _____

Date and Time_____

FLO _____

FLO _____

Appendix F

Current Recommended UK Autopsy Protocol for SUDI (from the Kennedy Guidelines (2004), Appendix III)

(GOSH = Great Ormond Street Hospital for Children; adapted from Weber and Sebire, 2009)

	Autopsy Protocol (adapted from the Kennedy Guidelines (2004))	Comments and Evidence
Clinical History	A precise account of the circumstances of death, including: • A detailed account of the sleeping arrangements (sleeping position, found in cot or co-sleeping on bed or sofa, risk factors associated with co-sleeping such as parental smoking, alcohol consumption and drug use). • Details about the child's clothing, the bedding used, and ambient room temperature. A detailed past medical history, including: • Details of the pregnancy and delivery. • Postnatal and antemortem history, detailing previous hospital admissions, previous apparent life-threatening events, recent and / or chronic medication, and health in last few days before death. A detailed family history, including: • Previous deaths of siblings. • Parental consanguinity. • Parental smoking, and drug and alcohol use. • Whether the family is known to social services A short reference to the resuscitation procedures employed by paramedics and / or A&E staff in hospital. A brief description of the examination in hospital by a consultant paediatrician. Records of any investigations performed in A&E and the results of these.	It is worth noting that there is currently no evidence to suggest that microbiological samples taken in A&E are better than those collected at post-mortem examination.

	If there are any clinical features that might suggest inflicted injury, sexual abuse or neglect, a joint post-mortem examination must be carried out with a forensic pathologist.	
Radiology	A full skeletal survey reported by a paediatric radiologist. If there are any fractures on skeletal survey, a joint post-mortem examination must be carried out with a forensic pathologist.	Fresh rib fractures are often missed on skeletal survey; careful inspection of the ribs is the best way to detect these, but the majority of fresh fractures are likely to be related to CPR if distributed anteriorly (Weber et al, 2009a).
External Examination	Careful inspection for signs of inflicted injury (eg bruises not explained by the clinical history, torn upper labial frenulum), sexual abuse (eg vaginal laceration) or physical neglect (eg dirty, unwashed, malnourished). Presence of petechiae on face, conjunctivae or oral mucosa, and presence or blood around nose and mouth. If there are features that might suggest abuse, a joint post-mortem examination must be carried out with a forensic pathologist. Document body weight, length and head circumference (compare to growth charts), presence of dysmorphism, and other relevant abnormalities. Consider use of photography to document important findings.	
Macroscopic Examination	Careful systematic inspection and prosection of all internal organs. Weights of all major organs. If the clinical history and pathological findings require a particular organ to be retained for further assessment, this should be discussed with the Coroner's officer and the appropriate authority obtained. In cases with no clinical evidence or macroscopic autopsy findings to explain death, it is strongly recommended that the brain is examined only after adequate fixation for one to two weeks. Note that the retention of organs may delay the funeral if parents wish that the organ(s) be retuned to the body after fixation and sampling. If head injury is suspected, the brain, spinal cord and eyes must be retained for specialist neuropathological examination (as part of a joint post-mortem examination with a forensic pathologist).	Organ weights are usually poor predictors of significant underlying pathology (eg heart weight is a poor screening test for the detection of myocarditis at autopsy and are likely to be diagnostically important in selected cases only (eg cardiomyopathy, adrenal gland hypoplasia, cerebral oedema), but the evidence is sparse. It is also worth noting that the weight charts used are often based on diverse and / or antiquated reference populations, making direct comparisons difficult. Note that there is currently no reliable evidence that organ weights / weight ratios will help differentiate between explained SUDI and unexplained SUDI / SIDS in individual cases.

		There is no published evidence that examination of the brain following adequate formalin fixation is better than examination and histological sampling of the unfixed brain during the initial post-mortem examination for the purposes of establishing a cause of death for the Coroner in cases with no past neurological history, and no features suspicious of abuse. There is a large volume of literature reporting on neuropathological findings in SUDI, much of which relates to subtle abnormalities of the brainstem, such as hypoplasia of brainstem nuclei and serotonergic aberrations, their detection of which are likely to require detailed examination of the brain by a specialist paediatric neuropathologist after formalin fixation. Whilst these abnormalities may be relevant to the pathogenesis of death in at least a subset of SUDI, their significance at present for the determination of cause of death remains unclear and further research is required.
Histology	Minimum blocks for histological examination: • Five lobes of lung (H&E, and Perls' method for haemosiderin). • Heart (free wall of left and right ventricle, and interventricular septum). • Thymus. • Pancreas. • Liver. • Spleen. • Lymph node. • Adrenal glands. • Kidneys. • Costochondral junction of a rib to include bone marrow sample. • Muscle. • Blocks of any macroscopic lesion, including fractured ribs. • Brain—four to six blocks, including cerebral hemisphere, brainstem, cerebellum, meninges and spinal cord; include dura if there is haemorrhage.	Histological examination is the single most useful investigation in the determination of a cause of death in SUDI (Fleming et al, 2000; Weber et al, 2008). However, there is no evidence base relating to 1) the macroscopic-microscopic correlation for different organs in SUDI, 2) which organs should routinely be sampled for histology, especially if macroscopically normal, to determine cause of death, and 3) how many samples should be taken from each organ for optimal diagnostic yield. There is much variation in the interpretation of pathological changes; for example, some pathologists may deem the presence of a focal pneumonia, in the absence of any other pathology, to be sufficient as cause of death, while others may argue that such a focal process is likely to have merely contributed to death,

		categorising such a death as unexplained in the absence of any other pathology. There is at present no standardised approach to such discrepancies. It is recommended that a Perls' stain is used for each lung section; the prevalence of intra-alveolar haemosiderin-laden macrophages (HLMs) is around tenfold greater in infants with other features of inflicted injury, even in cases without rib fractures. Therefore, although the majority of infant deaths in whom HLMs are found will be non-suspicious deaths, the presence of intra-alveolar HLMs should prompt a thorough search for other features of inflicted injury, and, if severe, such deaths may best be classified as 'unascertained' rather than unexplained SUDI / SIDS (Weber at al, 2009b).
Other Ancillary Investigations	If not already taken in the A&E department.	It has been our experience at GOSH that there is much variation about which samples, if any, are collected in A&E; moreover, pathologists are rarely informed about which investigations are performed or about their results. In addition, data remain lacking to demonstrate the superiority of taking samples in A&E to determine cause of death, particularly for the detection of infection.
Bacteriology	Blood, cerebrospinal fluid, respiratory tract, and any infective lesion.	At GOSH, we routinely sample the spleen as well, although the evidence-base for this is lacking. Interpretation of positive findings is difficult because of potential issues of contamination, post-mortem translocation and overgrowth, as well as possible agonal spread. Further research is required to distinguish cases in which the post-mortem isolates represent mere contaminants or 'post-mortem artefacts' from those with true infection. Sterile sampling technique is recommended to minimise the risk of contamination.

		Note that the mere presence of toxigenic bacteria, including toxigenic strains of Staphylococcus aureus, does not necessarily imply cause of death; a proportion of healthy infants will carry such toxigenic strains and its presence on post-mortem culture must be interpreted in the overall context of the case.
Virology	Post-nasal swabs or nasopharyngeal aspirate, lung, cerebrospinal fluid and faeces if indicated. Consider agreeing protocols with local medical microbiology departments to use PCR for organism recognition.	At GOSH, we routinely sample lung only, with heart and faeces if clinically indicated, but this, too, is not evidence-based. Interpretation of positive findings remains difficult, particularly in the absence of histological evidence of active infection. There is currently no evidence base as to which viruses to routinely test for and which tissue or fluid sample(s) to take for virological analysis. PCR is considered the more sensitive technique for virus detection, but the role of PCR over immunofluorescence in this context remains undetermined. That said, there is no evidence to support the ongoing use of immunofluorescence of post-mortem lung tissue (Weber et al, 2010).
Metabolic and Biochemical Investigations	Frozen section of liver, kidney, and skeletal and cardiac muscle, stained with Oil Red O for fat (mandatory in all unexplained unexpected infant deaths). Blood and bile spots on Guthrie cards for acylcarnitine analysis by tandem mass spectrometry if metabolic disease is suspected or if fat stains on frozen section are positive. Consider skin sample for fibroblast culture for enzyme assays. Urine, if present, for metabolic investigations.	The sensitivity and specificity of frozen section as a screening test for fatty acid oxidation defects remains undetermined.
Toxicology	Consider toxicology (peripheral / femoral blood, whole blood preserved in sodium fluoride bottle, urine, sample of liver, stomach contents, vitreous humour); request an illicit drug / alcohol screen, and specify other drugs as indicated from the history.	There is no doubt that toxicological analysis may reveal a cause of death in a small proportion of cases but its role in unselected SUDI cases remains undetermined.

Other		There is increasing evidence that cardiac channelopathies, in particular long-QT syndrome, may be associated with unexplained SUDI/SIDS. Furthermore, it has been suggested that a number of single nucleotide polymorphisms (SNPs) of immunoregulatory genes may be more likely to induce a 'cytokine storm' and sudden death with exposure to bacterial infection / bacterial toxins. However, at present, mutation analysis or testing for specific SNPs is not performed in the UK for diagnostic purposes, and further research is required.
Clinico-pathological Correlation	Summarise the clinical history, including risk factors for SUDI, and the main pathological findings, and, on the balance of probability: • Consider whether the death is attributable to a natural disease process. • Consider the possibility of accidental death (eg trauma, poisoning, scalding, drowning, accidental suffocation). • Consider the possibility of non-accidental injury or neglect (eg inflicted suffocation). • Identify features that may indicate a familial / genetic disease requiring screening and counseling of other family members. • Document the presence / absence of pathological processes that may contribute to the multidisciplinary clinicopathological evaluation of the death. If, in the light of initial post-mortem findings, there is no obvious or satisfactory natural cause of death, the initial 'cause' of death should be given to the Coroner as 'unexplained pending further investigation'. The final post-mortem report, including the details of all samples taken and the results of all further investigations, should be prepared and made available to the Coroner. The case will be discussed at the Local Safeguarding Children Board Child Death Overview Panel, and the pathologist should, if possible, attend and take part in these multiprofessional case discussion meetings.	

Appendix G
Medical Glossary

Abdomen—The part of the body cavity below the chest.

Acute—Of sudden or recent origin.

Acylcarnitine profiling—to test for fatty acid oxidation disorders, a form of metabolic disorder.

Adherent blood—Thrombosed blood stuck to a membrane, particularly the dural membrane covering the brain to form a subdural haematoma.

Anaemia—A deficiency of red cells in the blood or of haemoglobin, the red pigment in these cells is essential for the transport of oxygen.

Anaphylaxis—A state of shock, usually of sudden onset due to an allergic reaction.

Anatomical Pathology Technologist (APT)—A qualified person working in the mortuary who manages the day-to-day processes relating to all aspects of the mortuary service and assists the pathologist during post-mortem examinations.

Antepartum haemorrhage—Haemorrhage from the uterus before birth of a baby. There are a number of causes, particularly premature separation of the placenta (afterbirth) called placental abruption or *abruptio placentae*.

Anterior—Front.

Anterior fontanelle—A soft spot in the midline at the top of a baby's skull and towards the front where the bones of the skull have not yet fused together.

Anteroposterior—From front to back.

Anticonvulsant drugs—Drugs used in the treatment of seizures, particularly in epilepsy.

Apnoea—Cessation of breathing.

Apparent life threatening event (ALTE)—An episode in which an infant suddenly collapses unconscious and may require resuscitation. May be due to natural disease, such as congenital heart disease or seizure, but can also be due to airway obstruction that can be imposed. In about half the cases no cause is found.

Arachnoid mater—A delicate membrane covering the surface of the brain, beneath the dura.

Asphyxia—Lack of oxygen.

Autonomic regulation—This is the process of automatic regulation of many of the functions of internal organs by a network of nerves collectively described as the autonomic nervous system.

Autopsy—Examination of a body after death. Synonymous with post-mortem examination.

Axons—Long processes from nerve cells by which nervous impulses are passed from one nerve cell to another.

Bacterial toxins—Poisons produced by some bacterial organisms that can have sometimes serious or even fatal adverse consequences.

Bacteriological investigations—Various tests to identify bacteria and their products that may be important in identifying specific infective diseases.

Basal fractures—Skull fractures involving the base of the skull rather than the relatively thin curved bones forming the vault.

Bilateral—Both sides.

Bilateral retinal haemorrhages—Haemorrhages at the back of both eyes.

Bile—A green substance formed in the liver and stored in the gall-bladder. When released into the small intestine it has a role in the digestion of food as it passes from the stomach to the duodenum (first part of the intestine).

Biochemical processes—Complex chemical reactions involving particularly enzymes (biological catalysts) and proteins produced by cells in the body. They are responsible for all the biological processes by which life is sustained.

Bio-mechanical engineer—A scientist who studies the mechanics of movement and injuries caused by trauma.

Biopsy—A sample of tissue removed during life for examination to identify disease processes. This usually involves processing the tissue, embedding it in paraffin wax, and cutting very thin sections that are then stained and examined under a microscope. Other more sophisticated methods may also be applied to these tissue samples.

Bitemporal—Between the temporal bones on each side of the vault of the skull.

Blood culture—Culture of a blood sample in nutrient medium in which any disease-causing organisms can proliferate and be identified.

Bronchial swab—A pad of cotton wool on a stick that can be introduced to a bronchus to collect secretions that can then be cultured to identify any disease-causing organisms.

Buccal mucosa—The membrane lining the mouth.

Callus—Non-ossified tissue produced in the early phase of fracture healing.

Cardiac blood—Blood taken from the cavity of the heart.

Cardiac ion channelopathies—Genetic defects that can cause abnormal heart rhythms and which can result in sudden death.

Cardiovascular—Pertaining to the heart and blood vessels.

Carotid sheathes—The connective tissue surrounding the neck vessels.

Cerebellum—The back (posterior) part of the brain.

Cerebrospinal fluid—The fluid around the brain and spinal cord.

Cerebral hemispheres—The two halves that make up the main part of the brain.

Cerebral hypoxia—Reduction in the oxygen supply to the brain.

Cerebrovascular—Pertaining to the blood vessels supplying the brain.

Cervical—neck region.

Chromosomal disorder—Chromosomes are tiny bodies within cells that carry genetic material in the form of DNA. Abnormalities can cause diseases and malformations that can be hereditary.

Chronic—Continuing for a long time.

Clinical history—Information pertaining to the events and investigations leading to a diagnosis.

Clinicians—Those doctors looking after patients.

Clinicopathological correlation—The comparison and assessment of the clinical features and pathological findings to reach a more reliable diagnosis of a disease or injury.

Computed Tomography (CT)—A form of diagnostic imaging where a series of X-ray images representing slices through a body or an organ are taken for detailed study. The images can be converted by computer to provide an apparent three-dimensional composition.

Congestion—Engorgement of blood vessels.

Conjunctivae—The membrane covering the front of the eye and lining the eyelids.

Coronal slices—Parallel slices through an organ such as the brain.

Costochondral junctions—The joining points between the bony part of the rib and the cartilaginous part that attaches to the breast bone (sternum).

Cot death—Is the sudden and unexpected death of a baby for no obvious reason. The post-mortem examination may explain some deaths. Those that remain unexplained after post-mortem examination may be registered as Sudden Infant Death Syndrome (SIDS), Sudden Unexpected Death in Infancy (SUDI), or unascertained.

Cranial dura mater—A tough fibrous membrane lining the inside of the cranial cavity within the skull and covering the brain.

Cranial suture lines—The joining lines between individual skull bones. In babies and young children the skull bones are separated by narrow fibrous bridges (sutures) that gradually ossify and are obliterated as the child grows.

Cyanosis—Bluish discolouration of skin.

Cytogenetics—Chromosome analysis, also known as karyotyping.

Decalcified—The chemical removal of calcium salts responsible for the hardness of tissues such as bone. In preparing bone samples for histological sectioning, the tissue must be decalcified to allow very thin slices to be cut for microscopy.

Diagnostic imaging—Images using X-rays, CT (Computed Tomography) scans (see above), or MRI (Magnetic Resonance Imaging).

Differential diagnosis—Given a particular set of clinical and/or pathological findings there may be a number of possible diagnoses (the differential diagnosis). Often, by the application of further discriminatory investigations, a definitive diagnosis may be possible.

Diffuse—Extending throughout.

DNA markers—Specific sequences of DNA that may characterize a particular disease.

Duodenum—The first part of the small intestine between the stomach and the next part of the small intestine (the jejunum).

Dura mater—*See* Cranial dura mater above.

Dysmorphic features—Abnormal facial or other external appearances which may suggest an underlying chromosomal disorder.

Electron microscopy—By using a special instrument (the electron microscope) tissue can be examined using a stream of electrons of very short wavelength that allows much greater resolution than is possible with a light microscope. Even tiny sub cellular features can be studied with this technique.

Encephalopathy—Damage to the brain affecting function.

Endocrine—Pertaining to the endocrine glands that produce hormones.

Endotracheal tubes—breathing tubes that can be introduced into the trachea.

Engorgement—Stuffing a tissue with blood in distended (usually venous) blood vessels.

Epiphyses—The rounded end of a long bone. Beneath the epiphysis is the metaphysis which confusingly includes the growth plate, a band of active growth termed the epiphyseal plate. In adults, when growth has ceased, the epiphysal plates become completely ossified or fused.

Evisceration—Removal of the internal organs.

Exogenous stressors—Adverse factors from outside the body.

Femoral blood—Blood removed from the femoral veins. This is a better sample for toxicological analysis but it may be difficult to obtain a sufficient sample in a very young child.

Fetal—Before birth.

Fibroblast culture—This involves growing cells called fibroblasts in the skin, which can then be used for various enzyme tests.

Fissure—A thin indentation or a linear break in a membrane.

Forensic odontologist—An expert in the study of teeth in relation to various problems in forensic pathology, especially the identification of specific features of bite marks by which the biter can be identified.

Forensic pathologist—A pathologist skilled in identifying unnatural causes of death, injuries and their likely causes.

Formalin fixation—Hardening of tissues by placing them in a formalin fixative prior to their processing for histological sectioning.

Fossa—An anatomical hole or valley in an organ.

Fractures—Breaks in tissues, particularly bones.

Frenulum—A thin ridge of membrane. The term is most commonly used to describe the upper labial frenulum, a fold in the midline between the inside of the upper lip and the gum. Injury or rupture of this membrane is a characteristic non-accidental injury.

Frontoparietal suture—The suture line between the frontal and parietal skull bones.

Fundi—The back of the inside of the eye where the light-sensitive screen (the retina) on which images are focused by the lens is found.

Gastrointestinal—Pertaining to the stomach, intestines and related organs such as the liver and pancreas.

Gastro-oesophageal reflux—The junction between the gullet (oesophagus) and the stomach has a valve-like mechanism that usually prevents ingested material from returning to the oesophagus after it has entered the stomach. Defects in this valve may result in return of gastric content to the oesophagus.

Genetic disorders—Disease caused by a specific gene abnormality that may be hereditary.

Geneticists—Scientists expert in the study of inherited disease.

Genitalia—The sex organs.

Guthrie card—This is an absorbent card on which small spots of blood can be placed and allowed to dry. A Guthrie card is taken routinely from new-borns and the resulting blood spots can be used to make a wide variety of diagnoses by chemical or other analyses. Once dried, the cards are kept and can be used at any time. In paediatric autopsies, blood and bile spots on Guthrie cards can be analysed by mass spectroscopy for evidence of fatty acid oxidation abnormalities that are a rare cause of sudden death in young infants.

Haemorrhages—Bleeding.

Haematological—Pertaining to haematology, the study of blood and its disorders.

Haematoma—Blood clot.

Haematoxylin and Eosin (H&E)—A routine stain applied to histological sections to make structures visible under the microscope.

Haemosiderin-laden macrophages—are scavenger cells that have ingested red blood cells and converted the iron that is present in the haemoglobin into a substance called haemosiderin. This can be demonstrated in histological sections by applying Perls' stain that makes the haemosiderin an easily recognizable cobalt blue.

Histochemical—Pertaining to histochemistry. This usually implies the application of substrates on which enzymes in tissues can convert them to coloured products that can be recognized under the microscope. Deficiencies of the enzyme can be recognized by failure of this colour change to occur.

Histological—Pertaining to histology, the science of studying tissues at the microscopic level.

Histopathologist—A doctor expert in the diagnosis of diseases recognizable from often subtle abnormalities seen in histological sections examined under the microscope.

History—*See* Clinical history.

Homeostatic—Self-regulating.

Hypostasis—the gravitational pooling of blood in the soft tissues after death.

Hypothermia—Pathological lowering of body temperature.

Hypoxaemia—Decreased oxygen in the blood.

Hypoxia—Lack of oxygen.

Hypoxic damage—Damage due to lack of oxygen.

Immunohistochemical stains—The application of specific antibodies tagged with a visible marker to histological sections. If the particular antigen sought is present in the tissue, the applied antibody will attach to it and can be recognized by the presence of the visible marker.

Immunological—Pertaining to the science of immunology.

Intensivist—A doctor treating patients in intensive care.

Interhemispheric fissure—The gap between the two cerebral hemispheres.

Interocular distance—The distance between the inner ends of the eyelids.

Intracranial—Inside the skull cavity housing the brain.

Intracranial haemorrhage—Bleeding inside the skull cavity.

Intrapartum haemorrhage—Haemorrhage during the process of delivering a baby.

Intra-peritoneal haemorrhage—Bleeding in the cavity of the abdomen (the peritoneal cavity).

Intravenous catheters—Catheters placed within a vein.

Ischaemia—Insufficient supply of blood.

Jaundice—Yellow discolouration, particularly of the skin, by bile pigments. Often a sign of liver disease.

Kennedy Protocol for SUDI—A detailed methodology published in 2004 for investigating SUDI proposed by a Working Party chaired by Baroness Helena Kennedy. This was set up jointly by the Royal College of Pathologists and the Royal College of Paediatrics and Child Health in response to public concern raised over criminal cases involving sudden deaths in infants.

Kidneys—Organs on the posterior abdominal wall that filter the blood to produce urine, to remove waste products and maintain biochemical homeostasis.

Larynx—Voice box

Lesions—Any visible abnormality seen with the naked eye or under the microscope.

Liver—An organ on the right side of the abdomen involved in many vital metabolic processes. It is vulnerable to blunt force trauma applied to the abdomen.

Long QT syndrome—A rare form of cardiac arrhythmia (abnormal heart rhythm) that may be a cause of sudden death.

Lumbar puncture—A method to obtain a sample of cerebrospinal fluid (CSF) by introducing a needle between vertebrae in the lumbar spine below the lower end of the spinal cord.

Lumbar spine—The portion of the spinal column behind the abdomen, above the sacrum and below the thoracic spine, to which the ribs are attached.

Maceration—A change that occurs in the body of an unborn infant that dies in the womb. The most obvious change is a peeling of the skin exposing red underlying tissue. When seen at post-mortem it is an absolute sign that a baby is stillborn and has not had a separate existence.

Macroscopic—Visible to the naked eye.

Magnetic Resonance Imaging (MRI)—This involves placing in a machine that applies an intense magnetic field and radio waves to produce a very detailed, high resolution image, superior in most cases to that produced by CT scanning.

Mastoid-vertex-mastoid measurements—A measurement over the top of the skull from behind the ear on one side to behind the ear on the other side.

Medico legal autopsy—A term used both for examinations by pathologists performed for the coroner to establish the cause of death in a case reported to him or her, and for post-mortem examinations performed by a forensic pathologist at the request of the police under the direction of the coroner when the death is suspicious.

Meningeal swab—A swab taken at post-mortem from between the dura and arachnoid for bacterial culture to identify any possible disease-causing organisms.

Meninges—The delicate membranes covering the brain.

Meningitis—Infection of the coverings of the brain (meninges).

Mesentery—A delicate membrane by which the loops of intestine are suspended from the posterior abdominal wall.

Metabolic—Pertaining to the biochemical processes vital to keep an organism alive.

Metabolic disorder—Any abnormality of metabolism.

Metaphyseal fractures—A fracture of the metaphyseal portion of a long bone, usually at the epiphyseal growth plate. A characteristic non-accidental injury.

Microbiological material—Diagnostic samples taken for the identification of bacteria or viruses.

Microhaemorrhages—Small haemorrhages.

Mitochondrial disorder—A disorder that affects the biochemical processes inside the cells.

Munchausen syndrome by proxy—Fabricated or induced illness.

Myocarditis—Inflammation of the heart.

Naevi—Birthmarks.

Nasopharyngeal aspirate—Fluid removed from the back of the nose, usually for microbiological evaluation.

Neonatal—The first month of life (ie 28 days or less).

Neural arches—Posterior part of the vertebrae.

Neurological—Pertaining to the nervous system (brain, spinal cord, and associated nerves).

Neuropathologist—Pathologist who specializes in diseases of the brain and spinal cord.

Neuroradiologist—A radiologist who specializes in the examination of the central nervous system (brain and spinal cord), using X-rays, CT, and MRI scanning.

Neurosurgeon—A brain surgeon.

Non-ambulant—Not yet able to stand and walk unaided.

Occiput—Lower part of the back of the head.

Occult—Not obvious.

Oedema—Swelling of the soft tissues due to fluid retention.

Oedematous—Swollen with oedema fluid.

Omohyoid muscles—Strap muscles in the neck.

Ophthalmologist—A clinician expert in diseases and abnormalities of the eye.

Optic nerves—The big nerves that run from the eye to the brain.

Osteoarticular pathology—Pathology of bones and joints.

Paediatric—Of children.

Paediatric Pathologist—A pathologist specializing in disease of babies and young children.

Paediatric Radiologist—A radiologist specializing in imaging of babies and young children.

Pallor—Pale appearance, usually of the skin.

Palpebral fissures—The spaces between the upper and lower eyelids.

Parenchymal lesions—Abnormalities of the substance of an organ.

Parietal bones—Bones on each side of the vault of the skull.

Paroxysmal—Frequently episodic.

Pathogens—Organisms capable of causing disease.

Pathology—The study of disease processes.

Pathophysiology—Alteration from the normal metabolic processes occurring in disease states.

Patulous—Slack.

Perinatal—Around the time of birth, strictly up to <7 days of life, but often loosely applied to newborns in general.

Perineum—Area around the genitals and anus.

Periosteum—The tough fibrous covering closely applied to bones.

Peritoneal membrane—The membrane lining the peritoneal cavity within the abdomen as well as the individual abdominal organs.

Petechial haemorrhages—Pin-point haemorrhages that may be seen in the skin or in the membranes covering internal organs.

Physiological—Pertaining to normal metabolic processes.

Placenta—The afterbirth. This is a disc-shaped tissue closely applied to the inside of a mother's womb that regulates exchanges of substances between the mother's and the unborn child's circulating blood. At birth, delivery of the baby is followed by delivery of the placenta.

Pleural membranes—The membranes covering the lungs, the inside of the chest wall, and the diaphragm.

Pneumonia—Inflammation of the lungs, usually due to infection by a bacterium or virus, but occasionally due to inhalation of acid stomach content (chemical pneumonia).

Post-mortem—The examination of a body after death.

Postpartum haemorrhage—Bleeding after birth.

Posteriorly—At the back of.

Pulmonary haemorrhage—Haemorrhage from or into the lungs.

Radiology—The study of X-rays and other diagnostic imaging techniques.

Radiologist—A doctor specializing in diagnostic imaging.

Respiratory—Pertaining to the respiratory system (the lungs and airways including the nose, throat, windpipe (trachea), and bronchi).

Retinal haemorrhages—Bleeding into the retinae (the light-sensitive linings at the back of the eyes).

Retinae—*See* above.

Retroperitoneal haemorrhage—Haemorrhage behind the peritoneal lining of the abdominal cavity.

Rigor mortis—Stiffening of the muscles that occurs after death.

Sagittal sinus—A large vein that goes over the top of the brain on the underside of the skull.

Sagittal suture—A suture line between the two parietal bone in the midline of the vault of the skull.

Septicaemia—A diffuse infection in which infective organisms and their toxins are present in the blood stream.

Serotonergic pathways—Nerve pathways in the brain mediated by serotonin (a neurotransmitter substance).

Shaken baby syndrome (SBS)—A form of non-accidental head injury caused by violent acceleration/deceleration forces causing the brain to rotate back and forth within the skull. The description has been superseded by other less specific terms such as inflicted childhood head injury, because shaking is not the only circumstance in which this type of injury may occur. It is recognized pathologically by the presence of thin subdural haemorrhages, severe and extensive retinal haemorrhages, and brain swelling. Clinically, it occurs in young children, usually under six months, has a sudden onset, and almost always occurs in the presence of one person. In over half of affected babies, there is other evidence of non-accidental trauma outside the head.

Skeletal surveys (X-rays)—A complete and detailed radiological examination of the whole skeleton involving a number of different views to a protocol that would be used to identify any bony abnormality present. The same approach is used to examine post-mortem all babies dying suddenly and unexpectedly.

Space-occupying lesion (subdural haematoma)—Any pathological lesion occurring within the cranial cavity of sufficient volume to press on the brain and cause an increase in intracranial pressure. This may be a collection of blood in the subdural space (a so-called subdural haematoma).

Spiral fractures—A fracture of long bones caused by a twisting force.

Spleen—An organ on the right side of the body forming part of the lymphoid system. It is vulnerable to blunt force trauma to the abdomen to cause haemorrhage that may be slow and clinically inapparent until a significant loss of blood has occurred.

Sternohyoid, suprahyoid, sternomastoid, sternothyroid, muscles—These are all paired muscles on each side of the neck.

Subdural haematoma—A collection of blood in the subdural space often forming a space-occupying lesion.

Subdural haemorrhages—Bleeding beneath the dural membrane covering the brain.

Subdural space—The potential space between the dural and the arachnoid.

SUDC Paediatrician—A paediatrician specializing in the investigation of sudden death in childhood.

Sudden Unexpected Death in Infancy (SUDI) or Childhood (SUDC)—the death of an infant [under one year] or child (less than 18 years old) which was not anticipated as a significant possibility for example, 24 hours before the death; or where there was a similarly unexpected collapse or incident leading to or precipitating the events which led to the death.

Superficial abrasions—These are grazes or scratches involving only the superficial part of the skin and not penetrating the full thickness of the epidermis.

Superior orbital plates—The bony plates on top of the eyes.

Suprahyoid muscles—*See* Sternohyoid, etc, above.

Suture—A type of immovable joint.

Syndrome—An association of several recognizable symptoms, signs, or investigational results that together point to a particular disease process and possible diagnosis.

Systolic—The phase of the heart beat when the ventricles (the muscular lower chambers) contract to pump blood to the lungs and around the body.

Tentorium—A shelf of the dura within the cranial cavity that separates the cerebral from the cerebellar hemispheres.

Thoracic—Within the chest.

Thoracic pluck—A collection of organs including the heart and lungs taken out together as part of the routine procedure in a standard post-mortem examination.

Toxicology—The study of poisons and toxic substances.

Tracheal swab—A swab taken from the trachea, usually during a post-mortem examination, to obtain a sample for microbiological identification.

Transection—A cut right across a tissue or organ.

Transverse fracture—A fracture at right angles to the long axis of a bone.

Trauma—Injury caused by the application of force.

Vertex—Top of the head.

Virological—Pertaining to viruses.

Virology—The study of viruses.

Viscera—Internal organs.

Visceral—Pertaining to viscera.

Vitreous humour—The jelly-like substance within the eye.

Appendix H
Risk Factors for Suspicious Deaths

These factors if present may help in assessing whether or not a death is 'suspicious'.

Risk Factor	Present/Comment
History of violence to children	
Inconsistent accounts	
Mental ill health issues	
Previous atypical hospital visits	
History of alcohol abuse	
Child over 1 year old	
Child on child protection plan (now/previous)	
Known to Social Services/Children's Social Care	
History of drug abuse	
History of domestic abuse	
Criminal record	
RADI findings at PM	
Drugs present in deceased child	
Fractures	
Dead longer than stated	
Atypical bruises	
Also to be considered if relevant	
Sibling on child protection plan (now or previous)	
Previous sibling died	
Previous unexplained SUDI	
Time of death	
Circumstances of death	
Mode of death	
Blood on face	
Home environment/conditions	
Stressors, e.g. financial debt	
Family dynamics	
Interaction between parents	
Foreign body in upper airway	
Suicide attempt	
Comments made (verbal/text/written)	

Prior unusual or unexplained illnesses	
ALTE (apparent life threatening event)	
Signs of neglect, e.g. growth, hygiene	
Previous physical abuse	
Previous neglect	

Suspicious Death—'Although there is **no direct evidence** or grounds to suspect a specific criminal act there are however **factors** that raise the **possibility** that a **criminal act may** have **contributed to the death** and thereby merit a more detailed investigation of the circumstances of the death'.

References and Websites

A Local Authority v S [2009] EWHC 2115 (Fam) (8 May 2009).

Abortion Act 1967 (London: HMSO).

ACPO (2004), *Disclosure of Information in Family Proceedings (Police/Family Disclosure Protocol)* (London: Metropolitan Police).

ACPO (2006), *Murder Investigation Manual* (London: NPIA).

ACPO (2007), *Police/Family Protocol* (London: NPIA).

ACPO (2011), *National Decision Model* (London: NPIA).

ACPO Homicide Working Group (2011), *A Guide to Investigating Child Deaths* (London: NPIA).

ACPO Homicide Working Group (2011), *An SIO's Guide to Investigating Unexpected Death and Serious Untoward Harm in Healthcare Settings* (London: NPIA).

ACPO/ADSS/CPS (2003), *Protocol on the Exchange of Information in the Investigation and Prosecution of Child Abuse Cases* (London: CPS).

ACPO/NPIA (2008), *Family Liaison Officer Guidance* (London: NPIA).

ACPOS (2008), *Scottish Investigators' Guide to Sudden Unexpected Deaths in Infancy (SUDI)* (Glasgow: ACPOS).

Association of Anatomical Pathology Technology (AAPT), the recognized professional body for APTs employed in hospital and public mortuaries across the UK: <http://www.aaptuk.org>.

Attorney General's Reference (No. 3 of 1994) [1997] UKHL 31.

Bajanowski, T, Vege, A, Byard, RW, Krous, HF, Arnestad, M, Bachs, L et al. (2007), 'Sudden infant death syndrome (SIDS)—Standardised investigations and classification: Recommendations', *Forensic Science International*, 165, 129–143.

Batty, D (2003), 'Catalogue of cruelty', *Society Guardian*, 27 January. Available at <http://www.guardian.co.uk/society/2003/jan/27/childrensservices.childprotection>.

Batty, D (2007), 'Serial killer nurse Allitt must serve 30 years', *Guardian*, 6 December. Available at <http://www.guardian.co.uk/uk/2007/dec/06/ukcrime.health>.

Beckwith, JB (1970), 'Discussion of terminology and definition of the sudden infant death syndrome', in AB Bergman, JB Beckwith, and CG Ray, eds, *Sudden Infant Death Syndrome: Proceedings of the Second International Conference on the Causes of Sudden Death in Infants* (Seattle: University of Washington Press), 14–22.

Bichard Inquiry Report (2004) (London: HMSO).

Brandon, M et al. (2008), *Analysing child deaths and serious injury through abuse and neglect: what can we learn? A biennial analysis of serious case reviews 2003–2005* (Nottingham: DCSF Publications).

Brandon, M, Bailey, S, and Belderson, P (2010), *Building on the learning from serious case reviews: a two year analysis of child protection database notifications 2007–2009* (Runcorn: DFE). Copies of all reports can be downloaded free of charge at <http://www.education.gov.uk/research/>.

British and Irish Legal Information Institute (BAILII) website: <http://www.bailii.org>.

Butler-Sloss, Lady Justice E (1988), *The report of the inquiry into child abuse in Cleveland 1987*, Cmnd 412 (London: HMSO).

Byard, RW and Krous, HF, eds (2001), *Sudden Infant Death Syndrome. Problems, Progress & Possibilities* (London: Arnold, Hodder Headline Group).

Byard, RW and Krous, HF (2003), 'Sudden infant death syndrome: overview and update', *Pediatric and Developmental Pathology*, 6, 112–127.

Byard, RW (2004), *Sudden Death in Infancy, Childhood and Adolescence* (2nd edn, Cambridge: Cambridge University Press).

Casey, L (2011), *Review into the Needs of Families Bereaved by Homicide* (London: Ministry of Justice).

Child Accident Prevention Trust website: <http://www.capt.org.uk>.

Child Bereavement Charity: <http://www.childbereavement.org.uk> and Information and Support Line 01494 568900.

Child Death Helpline <www.childdeathhelpline.org.uk>; Free phone 0800 282986 or 0808 800 6019 for all mobiles.

Children Act 1989 (London: HMSO).

Children Act 2004 (London: HMSO).

Children and Young Persons Act 1933 (London: HMSO).

Children in Wales (2008), *All Wales Child Protection Procedures*. Available at <http://www.awcpp.org.uk/areasofwork/safeguardingchildren/awcpprg/proceduresand-protocols/index.html>.

Clothier, C (1994), *Independent Inquiry relating to deaths and injuries on the children's ward at Grantham and Kesteven General Hospital* (London: HMSO).

Cohen, M and Scheimberg, I (2009), 'Evidence of occurrence of intradural and sub-dural hemorrhage in the perinatal and neonatal period in the context of hypoxic ischemic encephalopathy: An observational study from two referral institutions in the United Kingdom', *Pediatric and Developmental Pathology* 12, 169–176.

Control of Substances Hazardous to Health (COSHH) Regulations. Available at <http://www.hse.gov.uk/coshh/>.

Coroners Act 1988. (London: HMSO).

Coroners Rules 1984. (London: HMSO).

Coroners (Amendment) Rules 2005. (London: HMSO).

Corporate Manslaughter and Corporate Homicide Act 2007. (London: HMSO).

CPS, *Non Accidental Head Injury Cases (NAHI), formerly referred to as Shaken Baby Syndrome [SBS]—Prosecution Approach (2011)*. Available on the CPS website at <http://www.cps.gov.uk/legal/l_to_o/non_accidental_head_injury_cases>.

CPS/ACPO Homicide Working Group (2011), *Guide for The Police, The CPS, LSCBs to assist with liaison and exchange of information when there are simultaneous Chapter 8 Serious case reviews and Criminal Proceedings*. Available at <http://www.baspcan.org.uk/files/SCR%20Guidance%20Document%20Final-%20John%20Fox.pdf>.

Criminal Attempts Act 1981. (London: HMSO).

Criminal Procedure and Investigations Act 1996. (London: HMSO).

Criminal Procedure Rules 2011. Available at < http://www.justice.gov.uk/guidance/courts-and-tribunals/courts/procedure-rules/criminal/index.htm>.

Crown Prosecution Service website: <http://cps.gov.uk/legal_resources.html>.

Department for Children, Schools and Families, *Why Jason died*. DVD and other childhood death resources at <http://www.education.gov.uk>.

Department for Education website: <http://www.education.gov.uk>.

Domestic Violence, Crime and Victims Act 2004. (London: HMSO).

DPP v Morrison [2003] EWHC 683, HC.

Family Procedure Rules 2010. Available at <http://www.justice.gov.uk/guidance/courts-and-tribunals/courts/procedure-rules/family/index.htm>.

Filiano, JJ and Kinney, HC (1994), 'A perspective on neuropathologic findings in victims of the sudden infant death syndrome: the triple-risk model', *Biology of the Neonate*, 65, 194–197.

Fleming, P, Blair, P, Bacon, C, and Berry J, eds (2000), *Sudden Unexpected Deaths in Infancy. The CESDI SUDI Studies 1993–1996* (London: The Stationery Office).

Fleming, P, Tsogt, B, and Blair, PS (2006), 'Modifiable risk factors, sleep environment, developmental physiology and common polymorphisms: understanding and preventing sudden infant deaths', *Early Human Development*, 82, 761–766.

FSID Fact Sheet (2010), *Cot Death Facts and Figures*. Available at <http://fsid.org.uk/page.aspx?pid=403>.

FSID Information Leaflet. *The Child Death Review. A Guide for Parents and Carers*. Available at <http://fsid.org.uk/document.doc?id=146>.

Geddes, JF, Tasker, RC, Hackshaw AK, et al. (2003), 'Dural haemorrhage in non-traumatic infant deaths: does it explain the bleeding in "shaken baby syndrome"?', *Neuropathology and Applied Neurobiology*, 29(4), 14–22.

Geddes, JF and Whitwell, HL (2004), 'Inflicted head injury in infants', *Forensic Science International*, 146, 83–88.

General Medical Council v Meadow (HM Attorney General intervening) [2006] EWCA Civ 1390 (26 October 2006).

Ghani and others v Jones [1969] 3 All ER 1700.

Goldsmith, Lord P (2004), *Review of Infant Death Cases 2004* (London: Attorney General's Chambers). Available at <http://www.lslo.gov.uk>.

Gould, SJ (2001), 'Sudden Unexpected Death in Infancy', *Current Diagnostic Pathology*, 7, 69–75.

Gould, SJ, Weber, MA, and Sebire, NJ (2010), 'Variation and uncertainties in the classification of sudden unexpected infant deaths among paediatric pathologists in the UK: findings of a National Delphi Study', *Journal of Clinical Pathology*, 63, 796–799.

Greater Manchester Police (2008), *GMP guidance on investigating unexplained and unexpected deaths in childhood*. Greater Manchester Police Chief Constable's Order 2008/52 Appendix B.

Guntheroth, WG and Spiers, PS (2002), 'The triple risk hypotheses in sudden infant death syndrome', *Pediatrics*, 110(5), e64.

Health and Safety at Work Act 1974. (London: HMSO).

HM Government (2004), *Every Child Matters: Change for Children Programme* (Nottingham: DFES). Available at <http://www.education.gov.uk/childrenandyoungpeople/sen/earlysupport/esinpractice/a0067409/every-child-matters>.

HM Government (2010), *Working Together to Safeguard Children. A guide to inter-agency working to safeguard and promote the welfare of children* (Nottingham: DCSF Publications).

HM Government (2008), *Safeguarding Children in Whom Illness is Fabricated or Induced* (Nottingham: DCSF Publications).

Home Office (1955), *Circular No 68/1955—Consolidated Circular to Coroners on Matters Other than Deaths from Industrial Accidents and Diseases* (London: Home Office).

Home Office (2005), *Circular 9/2005—The Domestic Violence, Crime and Victims Act 2004*. Available from <http://webarchive.nationalarchives.gov.uk> and <http://www.homeoffice.gov.uk/about-us/publications/home-office-circulars/circulars-2005/009-2005/>.

Homicide Act 1957. (London: HMSO).

Hopkins, G (2007), 'What have we learned? Child death scandals since 1944', *Community Care*, 11 January.

Huber, J (1994), 'Talk given in a panel discussion on the definition of SIDS, Third SIDS International Conference, Stavanger 1994', quoted in TO Rognum and M Willinger, 'The story of the "Stavanger definition"', in TO Rognum, ed, *Sudden Infant Death Syndrome, New Trends in the Nineties* (Oslo: Scandinavian University Press; 1995) 17–20.

Human Rights Act 1998. (London: HMSO).

Human Tissue Act 2004. (London: HMSO).

Human Tissue Authority Codes of Practice. Available at <http://www.hta.gov.uk>.

Human Tissue Authority Code of Practice 3: Post-mortem examination. Available at <http://www.hta.gov.uk/legislationpoliciesandcodesofpractice/codesofpractice/code3postmortem.cfm>.

Infant Life (Preservation) Act 1929. (London: HMSO).

Infanticide Act 1938. (London: HMSO).

International Classification of Diseases (10th Revision, ICD-10). Available at <http://www.who.int/classifications/icd/en/>.

Jones, D, Grieve, J, and Milne, B (2010), *Reviewing the Reviewers: The Review of Homicides in the United Kingdom*. Available at <http://www.investigativesciences-journal.org/article/view/5381/3749>.

Kennedy, H (2004), *Sudden unexpected death in infancy. A multi-agency protocol for care and investigation. The report of a working group convened by The Royal College of Pathologists and The Royal College of Paediatrics and Child Health* (London: The Royal College of Pathologists/The Royal College of Paediatrics and Child Health).

Kennedy, H (2004), *Sudden Unexpected Death in Infancy. The report of a working group convened by The Royal College of Pathologists and The Royal College of Paediatrics and Child Health* (London: The Royal College of Pathologists and The Royal College of Paediatrics and Child Health).

Krous, HF, Beckwith, JB, Byard, RW, Rognum, TO, Bajanowski, T, Corey, T, Cutz, E, Hanzlick, R, Keens, TG, and Mitchell, EA (2004), 'Sudden Infant Death Syndrome and Unclassified Sudden Infant Deaths: a Definitional and Diagnostic Approach', *Pediatrics*, 114, 234–238.

Laming, Lord H (2003), *The Victoria Climbié Inquiry. Report of an Inquiry by Lord Laming*, Cm 5730 (London: The Stationery Office).

Law Commission (April 2003), *Children: Their non-accidental death or serious injury (criminal trials). A consultative report*. Law Com No 279. Available at <http://www.justice.gov.uk/lawcommission/docs/lc279_Children_their_non-accidental_Death_or_Serious_Injury_Criminal_Trials_Consultative.pdf>.

Law Commission (September 2003), *Children: Their non-accidental death or serious injury (criminal trials)*. Law Com No 282. Available at <http://www.justice.gov.uk/lawcommission/docs/lc282_Children_Their_Non_Accidental_Death_or_Serious_Injury_Report.pdf>.

Levene, S and Bacon, C (2004), 'Sudden unexpected death and covert homicide in infancy', *Archives of Disease in Childhood*, 89, 443–447.

Limerick, SR and Bacon, CJ (2004), 'Terminology used by pathologists in reporting on sudden infant deaths', *Journal of Clinical Pathology*, 57, 309–311.

Lobmaier, IV, Vege, A, Gaustad, P, and Rognum TO (2009), 'Bacteriological investigation—significance of time lapse after death', *European Journal of Clinical Microbiology & Infectious Disease*, 28, 1191–1198.

Mayes et al. (2010), 'Risk factors for intra-familial unlawful and suspicious child deaths: A retrospective study of cases in London', *The Journal of Homicide and Major Incident Investigation*, 6(1) Spring 2010, 77–96.

Medical Act 1983. (London: HMSO).

Mental Health Act 1983. (London: HMSO).

Ministry of Justice (2010), *A Guide to Coroners and Inquests* (Coroners and Burials Division, Ministry of Justice).

Ministry of Justice (2011), *Achieving Best Evidence in Criminal Proceedings: Guidance on interviewing victims and witnesses, and guidance on using special measures* (London: Ministry of Justice).

Moon, RY, Horne, RS, Hauck, FR (2007), 'Sudden infant death syndrome', *Lancet*, 370, 1578–1587.

Munro, E (2011), *The Munro Review of Child Protection: Final Report A Child Centred System* (Runcorn: DFE).

National Archives, 'The official home of UK legislation' website: <http://www.legislation.gov.uk>.

National Center on Shaken Baby Syndrome website at <http://www.dontshake.org>.

New International Version of the Holy Bible, 1 Kings 3, 16–28. (Scripture taken from the Holy Bible New International Version Copyright c. 1973, 1978, 1984 by International Bible Society. Used by permission of Zondervan Publishing House. All rights reserved. The 'NIV' and 'New International Version' trademarks are registered in the United States Patent and Trademark Office by International Bible Society. Use of either trademark requires the permission of International Bible Society.)

Northern Ireland Department of Health, Social Services and Public Safety (2003), *Co-operating to Safeguard Children*. Available at <http://www.dhsspsni.gov.uk/show_publications?txtid=14022>.

NSPCC (2003), *Which of you did it? Problems of achieving criminal convictions when a child dies or is seriously injured by parents or carers* (London: NSPCC).

Offences Against the Person Act 1861. (London: HMSO).

Ofsted (2008), *Learning lessons, taking action: Ofsted's evaluations of serious case reviews 1 April 2007–31 March 2008* (London: Ofsted).

Ofsted (2009), *Learning lessons from serious case reviews year 2 (2008–2009)* (London: Ofsted).

Ofsted (2010), *Learning lessons from serious case reviews: interim report 2009–2010* (London: Ofsted).

Ofsted (2011), *The voice of the child: learning lessons from serious case reviews.* (London: Ofsted).

Osman v UK [2000] 29 EHRR 245.

Oxford Concise Colour Medical Dictionary (2010), (5th edn, Oxford: OUP).

Plunkett, J (2001), 'Fatal pediatric head injuries caused by short distance falls', *The American Journal of Forensic Medicine and Pathology*, Mar 22(1), 1–12.

Police and Criminal Evidence Act 1984. (London: HMSO).

Police National Legal Database (PNLD) website: <https://www.pnld.co.uk>.

Police Service of Northern Ireland (2010), *Service Procedure (SP 2/2010) Sudden Unexpected Death in Infancy*. Available at <http://www.psni.police.uk/service_procedure_0210.pdf>.

POLKA: POLKA is a secure online space for the policing community currently hosted by the NPIA to share insights, discover ideas, and suggest new ways of working including a DOCUMENT LIBRARY. POLKA can be accessed from the police national network within the Criminal Justice Framework.

Pryce, JW, Roberts, SE, Weber, MA, Klein NJ, Ashworth, MT, and Sebire, NJ (2011), 'Microbiological findings in sudden unexpected death in infancy: comparison of immediate postmortem sampling in casualty departments and at autopsy', *Journal of Clinical Pathology*, 64, 421–425.

Public Health Wales (2011), *The Procedural Response to Unexpected Deaths in Childhood (PRUDiC)*. Available at <http://wales.gov.uk/publications/accessinfo/drnewhomepage/drchildren1/2011/prudic/?lang=en>.

R v Adomako (1994) 99 Cr App R 362.

R v Anthony [2005] EWCA Crim 952 (11 April 2005).

R v Cannings (Angela) [2004] EWCA Crim 01 (19 January 2004).

R v Clark (Sally) [2000] EWCA Crim 54 (2 October 2000).

R v Clark (Sally) [2003] EWCA Crim 1020 (11 April 2003).

R v Harris, Rock, Cherry, and Faulder [2005] EWCA Crim 1980 (21 July 2005).

R v Henderson, Butler, and Oyediran [2010] EWCA Crim 1269 (17 June 2010).

R v Hunter, Atkinson and Mackinder (1973) 57 Cr App R 773.

R v Lane and Lane (1987) 82 Cr App R 5.

R v McNaghten (M'Naghten's Case) (1843) 10 C & F 200.

Rance v Mid-Downs Health Authority [1991] 1 QB 587 (PNLD D 6758).

Registration of Births and Deaths Regulations 1987. Available at <http://www.legislation.gov.uk/uksi/1987/2088/contents/made>.

Regulation of Investigatory Powers Act 2000. (London: HMSO).

SAMM (Support after Murder and Manslaughter) website: <http://www.samm.org.uk>.

Sebire, NJ, Weber, MA, Thayyil, S, Mushtaq, I, Taylor, A, and Chitty, LS (2011), 'Minimally invasive perinatal autopsies using magnetic resonance imaging and endoscopic postmortem examination ("keyhole autopsy"): feasibility and initial experience', *Journal of Maternal Fetal Neonatal Medicine*, August 10.

Secretary of State for Social Services (1974), *Report of the Committee of Inquiry into the Care and Supervision Provided in Relation to Maria Colwell* (London: HMSO).

Sidebotham, P, Atkins, B, Hutton, JL, et al. (2011), 'Changes in rates of violent child deaths in England and Wales between 1974 and 2008: an analysis of national mortality data', *Archives of Disease in Childhood*, 27 April.

Sidebotham, P, Bailey, S, Belderson, P, and Brandon, M (2011), *Fatal child maltreatment in England, 2005–2009*, published online at *Child Abuse & Neglect*, 35(4), 299–306.

Smith, K, Coleman, K, Eder, S, and Hall, P (2011), *Home Office Statistical Bulletin. Homicides, Firearm Offences and Intimate Violence 2009/10. Supplementary Volume 2 to Crime in England and Wales 2009/10* (Home Office: London).

Southall, P, Plunkett, C, Banks, M, Falkov, A, and Samuels, M (1997), 'Covert Video Recordings of Life-threatening Child Abuse: Lessons for Child Protection', *Pediatrics*, 100(5), 735–760.

Thayyil, S, Cleary, JO, Sebire, NJ, Scott, RJ, Chong, K, Gunny, R, Owens, CM, Olsen, OE, Offiah, AC, Parks, HG, Chitty, LS, Price, AN, Yousry, TA, Robertson, NJ, Lythgoe, MF, Taylor, AM (2009), 'Post-mortem examination of human fetuses: a comparison of whole-body high-field MRI at 9.4 T with conventional MRI and invasive autopsy', *Lancet*, 374, 467–475.

Thayyil, S, Chitty, LS, Robertson, NJ, Taylor, AM, and Sebire NJ (2010), 'Minimally invasive fetal postmortem examination using magnetic resonance imaging and computerised tomography: current evidence and practical issues', *Prenatal Diagnosis*, 30, 713–718.

The Stephen Lawrence Inquiry: Report of an Inquiry by Sir William MacPherson of Cluny (1999) (London: The Stationery Office). Available at <http://www.archive.official-documents.co.uk/document/cm42/4262/4262.htm>.

Timmins, N and Vallely, P (1985), 'Report featuring the deaths of Jasmine Beckford and Tyra Henry', *The London Times*, 4 December.

UNICEF, *Fact Sheet and information on UN Convention on the Rights of the Child*. Available at <http://www.unicef.org>.

United Nations General Assembly (1989), Convention on the Rights of the Child.

Vargas, SL, Ponce, CA, Hughes, WT, Wakefield, AE, Weitz, JC, Donoso, S, et al. (1999), 'Association of primary Pneumocystis carinii infection and sudden infant death syndrome', *Clinical Infectious Disease*, 29, 1489–1493.

Vaughan, J and Kautt, P (2009), 'Infant death Investigations Following High-Profile Unsafe Rulings: Throwing Out the Baby with the Bath Water?', *Policing*, 3(1), 89–99.

Weber, MA, Ashworth, MT, Risdon, RA, Hartley, JC, Malone, M, and Sebire, NJ (2008), 'The role of post-mortem investigations in determining the cause of sudden unexpected death in infancy', *Archives of Disease in Childhood*, 93, 1048–1053.

Weber, MA and Sebire, NJ (2009), 'Postmortem Investigation of Sudden Unexpected Death in Infancy: Current Issues and Autopsy Protocol', *Diagnostic Histopathology*, 15, 510–523.

Weber, MA, Risdon, RA, Offiah, AC, Malone, M, and Sebire, NJ (2009a), 'Rib fractures identified at post-mortem examination in sudden unexpected deaths in infancy (SUDI)', *Forensic Science International*, 189, 75–81.

Weber, MA, Ashworth, MT, Risdon, RA, Malone, M, and Sebire, NJ (2009b), 'The Frequency and Significance of Alveolar Haemosiderin-Laden Macrophages in Sudden Infant Death', *Forensic Science International*, 187, 51–57.

Weber, MA, Hartley, JC, Brooke, I, Lock, PE, Klein, NJ, Malone, M, and Sebire, NJ (2010), 'Post-mortem interval and bacteriological culture yield in sudden unexpected death in infancy (SUDI)', *Forensic Science International*, 198, 121–125.

Weber, MA, Hartley, JC, Ashworth, MT, Malone, M, and Sebire, NJ (2010), 'Virological investigations in sudden unexpected deaths in infancy (SUDI)', *Forensic Science, Medicine and Pathology*, 6, 261–267.

Wells, K (2005), *Goodbye, Dearest Holly* (London: Hodder).

Williams, C (2010), 'The Trouble with Paediatricians', *Medical Law Review*, 18(3).

Willinger, M, James, LS, and Catz, C (1991), 'Defining the sudden infant death syndrome (SIDS): deliberations of an expert panel convened by the National Institute of Child Health and Human Development', *Pediatric Pathology*, 11, 677–684.

Z and others v UK [2001] 34 EHRR 97.

Index